Marketing to Leading-Edge Baby Boomers

Brent Green knows a thing or three about marketing to Baby Boomers, and he proves it in this masterful and easily readable book. If you don't know what he has to tell you, there's a yawning void in your marketing education.

—Jay Conrad Levinson, lead author of the
Guerrilla Marketing book series

Brent Green has done a terrific job of defining the needs and aspirations of the "tip of the arrow." Many new insights . . . beautifully expressed.

—John Zweig, Chairman of Specialist
Communications, WPP Group

From beginning to end we feel the care and humanity of the author and know that marketing means more to him than selling product. It means meeting people where they live and engaging them so they leave the encounter feeling deeply nourished.

—Jed Diamond, Director of MenAlive
and author of *Male Menopause* and
Irritable Male Syndrome

OTHER MARKETING BOOKS FROM PMP

Marketing to Leading-Edge Baby Boomers

Perceptions, Principles, Practices, Predictions

BRENT GREEN

PARAMOUNT MARKET PUBLISHING, INC.

Paramount Market Publishing, Inc.
301 South Geneva Street, Suite 109, Ithaca, NY 14850
phone: 607-275-8100 • *toll-free:* 888-787-8100 • *fax:* 607-275-8101
www.paramountbooks.com

Publisher: James Madden
Editorial Director: Doris Walsh

Cover
Photography: Larry George, *www.larrygeorge.com*
Photo illustration: Kent Barnes, *www.kentdesign.biz*
Models: Carol Lyn Lucas and Jim Lucas, both Leading-Edge Baby Boomers
Cover photo illustration first appeared in the June/July 2004 issue of
Advertising & Marketing Review, www.ad-mkt-review.com Used with permission.

"Born To Be Wild," page 154. Words and music by Mars Bonfire.
Copyright © 1968 Songs of Universal, Inc. on behalf of Universal Music
Publishing, a division of Universal Studios, Canada LTD. (BMI) International
Copyright Secured. All Rights Reserved. Used by permission.

Paramount Market Publishing's books are available at special discounts
for bulk purchases for sales promotions or premiums. For more
information, contact Special Markets, Paramount Market Publishing,
301 South Geneva Street, Suite 109, Ithaca, NY 14850, or e-mail:
editors@paramountbooks.com

Library of Congress Catalog Number:
Cataloging in Publication Data Available

ISBN 0-9766973-5-1

For Becky Green

Contents

Acknowledgments

WRITING a business book is often a singular and intensely private outpouring of ideas. Sometimes it begins as a group project long before it comes to fruition on paper.

This book began in the spring of 1970 several months before, during, and the tumultuous weeks following the massacre at Kent State University. After Ohio National Guardsmen gunned down four unarmed students, the nation's colleges and universities could no longer function as normal. Outrage colored the soft hues of spring with crimson and fury.

Because of ominous threats of further campus violence, many universities wisely elected to shut down early that spring. Students at The University of Kansas had two choices: accept the grades they had earned through mid-term examinations, or take final exams and accept those grades. Many accepted the cumulative grades they had earned before the hasty shut down, preferring to avoid final examinations and term projects. This was also my choice, with the exception of one class.

That spring I had undertaken an ambitious exploratory project into a realm virtually untouched by intellectual inquiry. I designed and conducted an exploratory research study entitled *Loneliness at the University of Kansas*. This was my answer to a required term research project for an advanced placement course analyzing interpersonal communications and social psychology in complex organizations. My professor was the late Dr. Kim Giffin, then one of the most respected national authorities in the field of organizational development and interpersonal communications.

A charismatic, wise scholar, Dr. Giffin inspired me to undertake a sweeping exploration of loneliness, and perhaps uncover insights about its impact on students during an era of extreme social conflict and relentless alienation. Rather than accept the grade I had already earned pre-Kent State—that nevertheless would have been an A—I asked my professor if he would allow me to finish this paper.

Dr. Giffin agreed to accept the term project and review it after most of his colleagues already departed for summer break. I turned in the paper three weeks after shutdown. In interesting juxtaposition to the intellectual focus of the paper, I recall an empty campus exuding eerie, abandoned feelings, as I walked the term paper into the good professor's office. He returned the paper to me a few days later with an A grade and a simple note of encouragement: 'This is an excellent paper.'"*

Thus began my career-long search for greater understanding about the generation to which my birth date had given me unwitting inclusion, and ultimately, a fierce pride. I have never stopped being interested in the unique challenges that have confronted this generation and how society has come to perceive us, both the pros and cons.

Two other professors at KU influenced me greatly. Dr. Robert Shelton served as the university's ombudsman for eighteen years and is still teaching courses in the Department of Religious Studies. This intuitive, erudite man of peace rescued me more than once during those difficult Vietnam years that hung over college campuses as a black cloud. Dr. Shelton found the true balance between rigor and gentleness to focus my rambling mind and help me articulate my evolving ideas, values, and their ramifications. He ignited my lifelong quest to uncover truth and seek fairness in the name of peaceful coexistence. In May 2000, Dr. Shelton invited me back to KU to lecture one of his classes on the thirtieth anniversary of the Kent State tragedy. During this ninety-minute presentation, I impressed upon many of those wide-eyed students that their media-spun perceptions of the Vietnam era are much different from the realities of having been involved in the student antiwar movement thirty years earlier.

Another professor, a highly respected authority in social psy-

---

* This historical event has a contemporary legacy. KU established the Giffin Communication Research Award, given annually to a graduate student in communication studies excelling in a research project.

chology, opened a major door for an ambitious student. Dr. Howard J. Baumgartel agreed to sponsor an undergraduate psychology class that I had conceived, entitled "Topics and Problems on Humanistic/Existential Psychology." Behaviorists dominated the psychology department at KU during that time, so this class was a noteworthy departure from the department's prevailing and preferred psychology paradigm.

Dr. Baumgartel placed unusual faith in a novice lecturer by having the grit to sponsor a course probing such a controversial new view of the human psyche. He flexed his national reputation and brought to our class some of the leading minds of the time, including John Heider, author of the best-selling business book, *The Tao of Leadership*. Heider was then director of the Esalen Institute, the famous apex of the Human Potential Movement.

Perhaps the most significant event of an astonishing class was an intensive group inquiry facilitated by Abraham Kaplan. One of the top ten teachers in the United States, according to a 1966 article in *Time* magazine, Kaplan was a Guggenheim and Rockefeller Fellow. He had been a student of philosopher Bertrand Russell before he launched his extraordinary career as an educator. Kaplan wrote a number of scholarly inquiries, including *Pursuit of Wisdom: the Scope of Philosophy*.

More recently, I owe immeasurable gratitude to a wide circle of bright and demanding friends and colleagues who have challenged me during my frequent diatribes about the Baby Boom Generation. They have been kind to confront my assumptions and considerate to hear me out. They have added texture and depth to my evolving views of this generation.

Therefore, my heartfelt thanks go to my sister and brother-in-law, Julie and Joel Bethke; Madeleine Mellini; Carol Lyn and Jim Lucas; Paul Leibowitz Esq. and Julie Christian; Dr. Mark Crooks; Mark Joyous; Craig Cornish Esq.; Mark S. A. Smith; Dr. Ken Cinnamon; Dr. David J. Reibstein; Greg Dobbs; Lou Mellini; David Foster; Jim Rohrbach; Gordon Brown; Paul Franklin; John Darin; "Papa" Carl Faber; and, an intense young man headed toward a dazzling future, someone who has always been quick to offer the Generation Y perspective, Julian Harris Mellini.

A special thank you goes to Henry S. Blake III, who provided valuable insights about Boomers and who edited the eleven new chapters of the second edition. When we were just junior high school students, Henry ignited my passion for the language with his mature and critically acclaimed poetry and song lyrics.

The passion that I have felt all my life for justice and egalitarian values comes from a proud Kansas populist, an idealistic life-long Democrat who, as a federal employee and firebrand lobbyist, spent a career giving back to his community and fighting for equitable treatment of home buyers and retired employees. He is my father, Gilbert Green. Our family misses this principled, honest man, and we hope our best efforts can honor his gifts of fervor and high purpose, defiantly unfettered by critics or obstacles.

From my soft-spoken mother, Lucille Richards Green, I inherited an unquenchable thirst for creative self-expression and a patient and practical acceptance of diversity. She has also left indescribable emptiness in our family with her departure one day after my father's passing in July 2000.

Finally, although I recognize her on the dedication page, my deepest thanks goes to my life-partner, Becky Green, who has been extraordinarily patient with a writer in the house and the long hours of separation and aloneness. She has always encouraged me to pursue my wide-ranging passions, and she has been an invaluable resource for discussion and critique.

A note about an idiosyncratic grammatical convention in this book:
It is customary for "Baby Boomers," the "Baby Boom Generation," "Boomers," and the "Baby Boom," to be presented as common nouns, in lower case. It is the author's opinion, and, within the pages of this book, his artistic prerogative, to consider these generational descriptors as proper nouns, thus *names of particular or specific persons, places, things, or events.* This is a particular generation—as are the "GI Generation," "Generation X," and "Generation Y"—thus deserving upper-case designations for the various forms of generational identification.

Introduction

URING the next two decades, millions of Baby Boomers will reach retirement age. Never before in American history will so many people have arrived en masse at this life stage. Nevertheless, unlike the few preceding generations that had an opportunity to enjoy post-career retirement, Boomers will give this traditional period of reduced activity new meaning.

They will not be quiet, calm, or disengaged.

They will collectively redefine the connotations of aging and the purpose of life's closing years. They will set the stage for a long-term reorientation of American business to the value of the more mature population. They will bring to aging culture what they brought to youth culture when they boisterously became young adults four decades ago.

Not only will this life stage continue to be associated with fewer working responsibilities, as has been its tradition, there will be more free time to redefine the character of the country. Moreover, this generation's healthy materialistic appetite will feed a penchant for acquiring many new possessions, whether material, psychological, or spiritual.

Some Baby Boomers are retiring early, cashing in on good fortune bestowed by successful careers, and perhaps a robust slice of the trillions of dollars left behind by their parents' generation. Many more will forestall full retirement for economic reasons, financially unable to cope with a non-working future dependent on substantial retirement nest eggs and fortuitous investing throughout their careers.

As Baby Boomers arrive at the beginning of their golden years, they are unlike any preceding group of younger retirees. They will choose continuing education to transform hobbies into money-making occupations; many will seek mind expansion through exotic travel and educational pursuits; some will invest in luxury lifestyles with all the comfort trappings of the good life; and most will focus on the critical developmental challenges of this life stage: reconciliation with the past, and an ultimate search for meaning.

And the economic realities of America will change.

Around the collective quest will whirl thousands of new business opportunities, from yet unimagined lifestyle communities, to new technologies designed to minimize work and overcome the limitations of aging bodies. Medical breakthroughs will continue to revise understanding of human longevity and release untapped human potential from revitalized bodies and minds. A plethora of new products and services will spill out of America's companies to satisfy emerging needs for greater social relevance, spiritual integration, and comfort.

Demographers and futurists have been speaking to and writing about the impact of this phenomenon for years, with some predicting an economic Shangri-La and others cautioning national financial disaster. Both viewpoints have merit. Although the Baby Boom has an unparalleled number of successful, financially independent achievers, the generation also has a large segment that may be financially unable to cope with full retirement.

Since America's oldest segments have traditionally been the most aggressive about voting and lobbying for public financial support, it is reasonable to imagine increasing pressures on federal entitlement programs, already dangerously large. It is reasonable to predict a widening chasm between those of the generation who have resources and those who do not. It is reasonable to predict heightened conflict between an entitlement-hungry group and younger generations wanting their fair share of the American Dream. It is also reasonable to foresee that community service and stewardship will grow as many former social activists rediscover their fondness for giving and helping.

And the character of America itself will change.

The complex impact of this demographic shift can be reduced to two major economic forces. Millions capable of retiring and living the good life will form a luxury market for countless goods and services focused on the elderly. Millions more will confront financial limitations for the remainder of their lives, unable to afford society's bounty of luxuries; nevertheless, and ironically, they will be consumers of products and services designed to assist the less fortunate.

Whichever socioeconomic market you seek to develop, Baby Boomers have accumulated common cultural, sociological, and psychological experiences that drive their underlying motivations and influence their purchasing decisions. Individuals within this group vary widely and are conservative and liberal, male and female, straight and gay, Caucasian and of color, but when combined, this vast generation will bring to its retirement years many predictable and common attitudes about conducting business with companies.

Businesses that understand and effectively react to the nuances of this generation will prosper. Those that fail to comprehend the cultural and sociological underpinnings will suffer the economic consequences.

This book is dedicated to helping you understand how to communicate with Leading-Edge Baby Boomers in a meaningful and mutually beneficial way. Ultimately, it will help you achieve your business goals by showing you how to effectively target and market to a generation ready to bestow success on those who truly understand and act on its idiosyncrasies, values, dreams, and goals.

Reading this book promises something beyond an insightful and challenging analysis of a generation moving into retirement. You will discover some original ideas about how the Baby Boom is today shaping the future.

What happens next will be interesting, if not tumultuous.

PART 1

PERCEPTIONS

Strange new problems are being reported in the growing generations of children whose mothers were always there, driving them around, helping them with their homework—an inability to endure pain or discipline or pursue any self-sustained goal of any sort, a devastating boredom with life.

—Betty Friedan

Yippies, Hippies, Yahoos, Black Panthers, lions and tigers alike—I would swap the whole damn zoo for the kind of young Americans I saw in Vietnam.

—Spiro T. Agnew

For me, the lame part of the Sixties was the political part, the social part. The real part was the spiritual part.

—Jerry Garcia

CHAPTER 1

A Generational View of Aging

SIMILAR to parents naming their new baby, thought leaders from older generations choose a name for a newly arriving generation—whether members of the new generation eventually like the name or not.

A name can influence perceptions. People expect something different from someone with the name of Hershel than they do of Harrison. They have different ideas about Matilda than they do of Misty.

Names notwithstanding, every generation establishes a sense of its collective self, a cohesive identity that covers many dimensions, from core values to shared culture. As each generation proceeds through its unique chapter of history, the generational name comes to stand for something more than a simple, demographically convenient way to identify millions of people who share the proximity of contiguous birth dates.

Eventually, the given name becomes a cryptic headline in a newspaper or book title and represents a bundle of attitudes, experiences, images, defining moments, and shared vision about the future. The name becomes a package of values and expectations.

Sometimes generations achieve their unique identity within a period of just a few years out of the 100 or so during which the generation commences with the first birth and passes into history with the death of its last member. These defining months, or years, may reflect suffering or transcendence.

My parents' generation galvanized its identity between 1940 and 1945 during World War II, thus the "GI Generation." My older sister's generation has often been associated with a period of relative peace and economic prosperity, sometimes called the "Eisenhower Generation."

Experts periodically disagree about the most accurate name to identify millions of Americans born into a given cohort, and sometimes these names change as the generation confronts bellwether historical events.

Thus, pundits have identified overlapping and oppositional generational designations such as:

"The Depression Generation" vs. the "GI Generation"

"The Silent Generation" vs. the "Eisenhower Generation"

"Baby Bust," or "Thirteeners" vs. "Generation X"

"Millennials" or "Echo Boomers" vs. "Generation Y"

Oddly, the enduring name for one living generation that has experienced little naming inconsistency among pundits is "The Baby Boom Generation."

Authorities have also called Baby Boomers "The Sixties Generation," "Flower Children," "The Me Generation," and "Yuppies." A writer for *U.S. News & World Report* even called them "Zoomers."[1] However, the name "Baby Boomers" has become the accepted descriptor for this group, and has survived its many excesses and society's occasional hostilities.

As with most generations, the Baby Boom spans about twenty years. The generation came into being after years of economic depression, world war, and deprivation.

Its ranks began forming following the end of World War II, and ended one year and five weeks after the assassination of President John Fitzgerald Kennedy. The last member arrived a few seconds before midnight on December 31, 1964.

This short arc of history has cultivated different segments within the larger generational cohort. The *Leading-Edge Baby Boomers* are individuals born between 1946 and 1955, those who came of age during the Vietnam War. This group represents slightly more than half of the generation, or roughly 38,002,000 people of all races.

The other half of the generation was born between 1956 and 1964. Called Late Boomers, or Trailing-Edge Boomers, this second cohort includes about 37,818,000 individuals, according to *Live Births by Age and Mother and Race, 1933–98*, published by the Center for Disease Control's National Center for Health Statistics.

U.S. Live Births

1946 – 1955		1956 – 1964	
1946	3,411,000	1956	4,210,000
1947	3,817,000	1957	4,300,000
1948	3,637,000	1958	4,246,000
1949	3,649,000	1959	4,244,000
1950	3,632,000	1960	4,258,000
1951	3,820,000	1961	4,268,000
1952	3,909,000	1962	4,167,000
1953	3,959,000	1963	4,098,000
1954	4,071,000	1964	4,027,000
1955	4,097,000		
Total	**38,002,000**	**Total**	**37,818,000**

Source: National Center for Health Services

As these numbers attest, the generation is as much a phenomenon of proportion as of history. With over 75 million in its ranks, the sheer demographic size relative to other generations has influenced mass marketers to adapt products, pitches, and practices to their unique proclivities as Boomers have marched through life stages.

To complicate the task of generalization further, characterizations of the Baby Boom Generation by the media for the past 30 years have been disproportionately focused on roughly 25 percent of the generation whose parents were white-collar professionals with post-secondary educations. One of the results of this imbalanced coverage has been to underrepresent roughly 75 percent of the generation that grew up in households from poor, working-class, small family-farm, or small family-business backgrounds.[2]

Thus, when setting out to write about marketing to Baby Boomers as a discrete group, I am aware of the risks of over-generalization. I have reduced the immensity and impracticality of this task by choosing to focus my secondary research and analyses primarily on the Leading-Edge Baby Boomers, those born between 1946 and 1955.

The following marketing insights and recommendations most often embrace the part of the Leading-Edge segment that has realized at least a moderate level of educational and economic achievement, thus a group financially able to relish a wide variety of products and services that will be available during the next 10 to 30 years.

The potential market for this group ranges from 12 million to 20 million individuals, depending on the optimism of your calculator. Of course, in many instances, the insights and recommendations that apply to this segment will still be valid for the early retirement consumption habits of Late Boomers, those born between 1956 and 1964.

Individuals within this huge population of Americans have many differences. In common, they share a current transition into middle age and pre-retirement years. The formative experiences Baby Boomers share—from the tragedies of the Vietnam War to the memories of Watergate—have cultivated basic values and consumption habits amenable to generalization.

Although disagreements persist about the names and inclusive birth dates defining all living generations, the demographic descriptors I will also use to represent today's most significant generations are as follows:

The GI Generation *Born 1925 and earlier (Age 81 and older)*

The Silent Generation *Born 1926 to 1945 (Age 61 to 80)*

The Baby Boom Generation *Born 1946 to 1964 (Age 42 to 60)*

Generation X *Born 1965 to 1979 (Age 27 to 41)*

Generation Y *Born 1980 to 2000 (Age 6 to 26)*

As different as individuals within the Baby Boom Generation can be when compared side by side with terse generational summaries, common roots in late 20th century America have led to common marketing considerations.

Let us begin, then, with the first, most critical generalization:

What Baby Boomers have wanted during their march through life stages, the vast engine of American commerce has also wanted for the generation. What Baby Boomers will want in their waning years, business will also want. Marketing successfully to Leading-Edge Baby Boomers is a way to sell more products and services.

According to various research sources, consumers over age 50 now hold three-quarters of the country's financial assets. By 2010, nearly 33 percent of American adults will be over age 50, and they will have nearly $800 billion in combined economic power.[3]

Understanding Baby Boomers from a marketing perspective is not just good business. It is also a way to help members of the generation fulfill a nearly universal quest for meaning and value. In a society quick to condemn and loathe to forget Boomers' youthful excesses, it is a way to build new bridges and mitigate discrimination. It is a way to connect this generation to younger generations inevitably headed toward retirement and old age.

This book is part demographic and socioeconomic research interpretation, part common business sense, part recollection, part theory, part crystal ball gazing, and part idealism.

It's a message about business connectivity with a utilitarian purpose.

Reach this generation with powerful messages supporting relevant products and services, and you will bridge the generation gap. Your company will make more money. And you will grow in your appreciation of a generation intent on leaving behind a beneficent legacy.

I hope that when the final chapter about this generation has been written, America will be a better place to grow old for all the generations that follow.

CHAPTER 2

Of Statistics, Demographics, and History

THE post-World War II Baby Boom, lasting from 1946 to 1964, is more significant and far-reaching than numbers alone indicate. The statistics, however, have always portended something monumental and enduring.

During the nineteen-year span of the generation's birth cycle, 75.8 million Boomers joined the American family. At the end of this massive reproductive cycle in 1964, the generation represented 40 percent of the U.S. population. In that final year, over one-third of the nation was younger than twenty. There should be no doubt about why this cohort received a substantial amount of attention from older generations.

No matter how you slice and dice the numbers, the Baby Boom is a statistical anomaly in its forward march through American history, the so-called "pig in a python."

For example, at the peak of the boom between 1956 and 1960, 21.2 million Boomers fell from the beaks of storks, 150 percent more than the total number of births between 1941 and 1945. This late-1950's period experienced the largest population growth for any five-year period during the last century.[4]

In 1957, during the peak year of the boom, the *GI Generation* and *Silent Generation* gave birth to 4.3 million Americans. This annual birth statistic has not been exceeded before or since, and was closely rivaled just once (1990).

Today, the generation represents close to 30 percent of the population, including adults that in 2006 ranged in age from 42 to 60 years old. Adults at the older end of this spectrum, those in their late 40s and early 50s, will be of particular interest to companies with products and services focusing on retirement during the remainder of the first decade of the 21st century.

This Leading-Edge group is composed of roughly 38 million individuals, the youngest of which will turn 51 in 2006, while the oldest will turn 60 in the same year.

This means that a massive march toward retirement has begun in the minds of millions, including serious planning, thinking, and dreaming about this major life transition. Therefore, now is the time for businesses to think about capitalizing on the obvious.

However, statistics will never tell the entire story of this business opportunity, its implications, or how businesses can meet major demographic shift with products, services, and intelligent marketing communications.

The Baby Boom Generation has come to mean more than just a national statistical event; the collective concept is also a byproduct of its own history. Members of the Leading-Edge segment recall critical defining moments in their history that have created a common value set and even predictable consumption behavior.

Let's quickly review the benchmark historical events that influence this generation.

1956 Soviet Premier Nikita Khrushchev said, "History is on our side. We will bury you!" Baby Boomers learn about the threat of thermonuclear annihilation and master the art of playing "Duck and cover."

1957 The Russians launch Sputnik I and II, ushering in the space age, the space race, and the sobering possibility that America is not the world's technological leader.

1960 Pharmaceutical companies introduce "The Pill," giving women more control over their fertility.

1961 John Fitzgerald Kennedy is elected President of the United States, beginning a short period of buoyant optimism that America can prevail in technology and world leadership.

1962 American spy satellites observe Russian ships delivering ballistic missiles, and by implication, nuclear weapons to Cuba, moving the world to the brink of thermonuclear holocaust.

1963 Lee Harvey Oswald assassinates JFK in Dallas, Texas, ending the brief reign of Kennedy's Camelot, and permanently tarnishing Baby Boomers' childlike sense of optimism; Martin Luther King begins a new era of race awareness and relations by declaring: "I have a dream."

1964 President Lyndon Johnson declares his "War on Poverty," further igniting a Boomer passion for social justice, liberal politics, and community service; as if in contradiction to his nobler human motives, however, Johnson also significantly escalates the American commitment to a war in a faraway jungle country called Vietnam.

1966 In another stride toward "justice for all," the U.S. Supreme Court reaches its *Miranda* decision, thus giving those detained or arrested a better chance for fairer treatment by police and the courts; American troop strength in Vietnam escalates beyond 400,000.

1967 As if in contradiction to Martin Luther King's vision and hope for a more racially liberated society, race riots in Detroit kill dozens of citizens. A collective unease ripples through society regarding the meaning and attainment of equality in America.

1968 Robert F. Kennedy, then a leading candidate for the Democratic nomination for U.S. President, and Martin Luther King are assassinated just weeks apart; Vietnam War protests and riots at the Democratic National Convention in Chicago nearly close down the city while further souring American citizens' disposition toward antiestablishment Baby Boomers; Richard M. Nixon becomes President of the United States and mobilizes the sentiments of the Silent Majority.

1969 Realizing JFK's bold leadership vision for America in the space race with Russia, the United States lands the first man on the moon; a seminal rock festival called Woodstock begins near Bethel, New York, moving the hippie counterculture movement into hyperdrive; the Vietnam War reaches its peak number of committed U.S. soldiers.

1970 Vietnam War protests escalate throughout the country, culminating in the shooting deaths of four students at Kent State University in Ohio; colleges across the country close early to avoid further confrontations with angry students and protesters.

1971 Daniel Ellsberg publishes the "Pentagon Papers" in *The New York Times*, revealing critical flaws in U.S. Vietnam policy, its illegal and immoral implications, including deceptions of the American public, and also setting in motion a series of events leading to the resignation and disgrace of Richard Nixon.

1972 Early in the morning on June 17, 1972, police discover five intruders inside the headquarters of the Democratic National Committee at the Watergate apartment and office building complex in Washington, DC. The burglars were there, it turned out, to adjust bugging equipment that they had installed during a May break-in, and to photograph documents; this set in motion a complex cover-up by the Nixon Administration, and the triangular relationship between public officials, the media, and Baby Boomers is altered forever.

1973 The military draft ends, liberating male Baby Boomers from the threat of conscription; in the landmark decision, *Roe vs. Wade*, the U.S. Supreme Court legalizes abortion; a noose begins to tighten around Richard Nixon's neck; the last American troops leave Vietnam.

1974 President Richard Nixon resigns from office in disgrace; President Gerald Ford declares: "Our long national nightmare is over."[5]

To this parade of events, all of which provided new tests of American resolve and challenges to the generation's deepest values, you can also add all the strange changes in traditional culture and society. The prologue to my novel, *Noble Chaos*, captures the essence of collective confusion and dismay:

It was a time when all the old rules went away for awhile—
a short span when culture and society spun topsy-turvy.

Traditional American values were unfashionable. Political ide-alism became tantamount to personal survival. Our relation-ship to authority mutated to a fierce indignation.

Demonstrators swelled campus thoroughfares. Defiant black fists of rage rose mightily above the ghetto multitudes. Sweltering jungles and pastoral campuses became littered with the same young bodies. Resolute hitchhikers crossed the Canadian border to a conscientious freedom.

Every aspect of expected behavior in human relationships was questioned, re-defined, manipulated, and explored. We heard and read daily about Gay Rights, Black Panthers, the Women's Movement, Free Love, interracial marriage, the Woodstock Generation, altered consciousness, the Age of Aquarius, Students for a Democratic Society (SDS), Yippies, and open marriage.

We fought an unpopular war, popular beliefs, pollution of the environment, petty politicians, and perpetrators of the sta-tus quo. But most of all, we fought each other. There were blacks against whites, young against old, gays against straights, feminists against chauvinists, veterans against paci-fists, construction workers against students, liberals against conservatives, environmentalists against industrialists, Democrats against Republicans, and Native Americans against everyone. On all fronts, we fought for change.

The children of the World War II Baby Boom were 76 mil-lion strong. We were fortunate enough to be on the cutting edge of adulthood, to have lived passionately through that most poorly understood segment of recent history, and we found the changes mostly captivating and indelible. We grew up in syncopation with the coming of age of a nation. We were a collision of youth on the "threshold of a dream," locked in a war between tradition and change, revolution and counterrevolution, myth and disillusionment, love and hatred.

Gerald Ford's "long national nightmare" was not entirely over in 1974, but Baby Boomers slowly began to shift their focus to careers, achievement, and families. The generation's values, consumption habits, and full entry into middle-aged lifestyles started to change America again as Boomers became widely known as yuppies: young, upwardly mobile professionals, or young urban professionals.

The generation was becoming the great capitalistic prize. In addition, the bellwether events of childhood and adolescent years burrowed deeper into a collective subconscious as Boomers embraced the material world. The hallmark lessons from youth, however, remained indelible. When Boomers became a dominant force in the economic engine, as creators and producers, their numbers and history changed America.

Those common experiences, their lessons imparted, and the values they learned will have substantial impact on the methods and practices of business as Baby Boomers begin to leave behind their leadership positions and embrace the "quieter years."

CHAPTER 3

The Unpatriotic, Self-Absorbed Image

IMAGES of burning flags and draft cards still reside in the nation's collective memory, as do recollections of campus demonstrations, occupied buildings, and audacious confrontations between protesters and police at the 1968 Democratic National Convention in Chicago. Many Baby Boomers graduated into adulthood by following the unpopular path of disobedience and confrontation with authority. A segment of draft-age Boomers fled to Canada to avoid military conscription. An even larger segment, including allegedly two U. S. presidents, concocted creative ways to avoid armed combat through deferments or influence peddling and low-risk stateside jobs.

Boomer music and culture expressed widespread opposition to the Vietnam War and its potential of escalation throughout Indochina. Men grew their hair long and began to look as dissimilar as possible from the prevailing GI Generation norm of tightly cropped hair and formal business attire. Many added to this mixture of protest and politics drug experimentation, sexual promiscuity, and alternative lifestyles.

Is it any wonder that pundits and conservative political critics upbraided Leading-Edge Baby Boomers for being ungrateful and unpatriotic?

Although it is not my intention in this book to dwell on political issues, it is difficult to pigeonhole Leading-Edge Baby Boomer motivations and consumption behavior without exploring the period in their lives that engendered an unsavory image of the generation as a whole. Therefore, the following discussion is another view of this generation's political fervor during the Vietnam War era and the implications for today's marketers.

The period between 1967 and 1975 was a time of confrontation and political action by young citizens against a powerful ruling elite, one heavily dominated by underhanded politics, "guts and glory" military influences and corporate indiscretions. Leading-Edge Baby Boomers undertook these confrontations with no guarantee of impunity, and their discordant behavior led to substantive personal sacrifices surrounding family harmony, higher education, and careers.

Many young people so engaged (and I refer to those constructively involved in change, not the belligerent, foolish fringe) derailed their vocational pursuits during this period to focus on broader societal issues, from the war to the women's movement, and from racial discrimination to the environment.

One of the important points I would like you to consider is this: What society has come to recall as "the bad Sixties" is heavily based on media coverage of the radical fringe because covering controversy and confrontation in its most extreme forms is what the media do to attract viewers, listeners, and readers.

Some of the leaders destructive to the generation's overall image actually came from the older Silent or Eisenhower-era Generation. Prominent antiwar revolutionaries included Abbie Hoffman (born 1936), Youth International Party (Yippy) cofounder Jerry Rubin (born 1938), and even liberal-turned-conservative David Horowitz (born about 1938, extrapolated from his college graduation year). In the minds of many, these formerly outspoken radicals and their New Left compatriots came to represent the collective image of the Baby Boom cohort then of college age.

Edward P. "Ted" Morgan, a political science professor at Lehigh University, calls this phenomenon "decontextualization." In other words, the media have constructed a limited and biased view of the Sixties due to their own tendency to cover the most violent, reactionary, and confrontational events and people of the period.

News media isolated extreme events and their leaders from the true context and often underplayed the arbitrary actions by authorities that precipitated higher states of tension and counteroffensive behavior among students. Then media used these extreme events to represent an entire period, to cast a dark shadow on a larger population of young people, even the majority who contributed constructively to many socially evolutionary movements.

Somehow, the broader message of this generation's passionate democratic mobilization against the hegemonic political and social leadership then prevailing in America was lost in the simplifying, mitigating distillations of subsequent media reporting.

Another name for the resulting media phenomenon is "mobilization of bias," a factor which continues to this day. Currently, when some media choose to report about "the Sixties," they derive background coverage and image positioning from distorted archival reports. This perpetuates simplistic stereotypes and generalizations as valid truths.

The media, sometimes sympathetic to students and their political demonstrations, chose then, and often still choose, to reflect inaccurately the true context of the era. Media bias has led to a distorted construction of Baby Boomers as outlandish personalities, including notorious celebrities connected to student demonstrations. Some journalists and news accounts actually encouraged an escalation of militancy, theatrical expression, and revolutionary behavior.

Thomas Frank, author of *The Conquest of Cool: Business Culture, Counterculture, and the Rise of Hip Consumerism*, provides substantial evidence of mobilization of bias in his critique of business and the Sixties. He observes that mentioning the Sixties and associated images arouses in some "an astonishing amount of rage against what many still imagine to have been an era of cultural treason."

Although the Sixties era has been commonly positioned as a time of narcissism and social destructiveness, most young people in my experience consciously embraced a philosophy of non-violence while they opposed the horrific violence of racism, poverty, environmental assaults, and American bombardment of Vietnam in an undeclared and constitutionally illegal war.[6]

I write from personal experience to this point: Most Boomers were going about the business of earning college degrees or starting careers—albeit sometimes in slow motion because of the social struggles—while playing active roles in grassroots mobilization. They were far more motivated by a sense of obligation to others than by self-gratification.

Another interesting but complex concept has played a role in manufacturing what society now thinks of as the bad Sixties. This is the "theory of co-optation" or the tendency of the marketing industry to have quickly embraced young Boomers' powerful iconographic images and metaphors, transforming them into commercial messages. Thus, the symbols of the Cultural Revolution became distilled into come-hither selling images in magazine ads and television commercials. The creative revolutionaries in the advertising industry chose to mimic and mass-produce counterculture so that their corporate clients could cash in on the youth psychographic. The more ardent proponents of this theory even claim that the co-optation process helped to nullify the revolutionary aspects of the counterculture, thereby softening its threat to mainstream value consensus.

I believe, at the very least, that co-optation by the marketing industry—*my* industry—helped to synthesize in society's collective memory the most superficial, unsavory, cynical, pugnacious images of the student antiwar and democratic mobilization movements of the Sixties and Seventies. Businesses also made money through co-optation, which, by itself, is not necessarily a bad thing. When this commercially manufactured history *becomes* history, however, many start having a problem with the prevailing official record, as do I.

Part of the mission of this book, if you have not already guessed, is to help put the record on a balanced course so future pundits and policymakers can embrace a more realistic portrayal of a generation and its defining era—and subsequently can create more truthful and resonant marketing messages.

Most members of the generation do not appreciate businesses implying that Boomers lacked patriotism. Boomers will not reward companies that tell them that a quest for anarchy, or something close to it, was the underlying motivation for civil disobedience.

When marketers try to connect emotionally with the generation by appealing to nostalgia, they sometimes convey a message that Boomers were egregiously irresponsible, self-absorbed, and hedonistic during the Sixties. The imagery often communicates that Boomers were unpatriotic given the gravity of a nation at war and a society in upheaval. Marketers may reveal this underlying belief structure by using humor, such as the worn-out images of over-the-hill Boomers trying to recapture Woodstock or gray-haired free spirits that "head out on the highway" to a disconnected, self-gratifying existence.

Invalid assumptions can easily communicate a lack of respect and understanding.

It would be interesting if a valiant company undertook a different marketing approach surrounding this historical period, instead of just trying to capitalize on the decontextualized, depoliticized symbols and art forms that prevailed, including rock music.

The wrenching civil disobedience over U.S. Vietnam War policies caused many to sacrifice domestic tranquility for a higher purpose. Boomers shared a common goal of creating a more egalitarian and peace-loving society. They acted in the traditions of the nation's founders by confronting the ruling elite and holding these people more accountable. The worst rebels of the Baby Boomer Generation do not represent the true nature of the generation any more than the worst segregationists from the GI Generation represent the will and values of that cohort.

Not necessarily embracing either side of the Vietnam War debate, one potential message could recognize that many passionate people gave their best to fight injustice and inequality. In the process, they constructed more humanistic realities. They fought in Vietnam against the spread of communism, perhaps not always willingly, but dutifully; they fought on college campuses for greater human rights and a more inclusive nation.

Boomers came back to their communities from overseas and universities, inspired by a newfound populism, and they gave back to social service groups, nonprofit organizations, and grassroots organizing committees. They adapted with courage during a difficult chapter in American history, and they have become engaged citizens today who speak out, vote, and stay committed to doing good works in their communities.

The Boomer commitment to constructive confrontation and conflict informs their participation in the democratic process. This was their engagement then, and it is in the fiber of their collective character today. Their spirit of activism lives on.

Such messages would be a powerful way to link a responsible company with a huge cohort unwilling to be overly apologetic about this difficult time.

Tap these messages with sensitive marketing communications, and you will have latched onto a powerful motivational opportunity that can become a rousing future product reality.

CHAPTER 4

Challenging Negative Images of Aging

A S I AM writing this book, Baby Boomers are just waking up to the reality that they are the aging population to which many negative images are now applied. This fact came home to the author upon discovering a multi-page harangue against Boomers in a June 2000 *Time* magazine article entitled "Twilight of the Boomers." This tongue-in-cheek excoriation denounced Baby Boomers with plentiful references to mental deterioration, self-indulgence, estrogen replacement therapies, and exploding nursing home populations.

These stereotypes lurk in the background of contemporary marketing and reappear periodically. During the 30th anniversary celebration of Woodstock, for example, I recall Pepsi running a television commercial that touched almost all negative connotations associated with aging, and then connected them to Baby Boomers.

Two ten- to twelve-year-old boys watch the reunion from a hilltop and are horror-struck by the display of childish nostalgia among decisively middle-aged men and women, with Boomers appearing overweight, balding, and self-absorbed in their reverie.

One incredulous boy finally says to the other, "This is the anniversary of a historic event?" When his friend inquires about which one, the precocious boy confidently asserts, "Watergate."

The boy then asks with concern, "Do you think they'll go skinny dipping again?"

Frenetic, overweight dancers jerk and gyrate in front of them, and the other does not hesitate to exclaim, "I hope not!"

Let's reflect upon the underlying dynamic of these messages in another context. If you're a woman—and about half the readers of this book probably are—would you respond kindly to an advertiser who addresses you as "the weaker sex" and trots out images of your dutiful subservience to men and total absorption in domestic chores? Would you appreciate an advertisement that displays even the most final of final images, your unnamed tombstone that simply reads: "Wife"?

I cannot imagine women allowing this advertiser to communicate such denigrating images without raucous protests and calls for product boycotts. Furthermore, any cohesive and identifiable ethnic or cultural minority in the U.S. would resist and publicly condemn an advertiser that would associate its brand with negative stereotypes of the minority.

This is not done very often in America anymore—thank goodness.

The time is coming when Baby Boomers will not only react to negative stereotypes, even communicated in jest, but will also take aggressive actions against companies dimwitted enough to advance such offensive images.

Why would we?

Can we take a joke?

Marketers must understand that generational stereotypes, as amusingly as clever advertising agencies can communicate them, have had, are having, and will continue to have deleterious economic and social consequences. Baby Boomers are quickly learning about the penalty of what, right now, is socially acceptable denunciation of their value in society. As the *Time* article observes:

> If you're like the overwhelming majority of Boomers, your career has hit a brick wall, you haven't saved enough, your pension is underfunded, your health is deteriorating, even the medical advances that will probably extend your life will, in an especially cruel paradox, probably mean that late life will be meaner and more Spartan.

The Baby Boomer author, Daniel Okrent, concludes: ". . . your neighbors' children, simultaneously burdened with the cost of your aging and victimized by the one thing you'll hold onto—your political power—will boil with resentment."[7]

The article continues this speculation by making reference to Baby Boomers "getting squeezed on the job," experiencing "intergenerational conflict," and even "generational warfare."

Is it any wonder that Boomers will increasingly resent being cast in the role of self-absorbed, social piranhas—acceptable targets for denunciation, denigration, and wry debasement?

When drafting this section, I was not content to let the *Time* article stand as the lone unquestioned voice on this issue. I conducted online research for perhaps an hour to see if I could discover other commentaries that point toward the beginning of a new and special brand of Baby Boomer ageism, which I shall call "Genism."

Here are five representative examples:

Athens Banner-Herald: Age discrimination in both hiring and firing appears to be a growing problem for Baby Boomers, most of whom are now in their 40s and 50s, despite the protections of the Age Discrimination in Employment Act that dates to 1967. The Equal Employment Opportunity Commission, which enforces the law, said age discrimination is the fastest-growing category of complaints it receives, with 17,405 filings last year. Complaints about discrimination involving disabilities grew at the second-fastest rate.[8]

The Washington Times: A once proud nation of producers and entrepreneurs is being transformed into a country of gamblers and dimwits, as the Wall Street bankers and brokers are wagging the tails of the nation's business principals and shareholders.

Leading the charge to the precipice are America's modern day lemmings—the Baby Boomers—the "white slaves" of the New World Order. They are spending themselves out of house and home, lured by the thrill of the (gambling) game, and suckered into a false sense of prosperity by the paper gains of their stock portfolios.[9]

The American Prospect: With only one in three or four seniors able to afford appropriate care now, and with a widespread perception that the elderly are reaping more than their share of the social-welfare bounty, we are getting a taste of the conflicts that will come on a much larger scale.[10]

The Seattle Times: So where are the hip, happening Boomers, the scourges of the establishment? Napping on the La-Z-Boy watching *Seinfeld* re-runs. Boomers should be planning to use the next stage of life for the greater good. Instead they will wait to be catered to. Again, nothing new here.As they head into the sunset, nation's boomers are a bust.

—Lance Dickie, September 24, 2004

Michigan Booth Newspapers: Baby boomers will be like Velociraptors eating every health care dollar in sight," warned Hospice of Michigan President Dottie Deremo during a recent discussion on the nation's health care crisis. "We don't have a consensus in this nation about health care reform," she said. "Incremental change is not going to get us there." Meanwhile, those health care Velociraptors are getting hungrier every day."

—Rick Haglund, "Ravenous Baby Boomers Set to Devour Health Care Dollars," September 22, 2004

In my opinion, we are seeing a three-stage process unfold.

First, laying the foundation is denigration of Baby Boomers based on long-held contempt for this group's alleged self-absorbed and unpatriotic character, historically rooted in the Vietnam War era. Second, there is now an emerging employment and social ageism affecting those who are in their fifties—the Leading-Edge Baby Boomers. Finally, there are Orwellian predictions that hostility will grow and congeal as the generation reaches later stages of old age, a time when the generation may threaten to commandeer a disproportionate share of federal entitlement programs and taxpayer monies.

Clearly, it is in the generation's long-term interest to challenge marketers and media that perpetuate stereotypes, especially the special brand of Boomer ageism that links their self-absorbed, unpatriotic image from the Sixties with the traditional negative images of aging. This is an unprecedented double whammy. The price for ignoring this phenomenon may be greater than the Boomer Generation or society is willing to pay in the coming years.

This is not to conclude that Boomers totally lack a self-conscious sense of humor. We can poke fun at ourselves for our youthful naïvetè, archaic cultural styles, and oversimplification of reality during our teens and early adult years. As any comedian eventually learns, humor about a group is inevitably a very sharp, double-edged sword.

It is risky.

What may be belly-splitting funny to an advertisement's creators may also ring of disdain to a larger segment of the audience. Is it worth conveying stereotypes of one group to win the affection of another group—to become branded as prejudicial and not inclusive?

PART 2

PRINCIPLES

If you see in any given situation only what everybody else can see, you can be said to be so much a representative of your culture that you are a victim of it.

—S. I. Hayakawa

Age is whatever you think it is. You are as old as you think you are.

—Muhammad Ali

Our generation, like the one before us, must choose. Without the threat of the Cold War, without the pain of economic ruin, without the fresh memory of World War II's slaughter, it is tempting to pursue our private agendas—to simply sit back and let history unfold. We must resist the temptation.

—Bill Clinton

CHAPTER 5

Toward a Higher Marketing Consciousness

THE $750 Billion Question:

Do Boomers truly offer marketers a fertile business opportunity?

There is only one reverberating answer to this question: "Duh!"

Nevertheless, the question is being bandied daily in business media.

Marketing and media have a youth bias and we can partially thank Boomers for it. When they were younger, Boomers became Madison Avenue darlings by stimulating and popularizing youth marketing.

And it remains true today: marketers are obsessed with the 18-to-49 demo and its junior counterpart, 18-to-34. Boomers have become a neglected target audience, except by companies selling age-specific products and services. (Please, no Viagra jokes.)

People aged 50 and over haul in over half the discretionary income in the U.S. but are the targets of fewer than 10 percent of ad messages. When you consider that the nation's youth market is shrinking and the mature market is burgeoning, this reality is even more counterintuitive.

David B. Wolfe, author of *Ageless Marketing*, compiled data several years ago to reveal that people aged 40 and older outnumbered 18-to-39-year-olds—123 million to 84 million. By 2010, the imbalance will become 138 million to 87 million, an increase of 12 million.

In 2001, *Advertising Age* magazine concluded that of $8 billion spent in TV's upfront and scatter market, 55 percent targeted the

18-to-49 group. The remainder went to children (under 18) and adults 25-to-54.[11]

A youth-demo fixation appears to be driven by the "old brand-habit theory" instead of quantifiable evidence. This theory holds that brand loyalty hardens with age, and you can't teach old dogs new tricks. A recent study by AARP, the advocacy group for adults aged 50 and older, discovered that the majority of people over 50 are not overly brand loyal. Brand devotion varies more by category than by age.[12]

Of demos and psychos

To address the lingering questions about Boomer economic value, we need both a demographic and sociological perspective. As mentioned previously, those born between 1946 and 1955 are called Leading-Edge Boomers; those born between 1956 and 1964 are referred to as Late Boomers.

Most pundits agree that two sociologically distinct generations have been wrapped neatly in this nineteen-year package. The Leading-Edge Boomers are different from their younger brothers and sisters in some fundamental ways.

Members of the older group shared teenage encounters with the galvanizing experiences of the Vietnam War era and the "cultural revolution," including modern feminism, civil rights, and environmentalism. They came of age when pugnacious social and cultural forces crashed in on the Eisenhower era and John Kennedy's Camelot. Leading-Edge Boomers vividly remember the assassinations of JFK, RFK and MLK, as well as the debut of Four Lads from Liverpool on *The Ed Sullivan Show.*

Leading-Edge Boomers are most often associated with the protest movements of the Sixties, as well as over-publicized experimentation with "sex, drugs and rock n' roll." Late Boomers entered college after the Vietnam War ended in January 1973, and most experienced a more peaceful, less culturally chaotic time to start careers and begin families.

Leading-Edge Boomers are receiving a lot of attention right now because they are nearest to retirement, with bountiful implications for the housing, health, and hospitality industries, to name a few.

1946 1947 1948 1949 1950 1951 1952 1953 1954 1955 1956 1957 1958 1959 1960 1962 1963 1964

Meet Generation Jones: Boomers' Younger Brothers and Sisters

MANY GENERATIONAL OBSERVERS have recognized that a period of 19 years, the traditionally accepted span of the Boomer generation, is much too inclusive. Marketing guru David B. Wolfe, for example, believes that a true generational cohort occupies a much shorter duration than typically advocated by demographers.

In his book *Ageless Marketing*, Wolfe expands on the work of developmental psychologist Daniel Levinson by observing that "in terms of a person's sense of affinity with others and the ability to identify with and relate to them, a person's generation consists of people who are within six or seven years of his or her age."[13] Further, according to Wolfe, "This means that from a subjective perspective, the age span of a generation is 12 to 14 years."

This narrower view of the scope of a generation is also my conviction and why I have focused this book on "Leading-Edge Boomers," or those born between 1946 and 1955. Elsewhere in the book I've identified the younger cohort as either "Late Boomers" or "Trailing-Edge Boomers," consistent with traditional descriptors used by some demographers and social psychologists.

Jonathan Pontell, a visionary cultural historian and trends expert, identified the existence of a misunderstood generation existing between Leading-Edge Boomers and Generation X, and for this cohort he coined the term "Generation Jones." This self-confident and articulate 48-year-old Los Angeles-based marketing consultant has been gaining enthusiastic international support for his generational construct, as well as acknowledgement from unexpected observers such as President George W. Bush, political commentator George Stephanopoulos, comedienne Rosie O'Donnell, and Douglas Coupland, author of *Generation X*.[14]

Generation Jones has been the subject of several hundred media articles, including a cover story in *American Demographics* magazine. The Cambridge educated Pontell has been a frequent guest on national TV and radio talk shows, articulating his views about GenJones and its ascending importance in contemporary marketing thinking.

Pontell derived the new generational name from focus group research and numerous interviews, as well as years of personal reflection and his own sense of distance from older Boomers. He coined the term and defined Generation Jones in the late '90s.

In 1970s parlance, "to jones" means to have a deep yearning or habitual craving. This name addresses the younger cohort's huge expectations left unfulfilled and their disenfranchisement from full participation in the American Dream just as they were coming of age. Generation Jones refers to the idea of a large, but heretofore anonymous generation, and the name further addresses this cohort's extreme competitiveness, as in "keeping up with the Joneses."

Differing by three years with my conceptualization of the two cohorts, Pontell defines Generation Jones as those people born between 1954 and 1965.

The following discussion identifies some of the salient similarities and differences between these two generational cohorts, most often inadequately referred to as just Baby Boomers.

How do Leading-Edge Boomers differ from members of Generation Jones, demographically and culturally?

Leading-Edge Boomers were born between 1946 and 1955, while members of Generation Jones were born between 1956 and 1964 (or, according to Pontell, between 1954 and 1965). The two sub-generations or cohorts differ in some fundamental ways.

Members of the older group shared teenage and young adult encounters with the galvanizing experiences of Vietnam and the "cultural revolution," including modern feminism, civil rights, and environmentalism. They came of age when pugnacious social and cultural forces crashed in on the Eisenhower era and President John Kennedy's Camelot. They are most often associated with the protest movements of the Sixties, as well as over-publicized experimentation with sex and drugs.

Jonesers entered college and started careers after the Vietnam War ended in early 1975, and most experienced a more peaceful, less socially aggressive period. They began their young adult lives with ebullient expectations—a sense that "the world is my oyster"—but then they confronted sky-high interest rates, malaise during the Carter administration, and, because of their numbers, extreme economic competition. They were offered a plethora of credit cards from puberty onward; accordingly, many have accumulated enormous consumer debts. Many have had greater difficulty launching careers and creating long-term financial stability. Because of the increasing impact of immigration, Jonesers are much more ethnically and culturally diverse.

Popular cultural influences are also different between these groups. For example, Boomers rallied behind "Make Love, Not War," while members of GenJones chanted "No Nukes." Boomers displayed political engagement with the peace symbol; Jonesers wore POW bracelets. A significant defining event in the lives of Boomers was, of course, Woodstock. Jonesers gathered at *Live Aid*. Boomers often point to Bob Dylan as their poet and bard; Jonesers embrace Bruce Springsteen.

How does a marketer adjust strategies to accommodate the differences between them?

Beyond the collective personality differences between these two cohorts, one avenue is for marketers is understand the differences in life stage, although of course wide variability can exist within either cohort.

Leading-Edge Boomers are more likely today to be empty nesters. Many have lost one or both parents; and their careers are starting to slow down. They are thinking more actively about the next stage of life, whether this means retirement or starting a new career, moving to a new location or pursing unrequited dreams.

Jonesers are at the pinnacle of their career trajectories right now. Their children are still in school and living at home, and Jonesers are confronting serious concerns about retirement. They are still paying home mortgages, and many are struggling with large debts. They are just beginning to take on increasing responsibilities for their aging parents.

Marketing requires generalizations. Executives need to make assumptions about the major life events and challenges that are preponderant and relevant. For example, are prospects worried about paying for college education (Jonesers)? Is their biggest concern how to supervise quality care for institutionalized parents with rapidly failing health (Leading-Edge Boomers)? Is a sojourn to Europe likely to become a new traveling way of life (Boomers), or just a precious respite from a hard-driving career (GenJones)?

Are there any clear similarities between the segments?

Leading-Edge Boomers are typically impassioned idealists and social activists. Their younger siblings share idealism in many areas, but Jonesers are more pragmatic—some would say, realistic. Nevertheless, both cohorts share many values. Both famously distrust large institutions and government and both value personal freedom and individual self-expression.

Jonesers may have been too young to recall much about the Sixties, but they were old enough to be influenced by the detritus left from civil rights, Vietnam and Watergate. Further, because of the long-term impact of many social movements that dominated the Sixties and early Seventies, both groups firmly respect racial and cultural diversity, believe in safeguarding the environment, honor religious pluralism, insist upon equality between the sexes, and seek personal expression and individual liberty as central to the American experience.

Is there any validity in targeting them as one segment?

In many areas, Jonesers are closer to Generation X in terms of worldview and collective personality. Jonesers have their own life experiences that are different from their older siblings, and marketers can reach this cohort with distinctive messages appealing to their current lifestage, aspirations, and needs. Working with political and research consultants, Pontell has isolated many unique values and needs harbored by the Gen-Jones cohort.

However, intergenerational values and purchasing decisions are sometimes similar, particularly about such product categories as automobiles, furnishings and travel. Marketing messages that address broader values and themes can reach across the generational spectrum. These common values include personal development, psychological growth, health and wellness, environmental sustainability, social responsibility, egalitarian principles, and making a difference or creating a legacy.

Which industries stand to benefit most from Leading-Edge Boomers and from Generation Jones?

Leading-Edge Boomers are obviously closer to retirement—or at least closer to slowing down their careers, voluntarily or not—so some of the most promising industries include health care, financial planning, travel and tourism, and retirement housing. They're in the market for downsized primary or second homes, long-term care insurance, personal growth experiences, and education about entrepreneurship. They're also becoming insatiable grandparents.

Jonesers are still mostly in their forties, so their focus is on such areas as education for their children, further career development, learning how to master new productivity technologies, and family vacations. They're in the market for sophisticated home theaters, spa vacations, the latest electronic communication devices, and educational experiences for their adolescent children.

What should marketers keep in mind when pitching to Leading-Edge Boomers vs. GenJones?

As discussed elsewhere in this book, the validity of generational marketing as a segmentation approach begins with an interesting theory by German sociologist Karl Mannheim (1893–1947). As Mannheim observed, social and cultural events during the impressionable years of adolescence can foment and solidify a generation and its shared outlook, thus shaping subsequent life experiences with a collective consciousness.

The *zeitgeist* phenomenon—that is, the shared feeling for an era and the unique spirit of a generation—is not equally magnified for every generation. Those who become young adults during a more quiescent period are less likely to experience as strong a sense of generational connectivity, ergo the term "lost generation."

The coming-of-age era for Leading-Edge Boomers continues to mobilize and motivate this cohort today. Boomers respond to messages that call to their idealism, their desire for constructive social and political change, and their struggle to answer a universal question: "Is there something more?"

While Jonesers may have had a taste of Watergate, they came of age during a politically calmer time. Jonathan Pontell has flagged this group as being in a constant state of yearning for something more. Because of the influences of high inflation and career lassitude in their early careers, Jonesers were initially more focused on material values than their older brothers and sisters, but as they've aged they are reconnecting with less material values such as purpose, personal growth, and self-fulfillment.

Nevertheless, studies show that Jonesers score higher on concerns about job stability and financial success than their older siblings. They're more pragmatic and focused. They respond to messages that offer practical solutions to economic problems, messages that promise competitive advantages and deliver escape from ever-present stress.

Marching across the threshold

Every 8 seconds, another Boomer turns 50. That's 10 to 12 thousand per day and 4 million per year. America is getting older every month, and we can count on one-third of the U.S. population being over age 50 by 2010.

What's so fascinating about this? Well, in the entire history of the U.S.—and all of Western civilization, for that matter—there's never been such a dramatic march to maturity.

A century ago, most people did not reach retirement age; they died.

The average life expectancy at birth for someone born in 1900 was 47. By 2000, average life expectancy at birth increased to 76.5 years. Perhaps the single greatest achievement of 20th-century science was the addition of two full years to average life expectancy for every passing decade.[15]

Global pharmaceutical giants have 750 new drugs under development to target the aging process.

Now *AARP The Magazine*, the world's largest circulation magazine, heralds "60 as the new 30." Former youth icons cross the maturity threshold monthly, from Billy Crystal to Lauren Hutton. It's astounding to consider that members of The Eagles and Fleetwood Mac, defining rock supergroups of the Seventies, are targets today for senior discount programs.

Two-thirds of all those who have lived past age 65 are alive today, presenting a daunting view of the future. Global pharmaceutical giants have 750 new drugs under development to target the aging process and expand our mortal timeline even further.[16] A culture once dominated by youth values is transforming to the psychological agendas more characteristic of older adults.

This population and cultural shift is so large and all-encompassing that it as difficult to notice the change in direction, as if trying to perceive the *Queen Mary 2* turning in the middle of the Atlantic while you're blithely dancing the night away.

As historian and social observer Theodore Roszak observed, "The future belongs to maturity."

Beyond trends, toward transformations

Boomers have proven that they don't just occupy life stages, they transform them. Ken Dychtwald, Ph.D., author of several books on the subject, including *Age Power: How the 21st Century will be ruled by the New Old*, points out that Boomer trends become social phenomena and cultural obsessions. Allow me to elaborate.

When the multitude of Boomer children overwhelmed mealtime during the Fifties, a company called Gerber introduced portioned and prepared foods for babies and toddlers—such memorable delicacies as pulverized spinach in a jar.

When the nascent medium of television enraptured preschoolers with the *Mickey Mouse Club*, mass marketers found in TV the perfect medium to propel galactic fads such as Hula Hoops and Silly Putty.

When Boomer teenagers developed a taste for carryout food and its conveniences, McDonald's grew from one humble California store to a national French-frying juggernaut.

When GM became a metaphor for Big Brother during the anti-authoritarian Sixties, Germany and Japan, America's World War II arch-enemies, captured the automotive market with VW Beetles and Toyotas.

When Boomers decided to lose the extra pounds from consuming so much fast food, jogging became a craze, and Nike became a Fortune 500 company.

One question fellow Boomer Dychtwald poses is worth further contemplation. Considering the paradigm-busting history of the Boomer generation, why would anyone apply yesterday's thinking about aging and retirement to tomorrow's possibilities?

It is ludicrous to expect members of such an outspoken generation to accept their parents' standards for retirement life. It is equally ludicrous to foresee them sauntering passively into a golfing sunset, estranged and disenfranchised. Recall the battle cry many Boomers enjoined during Vietnam: "Hell no, we won't go!"

Today's economic and social realities portend a different kind of retirement era, one driven by activism more than resignation. We're on the threshold of an entirely new life stage—a third age.

Showing the money, taking the money

Consider the economic clout held by Boomers and older generations. Today, American adults aged 50 and over represent 38 percent of the population. That share will explode to 47 percent by 2020. According to data collected by the U.S. Census and Federal Reserve, the 78 million Americans who were 50 or older as of 2001 controlled $28 trillion, or 67 percent of the country's wealth. In 2000, households with someone in the 55-to-64 age group had a median net worth of $112,048—about fifteen times the $7,240 reported for adults under age 35.[17]

Concerning the dim-witted question leading this chapter, adults over age 50 control more than $750 billion of all household discretionary income; mature consumers outspend younger adults by a factor of two to one.

A huge generation guarantees attractive and sizeable market segments for all comers, whether business-to-consumer or business-to-business. A generation accustomed to experimentation and an abundance of brand choices since infancy does not support the myth that brand loyalty hardens with age. A generation warily observing its parents age is also learning about the unattractive aspects of maturity, longevity, and retirement.

Another salient fact about the Boomer generation is the same conclusion marketers must grasp when targeting any segment. Segmentation is still based on descriptive generalizations. The Boomer generation is not a homogeneous market. Nearly one-third of the generation is not prosperous today, or even marginally comfortable; 25 million Boomers are broke. This is gloomy news, but people without liquid assets still consume a plethora of products and services designed to address their economic handicaps.

Furthermore, according to MetLife's Mature Market Institute, almost 17 percent of the generation is not Caucasian, with 12 percent African American, 4 percent Asian, and nearly 1 percent Native American. Almost 10 percent of the generation is of Hispanic origin, while representing several different races. Over 12 percent of the generation has never married, versus 4 percent of the GI Generation. Around 14 percent of Boomers are divorced, versus just under 7 percent of their parents' generation. And Boomers are one of the most educated generations in American history, with over 88 percent having graduated from high school, and almost one-third having attained a Bachelor's or higher graduate degree.

The Boomer business opportunity is without question a huge opportunity, and as I'm writing this paragraph, many businesses are finally considering these untapped possibilities. I suppose that what seems to be evangelism today will someday appear more like preaching to the choir. But, for right now, the challenge to educate and enlist continues; too many just don't get it.

CHAPTER 6

A Theory of Bipolar Metavalues

BOOMERS seek value in their product and lifestyle choices. They also color those choices with their core values.

This simple idea underscores most of marketing communications. It's neither a new insight nor particularly revolutionary. It is, however, the essential test that all marketing communication strategies must ultimately pass. With few exceptions, we can only sell to our customers what they value.

As David B. Wolfe, author of *Ageless Marketing,* observes: "The most effective marketing is the marketing that helps people process their lives."

We process the events and choices in our lives based on our values. Some values are enduring and can find expression during various stages of life; other values emerge with changing circumstances and the influence of the aging process or, as Wolfe refers to it, season of life.

Dr. Abraham Maslow, the eminent humanistic psychologist, believed that humans cannot achieve true psychological health and personal freedom unless they grow to embrace such values as wholeness, perfection, completion, justice, aliveness, richness, simplicity, beauty, goodness, uniqueness, effortlessness, playfulness, truth, and self-sufficiency. These are the metavalues, or values that become the foundation for all other values—a set of higher guidelines for living that exceed expediency or whim.

This book makes a case for the importance of Boomers' coming-of-age values, those firmly held beliefs and attitudes that formed during their tumultuous teens and early adult years in the second half of the twentieth century.

The validity of generational marketing as a segmentation approach begins with an interesting theory posited by German sociologist Karl Mannheim. "Zeitgeist" is a shared feeling for an era and the unique spirit of a generation. As Mannheim observed, social upheaval during the impressionable years of adolescence can foment and solidify a generation and its collective outlook. Mannheim similarly observed: "Early impressions tend to coalesce into a natural view of the world."

Just as the lessons of depression-era economic deprivation live on with the children of the twenties, the Leading-Edge Baby Boomers—those born between 1946 and 1955—carry with them an indelible sense of intra-generational connectivity, a quixotic attraction to a chaotic period when effusive societal change was the norm.

The coming-of-age era of their lives—those fragile years that for Americans fell roughly between San Francisco's Summer of Love in 1967 and the end of the U.S. involvement in the Vietnam War during January 1975—continues to mobilize and motivate Boomers today.

Although Mannheim's theory has never been proven empirically, neither has been Abraham Maslow's hierarchy-of-needs model of psychological development. Maslow's powerful interpretation of human needs has been widely adopted, has unassailable construct validity, and continues to explain many complexities of human behavior.

The zeitgeist phenomenon is not as magnified for every generation; those becoming young adults during a quiescent period are less likely to experience such a strong sense of generational connectivity. I'm convinced that Leading-Edge Boomers lived through one of the most powerful, indelible zeitgeists of the 20th century . . . thus leading to many common values, as well as an idealistic attraction to music, art, and cultural phenomena of that time.

Boomer metavalues are unique in that they have always involved conflicts. For example, most Boomers will agree that government authority is a fickle mistress: too little and she is wildly unpredictable, too much and she becomes a prison warden. So this Boomer metavalue becomes the competing allure of authority and independence. Boomers want both, rarely all or none.

It is logical, therefore, to present Boomer metavalues as they exist on a choice continuum, a struggle between often competing forces. Similar to the challenge of bipolar emotional states that causes the sufferer to waver from depression to mania, Bipolar Metavalues sometimes push the individual to extremes in competing value choices. Sometimes these opposing values compete within the psyche of an individual, depending on mental framework and immediate circumstances. The following discussion identifies some of these metavalues and juxtaposes them with today's challenges in line with sometimes conflicted critical life choices.

Authority	Independence
Accountability	Laissez-faire
Community	Anonymity
Spontaneity	Discipline
Engagement	Detachment
Generosity	Material Gratification
Health	Hedonism
Transcendence	Temporality
Unity	Diversity

Authority/Independence

Then Boomers have always had a tentative relationship with authority because it is in their nature to question authority. This is the generation that challenged the government, corporations, national priorities, and traditional religious institutions. Boomers often defined the national debate around women's rights, race relations, and U.S. foreign policy. Their collective quest was personal choice and freedom of expression, or, in the vernacular of the time, "Do your own thing."

Boomers have evolved in their lives to become the sources of authority they once questioned.

Yet, the generation grew up surrounded by authority in a

post-World-War-II era. GI Generation parents and teachers expected dutiful pledges to the flag during grade school. Many elementary school age Boomers learned moral values from structured organizations such as the Boy Scouts and Girl Scouts. Children of the Fifties grew up addressing their elders with formal surnames, and rarely did Leading-Edge Boomers experience hostile confrontations in the school classroom between students and teachers. I remember just one instance throughout all my elementary and secondary education when a student openly confronted a teacher and did not quickly back down. Television shows of the 1950's such as *Father Knows Best* and *The Adventures of Ozzie & Harriet* portrayed mostly respectful children and gently authoritative parents, yet gave tacit permission to mild antiauthoritarian behavior though such harmless characters as Beaver Cleaver and young Dennis in *Dennis the Menace*.

Now Boomers have evolved in their lives to become the sources of authority they once questioned: corporate executives, political leaders, and pundits. Political ideology is a major theme in the national conversation with increasing conflict between conservative and liberal factions. Authority and independence find expression on either side of the political debate. Conservatives seek less government intervention and taxation to allow free markets to flourish; they pursue greater independence from government regulations on businesses. Liberals seek greater authority over multinational corporations to protect the rights of workers. They seek independence for middle-class Americans from the potential tyranny of corporations dedicated solely to the bottom line. They fear an American plutocracy dominated by a handful of wealthy power brokers.

As Boomers age, they face many new challenges on the authority/independence value spectrum. Should Social Security be strengthened to supplement the income of so many who are deficient in retirement savings, or should we remove the handcuffs of this extraordinary entitlement

burden to create privatized retirement accounts? Will eldercare evolve to embrace home health care and other ways to
enable Boomers to remain self-directed in their daily lives, or
will nursing homes remain as the only realistic choice?
Where does society draw the lines between freedom and personal expression, moral and immoral behavior?

Marketing implications

This metavalue raises interesting possibilities: communicating
the metaphorical freedom of the open road while suggesting respect
for traditional sources of authority. This idea reflects at least one
brand strategy of Harley-Davidson, in a nutshell. The Harley rider
personifies the modern maverick, but who can forget Harley clubs
riding in packs to honor the American flag following the September 11, 2001 attack on the World Trade Center? The authority/
independence metavalue can also find realization in brand personalities for products as diverse as cellular telephones and insurance
annuities. Brands that speak with authority yet appear absent of
arbitrary control can connect with authority-minded, indepen-
dence-craving Boomers.

Accountability/Laissez-faire

Then Boomers entered adulthood during a storm of conflict over
accountability, both of institutions and government. With the
assassinations of John Kennedy, Bobby Kennedy, and
Martin Luther King, plus an omnipresent jungle war
framing their early years, Boomers faced fundamental concerns over the veracity of political leaders and their
dedication to serving the people. Boomers perceived many
inconsistencies between the nation's high-minded founding
principles and the application and realization of these principles during a time of growing outrage and conflict. Nevertheless, idealism reigned.

The student movement, especially SDS (Students for a
Democratic Society), demanded candor and communication
from the administrations of both Lyndon Johnson and
Richard Nixon. SDS demonstrated for greater accountability.

Members asked the government to step up to higher standards of performance.

However, when frustrated with individual initiative—a sense that challenging the status quo changes nothing—college students of the Sixties searched for other principles by which to live. Their reaction sometimes seemed to become a collective, "Whatever."

Laissez-faire thinking—a choice not to interfere in the affairs of others—to "do your own thing"—reflected a counterbalancing movement to live and let live, to withdraw from engagement with sources of authority.

> As they face the coming struggle between federal entitlements and a growing national debt, Boomers have difficult choices.

This end of the spectrum of the accountability/laissez-faire metavalue led many Boomer college students to seek counsel from philosophers such as Emmanuel Kant and Frederich Nietzsche. They embraced the idea that humans are ultimately isolated in a hostile universe and the only true value is freedom of choice—so, if the government leaders are so insane . . . whatever. Rather than confronting the atrocities they perceived, and the call for greater accountability in institutions and government, they sometimes wallowed in alienation. They felt like strangers in a strange land.

Now   As they face the coming struggle between federal entitlements and a growing national debt, Boomers have difficult choices. One faction will hold the government accountable for runaway deficit spending and demand severe cuts.

In late February 2004, then-Federal Reserve Chairman Alan Greenspan announced that the country cannot afford the retirement benefits promised to Baby Boomers and pressed Congress to trim them. Greenspan's position was echoed by the Alliance for Worker Retirement Security, a coalition of more than 40 employer groups. "Social Security's pending crisis can no longer be pushed off to future generations," Derrick Max, the group's executive director told the Associated Press.[18]

Another faction will ask more of government as an increasing number of retirement-age citizens fall short of meeting their retirement financial needs. The head of AARP, William Novelli, concluded that Greenspan's trimming proposals "would be unfair to Boomers and younger workers, pulling the rug out from under their retirement security."[19] The perception follows: large print giveth while small print taketh away.

This debate may lead some to consider combative engagement and others to withdraw in futility. Where does personal responsibility begin and government accountability end? What is the function of government in a mature society when it comes to taking care of its oldest citizens? These are the bold questions that will demand answers in the next twenty years.

Marketing implications

Many Boomers have struggled recently with the metavalue of accountability/*laissez-faire*. Stock market manipulation by a number of high-profile corporations, and the resulting crash of the markets, has forced many pre-retirees to consider the proper balance between government regulations and undeterred, freewheeling capital markets.

Business recently discovered that trust takes years to earn and can evaporate in days or hours. Companies pursuing trusting business relationships with Boomers need clear messages that communicate high ethical standards, including mitigation of conflict of interest, accountability among employees, and forthright communications to the financial community. Otherwise, many Boomers will withdraw, literally and metaphorically.

Trust takes years to earn and can evaporate in days or hours.

Corporations will be expected in the future to focus on win-win business strategies—not only for their shareholders but also for their customers, employees, and global stakeholders. Those with effective corporate governance based on this metavalue—a healthy balance between financial accountability and an unfettered free-enterprise system—will have greater competitive advantages, thus attracting and retaining talent and generating positive reactions in the marketplace.

Community/Anonymity

Then Children during the Fifties and Sixties lived with massive numbers of peers at every turn and thus were confronted with the task of sharing resources. This often included standing in line and placement in large classes throughout their primary and secondary education. Television fostered a sense of community through programming such as *The Howdy Doody Show* and the *Mickey Mouse Club*. Children saw themselves as part of a much larger group, connected by common culture and concerns. Yet, the media culture also praised the individual, the notion of standing tall for oneself while confronting life's adversities. Television programs such as *Lassie*—the story of a solitary boy and his amazing collie—and *Have Gun, Will Travel*—the story of a maverick, justice-seeking Old West gunfighter—fostered the idea of individual initiative, creating a powerful sense of self as separate from the group. Then, as the children of the Baby Boom became teenagers and young adults, the idea of community was defined by such cultural events as Woodstock and communal living arrangements. Alternatively, the idea of the autonomous person found realization through images of the solo American backpacker hitchhiking across the United States or throughout Europe.

Now Retirement creates a new challenge for Boomers. Community living strategies, such as continuing care retirement communities, insure safety, cost sharing, and a sense of connection to others at potentially the loneliest time of life. Yet, many feel the call of the open road and want to get away from the maddening crowd. They feel compelled to escape from the complexity of relationships and the challenges of teambuilding that perhaps dominated former careers. These are the Boomers who today are buying 35-acre ranches in wide-open spaces such as Wyoming and Montana.

Marketing implications

Companies can build brands and brand messages to appeal to both poles of the *Community/Anonymity* metavalue. Recognizing the need for community, motorcycle manufacturer Harley-Davidson sponsors H.O.G.—Harley-Davidson Owners Group—which fosters community and connections among riders in events such as a famous one in Sturgis, South Dakota.

Started in 1983, H.O.G. today includes 1,157 chapters, with 800,000 members worldwide. The company captures the essence of this metavalue on its member website, first by showing a multi-generational group photo, somewhat dominated by middle-aged riders, and then by encapsulating the slogan *Live to Ride, Ride to Live.* The bike's saddle becomes part of the destination. At the same time, we can applaud Harley-Davidson for its personification of the lone eagle, the single detached rider heading down the highway to nowhere in particular.

An overriding marketing theme makes the motorcycle manu-facturer's insights about its customers more clear-cut: *Express your-SELF in the company of others.* (Typographical emphasis added). Deeper in this website, the appeal to Community/Autonomy achieves even greater clarity: *What does the future hold? No one can say for sure, but from here the road ahead looks long, wide open, winding, and scenic—with lots of new friends to make along the way.*[20]

Spontaneity/Discipline

Then The Sixties and Seventies are often associated with the *Age of Aquarius*, a time of tribal awareness when Boomers felt enti-tled to pursue whim and answer the call of constant change. Relationships changed overnight. Styles and fads ebbed and flowed almost monthly. The cultural calendar followed breaking news events, coupled with the latest hit rock album. Discipline took a bow and exited the stage. Some dropped out of college, traveled the country, sampled alternative liv-ing arrangements and assumed fleeting identities. Sometime after the end of the Vietnam War, however, discipline returned with rigor. Boomers burned the midnight oil at jobs and became intensely focused on career achievement. Dilettantes returned to school. Others built businesses from former hippie preoccupations such as organic gardening, candle making, blended juices or natural oatmeal cookies.

Now Expect that Boomers may return to some of the spontaneity of youth, especially those who have educated their children and are confronting the tedium of worn-out careers and tired marriages. Because middle age is a season of reassessment, often accompanied by disenchantment, it is reasonable to predict that once predictable lives will become less predictable. Discipline imposed by career focus and child rearing may soon become less of a priority. This is often a time of life when people divorce, change careers, or return to school. Spontaneity leads to change. Discipline leads to commitment. In midlife, both forces can and do influence significant personal changes.

Marketing implications

The travel industry is breaking the business code for this metavalue. For many Boomers, the carefully planned two-week vacation is long gone. Major airlines now actively market bargain getaway mini-vacations. United Airlines bombards its Mileage Plus customers with value-rates for trips lasting no more than four days domestically and up to ten days internationally. A couple can decide on Wednesday to leave behind the summer heat of Dallas and be hiking in the Rocky Mountains two days later. They will return to Dallas the following Monday or Tuesday, and still qualify for this bargain, short-term fare. On the other hand, the same airline rewards disciplined use of its frequent traveler card, with truly useful rewards accumulating at a grindingly slow pace for typical airline travelers. Perhaps one route to this metavalue is the timeworn notion that discipline leads to spontaneity.

Engagement/Detachment

Then Think of the Vietnam War era and in your mind's eye you may see the image of impassioned college students marching down a campus thoroughfare, carrying signs of protest. Civic engagement, as oppositional as it became, was the theme of the time. Protesting is a form of engagement, as much as protest events are often berated by opponents of controversy. College students of the mid-Sixties to the mid-Seventies learned important lessons outside the classroom about organizing, delegating, setting agendas, managing group discussions, leading consensus, and opposing critics. Another image of the time that comes to mind is a farmhouse somewhere in the middle of nowhere, previously abandoned by the urbanization of America, but reoccupied by young college dropouts. Their only preoccupation seems to be growing organic vegetables and cannabis. These former middle-class kids have chosen the route of separation—an alternative to an uptight, bureaucratic society.

Now Marc Freedman, in his landmark book *Prime Time, How Baby Boomers Will Revolutionize Retirement and Transform America*, predicts a coming renaissance of civic engagement, a revitalized Boomer generation involved in eliminating many social problems through voluntary contributions of time and talent. This book is an articulate prediction and an impassioned plea for Boomers to do the right thing by joining and giving. Whether or not this comes true to the extent envisioned by Freedman depends on many complex factors, not the least of which is the Boomer tendency to detach from the hectic pace and pressures of modern living. Will there be an exodus to Central and South America, where expatriated Americans slow down and leave to memory the many complex problems of their native land? Will they choose to slow down or, like former president Jimmy Carter, will they spend retirement in service of others?

Marketing implications

Actually, engagement and detachment mix much better than oil and water. I remember one day of physical agony when I clawed and tripped to the top of a fourteen-thousand foot mountain in Colorado called Quandary. My quandary was whether or not I could

keep up with my client, fifteen years my junior, who most succinctly could be described as a mountain moose.

Near the top of this peak, we came across a group of cheerful
workers who were reclaiming the fragile areas surrounding the
trail. About half the workers were either retirees or old enough to
be. I observed how each seemed to be working solo, relishing
the vigorous work two-and-a-half miles above sea level; they were
alone but engaged. Marketers can appeal to this metavalue by
giving people solo challenges that serve a larger group purpose.
Many nonprofit organizations are adapting their annual fundraising campaigns to become tests of physical endurance,
from walking marathons to bicycling tours through the Rocky
Mountains.

Generosity/Material Gratification

Then One day while driving from Topeka, Kansas, to a farm near
Manhattan and Kansas State University, my driving companion turned onto Interstate 70 from a county road. On the
access ramp stood a forlorn-looking vagabond, a young man
about our age who was ostensibly thumbing his way across
the country. He held up a hastily made sign with a single
word neatly printed: Denver. He looked approachable, the
kind of person who appeared safe to pick up during a time
of so much hitchhiking among young people. However, my
friend, who was driving the car, held up his left hand with
the thumb and index finger about an inch apart, a curious
gesture suggesting that we were only traveling a short distance. My friend's nonverbal message said, "We're turning off
soon, but if we were traveling farther down the road, we'd
be happy to give you a lift. Peace, brother."

What is remarkable about this trivial event, and why I
still remember it, is what it symbolized: a buoyant generosity that included a desire not to offend even a hitchhiking
stranger, a lingering promise of helpfulness: "Sure, you can
crash at my pad."

People helped each other out during this time of peace

worship and brotherly love, sometimes in extraordinary ways. On the contrary, Boomers famously accumulated possessions in a time of anti-materialism. Lava lamps cost good money; so do candles and incense. One of the nation's most economically prosperous generations has never been shy about self-gratifying materialism, or ego satisfaction.

Now This generation has not been lauded for its generosity, even though many civic and community organizations depend on Boomers for their annual drives. Especially since the events of September 11, 2001, many public service organizations have struggled with declining membership and languishing fundraising campaigns. With predicted shortfalls in retirement accounts and the possibility of extended careers, civic organizations are wary of the financial future. Many Boomers do have civic spirits that endure in spite of short-term financial hardship, but many turn away from service to others when it might mean curtailing a few rounds of golf or not purchasing the next generation of computer or the latest electronic gadget.

Marketing implications

Nonprofit organizations are making excellent strides at rewarding Boomer generosity with material satisfaction. Public television has mastered this art by collaborating with pundits and artists and offering tangible, value-added rewards for contributions.

For example, Rick Steves has helped bring Europe to the living rooms of adventure-travel-craving Boomers for almost two decades. Rick advocates smart, independent travel throughout Europe, with an eye for the budget conscious. His 82 television episodes are candid, humorous, and memorable. In addition to producing a library full of videos, he has also written 27 European travel books. These valuable information resources on the best of European travel have become attractive gifts in exchange for contributions to public television. During periodic fund drives, Rick often travels to local stations and promotes his tapes and books as gifts in return for donations.

Health/Hedonism

Then   When we started the first semester of our second year in graduate school, my new roommate Steve had an immediate impact on my grease-loving appetite when he began preparing sophisticated vegetarian meals for us. In spite of my tendency to fry bacon and eggs on Saturdays in opposition to Steve's stern admonitions, I nevertheless became more conscious of food and how what I eat might determine my future health and longevity. Most people who were college students at the time will wince when reminded of a bodacious hangover following a night of too many tequila shooters or pitchers of beer, or both. Yet, those same hedonists often confronted their morning-after hangovers with handfuls of vitamins and exotic blended vegetable juices. We partied and then repented with equal abandon.

Now   Steve, with his once-upon-a-time quirky attitudes about eating greens and grain, was typical of the future customers of General Nutrition Center and Whole Foods, as well as thousands of boutique health food stores that have set up shop across the land. The ethos of natural and wholesome food has become ubiquitous and today has been realized in almost all aspects of contemporary society. (See also, *LOHAS: Genesis of a New Market Segment.*)

Marketing implications

Even at a neighborhood convenience store such as 7-Eleven you can find products packaged for their alleged healthfulness, from exotic, vitamin-infused bottled waters, to nutrition bars just a few shades different from candy bars. The message today is that wholesome, healthy food can be good for you and at the same time

> Most foods and beverages today sell better if they promise to spoil you *and* sustain a healthy lifestyle.

gourmet, prudent and even lavish. New products appear at the neighborhood health food store almost weekly proclaiming exotic flavors. Traditional grocery stores have opened entire sections communicating the culture of *Do-It-Yourself Health*. Most foods and beverages today sell better if they promise to spoil you *and* sustain a healthy lifestyle. Even alcoholic beverages have evolved to include exotic blends of fruit juices and other ingredients associated with healthfulness.

Transcendence/Temporality

Then The Sixties and Seventies became infused with matters of the spirit, cross-cut by a God-Is-Dead nihilism. This meta-value became apparent perhaps most famously with The Beatles' adoption of Maharishi Mahesh Yogi, the Indian transcendental meditation guru who introduced scores of American college students to the possibilities of enlightenment without years of rigorous self-discipline and arduous dedication to meditation. Christianity also found some of its earliest born-again bearings with the popularization of traditional beliefs in such hit songs as the Doobie Brothers' 1972 hit song, "Jesus Is Just Alright." The punchy lyrics promote spiritual separation with the decidedly temporal merchandising of hard-hitting rock 'n' roll:

> *Jesus, he's my friend; Jesus, he's my friend*
> *He took me by the hand; led me far from this land . . .*[21]

Yet, within a few years, John Lennon, the often spiritually motivated elder Beatle, enjoined his generation and Americans to consider the perspective of an agnostic:

> *Imagine there's no heaven,*
> *It's easy if you try,*
> *No hell below us,*
> *Above us, only sky . . .*[22]

Boomers sometimes addressed their confused lives during a confusing chapter of history with the finality of existential philosophy. Others experienced spiritual satisfaction through mesmerizing journeys into obscure, non-Western realms of Eastern and Native American mysticism. Still others allowed God to die, giving permission to living for today.

Now Perhaps one of the most significant cultural events of 2004 was the release of *Passion of the Christ*, actor and director Mel

Gibson's portrayal of the last 12 hours in the life of Jesus. Mixing traditional Christian scriptures with the powerful medium of cinema, Gibson raised imposing new questions about one of humanity's most significant historical events: the crucifixion of Jesus Christ. Ironically, Gibson's own persona prior to the release of this film had been one of an angry, violent opponent of evil, a lethal-weapon-carrying iconoclast, unflinchingly nonchalant about exacting the death penalty on enemies who crossed his path.

Born January 3, 1956, technically three days too late to qualify as a Leading-Edge Boomer, Gibson today personifies all the extreme possibilities of temporal achievement: fame, wealth, and enormous cultural power. But within the psyche of this famous actor is a dualism characteristic of some of today's Boomers: material wealth and spiritual starvation.

In an interview on the ABC network newsmagazine *Primetime*, Gibson revealed to host Diane Sawyer that his many personal and professional conflicts could only find resolution through accepting powerlessness over addiction and the power of traditional Catholic scriptures.

"Pain is the precursor to change, which is great," Gibson said in the interview. "That's the good news." Psychic pain had led him thirteen years earlier to confront his addictions and then to achieve resolution by financing, producing and directing his gruesome, spiritually compelling movie.

Marketing implications

Modern Americans and especially modern Leading-Edge Boomers often struggle with the lure of material wealth and a corresponding sense of spiritual poverty. American culture encourages them to consume material goods, as did President George W. Bush following the September 11 tragedy. Spiritual society asks Americans to be less concerned about material gain and its transitory satisfactions. The power of these dualistic forces can find meaning with products and services that satisfy materialism while driving Boomers toward spiritual renewal.

Athletic shoe manufacturer and marketer New Balance captures the essence of this in a magazine advertisement headline: "The distance between two points is not the point." The message: buy its brand of running shoes to enable yourself to be less concerned about the trappings of a material world. Run to self-realization. Run to connect with the transcendental. Run to yourself.

Unity/Diversity

Then Woodstock, the famous August 1969 music and art fair near Bethel, New York, has been given way too much attention as a defining moment in the history of Leading-Edge Boomers. Three novice organizers pulled together nearly half-a-million people for three days without violent incidents. Certainly, it was unprecedented. Given the massive problems of sanitation and basic services for such a large crowd, the implications of this festival of "peace and love" are noteworthy.

Woodstock created a new myth with its utopian overtones: the idea that we're all the same. We're all human beings, whether man or woman, black or white, or somewhere in between. We can come together and be together. However, the reality of Woodstock was diversity: anti-war protesters vs. Vietnam vets; Black militants vs. rednecks; anti-gays vs. gays and lesbians; drug legalization advocates vs. anti-drug advocates; and anti-government advocates vs. pro-government advocates.

Now Myth sterilizes reality, making reality safer and less contaminated with inconvenient anomalies. The stories about Woodstock, imagined, hoped for, or drug induced, created a common perception that this generation is homogeneous when it comes to its core beliefs and values. Yet, Boomers are no different from any other generation when it comes to the divergence of wealth and poverty, privilege and paucity, politics and points-of-view. We share common cultural ties, and we often resonate harmoniously around the same social themes, but we have grown up to become more autonomous in the way we think and express ourselves.

Marketing implications

When you're talking about "my generation," tread softly with your assumptions about what "we" feel. We didn't all once own VW Beetles or choose to wear sandals made from automobile tire retreads. These sweeping assumptions are often stereotypes that have been sugar-coated to make them palatable. It is best to market to the values resting beneath the cultural and sociological generalizations.

For example, if you wish to portray that Boomers appreciate the lure of the open road as if to hearken back to our time of youthful wanderlust, the underlying value is personal freedom. We cherished having choices, and we still do. When we were young and naïve, those choices led to erratic experimentation. Today we face more mature trails aiming toward personal freedom as we contemplate the journey into and through retirement.

We change with the events in our lives; we evolve as our values become tested by triumph and tragedy. Bipolar Metavalues often influence us to choose a satisfying color of gray amid the extremes of black and white, and the most desirable shades change in intensity and hue as circumstances change.

A marketing colleague of mine once emphatically promised to deliver results to a client with a direct marketing strategy, no matter how uncontrollable the forces that might come to bear on the situation as the program unfolded. My colleague had no control over the price of the product or the actions of competitors.

I was incredulous.

Promising marketing results in the form of bottom-line sales is akin to a doctor promising a cure or an attorney promising success in court. Professionals cannot guarantee anything but their professionalism. My colleague was nevertheless fully committed to his bottom-line promise until his campaign did not deliver as promised. I asked him again about his guarantee of success.

He shrugged. "My commitment changed with the changing circumstances. The client did not hold up his end of the bargain."

I thought this was rather shallow at first. Why commit to something if you can so easily toss away the commitment? Then I was reminded that all Bipolar Metavalues, no matter how intractable on the surface, are fluid and follow a continuum between extremes.

CHAPTER 7

On Booming Competition

THE baby boom following World War II began like this: Maternity wards spilling into hospital hallways—motherhood arriving in the middle of an infant traffic jam. Gerber Baby Food became a household brand. So did Dr. Spock.

Public schools were ill equipped to handle the rising tide of students. I remember shivering in an American History classroom tucked away in a hastily erected pre-fabricated building next to Capper Junior High School in Topeka, Kansas. The main school building could not contain a swelling student body. This also happened in high school: rushed temporary classrooms housing annexed classes. Public schools became a good market for the manufactured housing industry.

When it came time for college, admission standards seemed to become more selective with the growth of each high school graduating class. Stanford admitted 80 percent of its applicants in the mid-1950s, but ten years later the rate fell below 30 percent.

During summer breaks, Boomers scoured the want-ads for summer jobs. My indoctrination into the world of work began at age 14 sweeping the floors of a department store. After that I washed dishes at a state fair, carried out groceries, hustled as a soda jerk in a drugstore, unloaded 100-pound bags of Ethiopian pea beans from boxcars, and flagged traffic for a highway construction crew. All of these jobs were before I turned 18.

In the summer of 1969, I counted myself lucky to land a job selling encyclopedias door-to-door in southern Texas, even with unpredictable income and sweltering late-afternoons spent canvassing rundown neighborhoods. My sales colleagues hailed from elite colleges across the nation, including Harvard and UC Berkeley. None of us wanted to sell encyclopedias, but a dismal summer job market demanded flexibility.

Career jobs were then elusive. My first position after graduate school was with the State of Kansas Department of Rehabilitation as a rehabilitation counselor— a professional responsibility paying less than most clerical jobs. Boomer worker bees were more plentiful than responsible job opportunities and good starting pay.

As Leading-Edge Boomers reached the middle stage of their careers, many found themselves without a clear career horizon. Factory work immigrated overseas. Middle management jobs disappeared faster than the explosion of a dot-com bomb. Millions today face the uncertainty of a downsizing economy and upsizing job competition. Many are underemployed as people with graduate degrees take low-paying service jobs. With yet another Boomer turning age 50 every seven seconds, the future promises a glut of dispossessed and disenfranchised mature citizens, many financially incapable of affording retirement.

Outspoken critics will propose all kinds of reasons to explain why so many people have inadequately prepared themselves for their retirement. They'll remind us of Boomer narcissism coupled with a live-for-today mentality. They'll analyze collective credit-card debt as a clear symbol of irresponsible personal financial management. They'll overlook anomalies such as how high school counselors of the time encouraged students to pursue teaching; the demographic trend indicated a huge need for educators. By the time many Leading-Edge Boomers graduated from college, teachers faced layoffs. The meal had passed through the python. Teachers were in surplus.

What is unlikely to come under close scrutiny is a post-World War II society that focused more on economic expansion and fertility than it did on the long-term social consequences of an unabated fertility rate. At the apex of the boom in 1957, American women on the average were delivering 3.7 live births.

The real obstacles of a crowded workplace and highly competitive job market with limited opportunities will not factor into the critics' calculation of blame.

The Boomer glut presents an unprecedented generational problem. Too many people are competing for limited resources, whether snagging rock concert tickets or securing long-term health care. And since their arrival onto the American stage beginning in January 1946, Boomers have paid the price: diminished advancement opportunities, insufficient rewards for hard work, and employment disruption due to layoffs from job exportation (off-shoring), and corporate downsizing.

Then there is the nature of the economic system that nurtured a super-sized generation. Boomers grew up in an international order of market-driven economies, where a cacophony of marketing messages nudged them to consume. From the beginning of their long journey through TV land, they became molded and shaped by companies asking them to buy more and dispose quickly so they could buy more. Patriotism implied consumption, not frugality.

Soon it's going to be easy to blame millions for inadequate retirement assets. It's going to be convenient to criticize those who must become dependent on the largess of social service organizations and shrinking federal and state entitlements. If only those lazy Boomers had worked harder, planned better, saved more.

CHAPTER 8

Living Younger Rather than Older

IN ITS outspoken march from the 1950s, 1960s, and into the 1970s, the Baby Boom Generation created the first youth culture in America. When this massive cohort reached young adulthood, its music, dress, attitudes, and social agenda dominated mass media. Youthfulness achieved full expression through bell-bottom jeans, long hair, rock and roll, communal gatherings, hitchhiking, European backpacking, liberal politics, noncommittal sexuality, confrontations with authority, drug experimentation, and constant role testing.

In their hearts, Baby Boomers have never stopped being young.

In their hearts, Baby Boomers have never stopped being young if the fundamental hallmarks of youth are experimentation and unconventional thinking.

They never will.

In a June 2002 article, *Seattle Post-Intelligencer* columnist Bill Virgin observed: "...evidence, to the contrary, they (Baby Boomers) are not getting old, dammit. Yes, they'll spend money on the medical marvels to stem the tide of aging, but far more than previous generations, they'll buy products oriented toward the young, and they'll insist anything marketed to them not be sold to them as old people."

Critics have often observed that either Baby Boomers refused to grow up when the time came, or they were much slower than preceding generations to cast away the trappings of youth.

There is truth in each of these observations.

Some today refuse to relinquish, by any measure, the youth-defining expressions of yesteryear. When you visit Venice Beach, California, or Boulder, Colorado, you will find enclaves of graying hippies who seem locked in a time warp. They still dress and sometimes behave as if today is just another day in the never-ending *Age of Aquarius*.

On the other hand, a much larger portion of the Leading-Edge segment still listens to classic rock music and continues to question, even challenge, arbitrary authority. Members of this larger group may look middle-age in the classic sense, gray hair and body fat included; they may drive mammoth SUVs; and they may appear to be well-adjusted adults in the traditional sense.

Behind closed doors, they pull out and play their Jethro Tull CDs and party hardy with friends. They still have an endemic disrespect for authority. Popular culture from the Sixties and Seventies still finds its way into candle-lit living rooms, on European sojourns, or with the guaranteed popularity of retrospective movies such as Oliver Stone's, *The Doors*.

AARP conducted a nationwide survey of Baby Boomers between April and June 2002. The survey involved 25-minute telephone interviews with 2,127 Boomers, age 38 to 57. Then, to create an understanding of how Boomer attitudes about important life issues compare and contrast with other age groups, the researchers surveyed 781 Americans age 18 to 37, and 758 Americans age 57 and older. A companion study used focus group interviews with Boomers in three U.S. cities.

Among many interesting findings, this study confirmed that Boomers are chronologically in midlife, but the generation's attitudes about critical issues such as how often they think about the future more closely resemble those of younger adults. (Boomers 64 percent, younger 78 percent, and older 41 percent).

One survey question asked, "Five years from now, do you expect things in your life will be better, the same, or worse than they are right now?" The youngest segment, aged 18 to 37, revealed the most optimism with 93 percent feeling that the future will get better. Right behind them, 77 percent of Boomers keep the same optimistic outlook, while only 41 percent of adults over age 57 see the future through such rose-colored glasses.

Forever Young is the Boomer way of life. And why should anyone give it up? The cohort's youth culture has been the wellspring of idealism, the fountain of relentless energy to make the world a better place, and often the source for continuing challenges to the status quo. It has fostered and still attempts to cultivate women's liberation, racial integration, and economic equality for all segments of society. It has forced the U.S. government and multinational corporations to be mindful of their accountability in a watchful society.

Youthful ideals and their expression persist and idealism will emerge again as the generation faces the challenges and conflicts of aging.

CHAPTER 9

Mitigating the Signs of Aging

WITH the help of mass marketers and media, Baby Boomers defined youth in a new way, not only as an existential fact, but also as an ideal to be preserved and glorified.

Mother Nature sees things differently, and more than three decades of wear and tear have left their telltale signs. No matter what augmentations of their physical bodies they embrace, most still look middle-aged. The less fit of the lot, or the genetically challenged, look downright old.

However, many Baby Boomers concerned about ageism and the deleterious consequences of physical aging have adopted aggressive personal regimens to maintain as many youthful qualities as possible. Perhaps this explains why many Boomers work out so frequently, why fad diets have never been more popular, or why so many have taken the ultimate youth-defying plunge with corrective plastic surgery.

The best way to understand what is important to this group from a physical perspective is to reflect upon some icons from the generation. For example, I am thinking of musicians Mick Jagger, Cher, and Sting; news anchors Charlie Gibson and Diane Sawyer; and actors Goldie Hawn and Kurt Russell. Granted, these people are in the public eye and have vast resources to invest in maintaining a more youthful appearance, but they are still icons and show their peers how these investments can pay off.

One might argue that The Rolling Stones' Mick Jagger's deeply lined face is anything but youthful in appearance, and that argument is correct. However, what he has done successfully is maintain the aura of youth through long hair, a trim body, incomparable energy on stage, and some of the most invigorating rock and roll music in history. There is a difference between appearing older and being older as a way of self-expression. Jagger overcomes the wrinkles of age with the verve of youth. (Jagger, by the way, was born July 26, 1943, but for sake of the discussion here, his lifestyle habits and rock music influence clearly admit him to the Leading-Edge club.)

This is the critical point: whichever way a Boomer chooses to maintain a modicum of youthful attractiveness—whether with a face lift or yoga-enhanced suppleness—it's the widespread objective that counts. Boomers may be grayer and slower than during those

> Whichever way a Boomer chooses to maintain a modicum of youthful attractiveness—it's the widespread objective that counts.

bygone youthful days, but most admire those who do not easily give up ground to Mother Nature. Boomers still appreciate and honor those who remain energetic, physically active, and are in touch with contemporary styles.

A recent segment on ABC's *Good Morning America* probed the choice made by several Baby Boomers to have facial plastic surgery. The reason they did this, as proposed by host Diane Sawyer, was to be more employable in a highly competitive marketplace.

The male interviewee, an advertising executive who is 51, claimed to have received a promotion to senior vice-president soon after surgery to eliminate puffiness and lines around his eyes. Even Diane Sawyer commented that his before photo "... didn't look that bad!" The adman reacted by justifying his surgery as a choice not so much to look better, but to feel better. Feeling better about one's appearance, so he argued, puts out a positive energy that leads to positive consequences.

Whether Baby Boomers embrace age-defying strategies to look or feel better, their actions are both a proactive step toward better self-image, and a reaction to negative perceptions in society about the aging process.

Therefore, it is critical that marketers embrace these ideals about graceful aging through youth maintenance when positioning products for the mature market. If you want a stronger relationship with Boomers, use age-appropriate spokespeople who may appear middle-aged, but who exude a zest for living and an engagement in what is hip today.

The last thing a marketer should do is poke fun at beer bellies, balding pates, or age-related disabilities. This may get hoots among the nymph-like creative people who develop advertising programs in large advertising agencies, but it offends the target audience.

Boomers can laugh at themselves and lament their spent youth with a measure of humorous detachment, but this does not mean they run to the store and buy products as a result of a communication strategy built around the idea that they are a funny group of over-the-hill, wannabe hipsters.

From a superficial perspective, old age is inevitable, and with the ravages of time come the consequences of aging: graying hair, sagging skin, wrinkles, and loss of muscle tone and mass. Baby Boomers cannot change these facts of aging, but many will focus on mitigating physical manifestations until the end of life.

The cosmetics industry has been quick to take notice. Many are, and will continue to embrace cosmetic fixes, ranging from dyeing hair to wrinkle management, and from vitamin therapies to day spas. Some of the more affluent will invest in bolder body management regimens such as facelifts and tummy tucks.

For many, physical fitness will be a consuming passion, with several hours a week devoted to aerobic equipment and weight training. Yoga and meditation will help many achieve the goal of the physical-emotional-spiritual balance that has been a consuming passion throughout their adult lives.

However, when the end of life gets nearer, and clear-cut signs of aging are unavoidable, Boomers will still seek ways of expression suggesting youthfulness. The intrepid survivors will find clothing styles that evoke independence, the hallmark of youth.

Some choices could recycle the past. Perhaps men will adopt flattering, longer hairstyles and women will wear clothing such as the once-popular granny dresses, that hides flab, while enhancing the illusion of youthful curves. Other styles have yet to appear, but inevitably will include denim, leather, and soft cotton—the natural

How Boomers Are Revolutionizing Health & Fitness

OVER THE LAST three decades, Boomers have made substantial monetary contributions to health and fitness companies. However, many of the leading fitness brands have forgotten their legacies, recently ignoring the generation that propelled early growth.

Health & fitness companies are learning that the motivations driving Boomers today are very different from those that were once the foundation of industry marketing. Instead of marketing to externally-directed values, such as physical appearance and romantic conquest, Boomer-focused innovators address internally-directed values such as age acceptance, gains in stamina and energy, and forestalling age-related illnesses.

Curves has created a culture where members perceive that they're helping each other. The burgeoning fitness franchise has discovered the power of "dialogue over monologue." Curves further addresses its clientele of middle-aged women by facilitating formation of support communities. The company plays classic rock music to create an uplifting user experience.

Then there is the rising importance of a new consumer segment entitled *Lifestyles of Health and Sustainability*, or LOHAS. As discussed elsewhere in this book, the group is an economic powerhouse, purchasing over $350 billion in goods and services annually. Over 26 million members of the LOHAS segment are also Boomers, born between 1946 and 1959, or members of the Silent Generation, born between 1940 and 1945.

LOHAS consumers differentiate themselves by preferring brands that meet value-driven expectations for wellness, self-development and healthy living. They gravitate to fitness programs integrating "body, mind and spirit," such as PIYO, a blend of Pilates and yoga.

Other intrinsic fitness drivers include the need to remain mentally and physically active for the purpose of being productive and useful. Boomers' most preferred exercise methods include walking, bicycling and weight lifting. Yet, this technology loving cohort resonates with the work-out advantages of high-tech machinery.

Boomers will increasingly pursue fitness as a way to obviate the cosmetic impact of aging. Less obvious will be emerging fitness motivations such as staying vigorous for grandchildren, undertaking intense physical preparation for adventure vacations and learning expeditions, and to improve cognitive health and memory.

fabrics from a time when casual attire was the only fashion statement worth making.

Rock music from classic artists such as Bruce Springsteen, The Eagles, Fleetwood Mac, and The Rolling Stones will follow Boomers to their graves, but Boomers will also be interested in emerging artists like Norah Jones and David Gray.

Boomers will seek youthful attractiveness through chemistry and surgery, and when that fails, they will absorb youth by association with icons, values, contemporary culture, and continuing engagement with the surrounding world.

CHAPTER 10

Industries Targeting Baby Boomers

THE smart money in the near future will be on businesses promoting products and services designed to address the changing agendas of aging Boomers. They will seek products and services that promote better health, address the complexities of aging, encourage productive leisure, maintain community engagement, and augment their active lifestyles.

The following list suggests some of the next decade's hotter categories:

Nutraceuticals: Designer foods and supplements infused with nutritional supplements known to mitigate the effects of aging, such as Vitamins A, C, E, and beta carotene

Fitness centers: Fitness facilities specializing in exercise and relaxation programs for older people; expect these facilities to include joint-friendly aerobic equipment, yoga classes, and relaxation programs

Bionic aids: Eyeglasses that hide bifocals, hearing aids that are virtually invisible, and other forms of bionic aids that control and hide, rather than exacerbate, the appearance of disabilities

Sports medicine products: Home remedies to help Boomers better manage minor muscle and skeletal injuries from sports participation

Home health care: Businesses and organizations focused on helping Baby Boomers remain at home by providing assistance services such as prepared meals, food delivery, homemaking, support with activities of daily living, and social connections

Cosmeceuticals: Cosmetics formulated with anti-aging ingredients, such as antioxidants and intense moisturizers

Women's apparel: New fashions that enhance and embellish mature figures; new styles that reveal mature beauty, reflect midlife confidence and adapt to sophisticated, casual lifestyles

Men's casual fashions: Blue jeans, leather apparel, soft cotton sweat suits, and any garment design to project a more youthful, carefree attitude

Psychological services: More optimistic mental health services to help Boomers through the aging process.

Retirement communities: Smaller, well-designed homes with conveniences such as media rooms, home offices, and single-story living. Thinking ahead, many Boomers will also relocate to homes that have been designed to accommodate wheel chairs and other physically disabling conditions.

Continuing care retirement communities: Within ten years, a segment of the generation will anticipate the final stages of life by moving into communities that offer independent living options but also provide assisted living and skilled nursing care.

Investments and financial planning: Lacking traditional company retirement benefits, many Boomers are fully responsible for managing and protecting their retirement assets, so they will seek counsel about how to address this complex and dynamic aspect of their lives.

Insurance: The insurance industry will continually find new ways to build products for aging Boomers, with long-term health care insurance for extended nursing care taking a leading role.

Adventure and educational travel: As has been noted, Boomers are seekers and explorers; those with the means will roam widely, coupling travel with exciting adventures off-the-beaten track and learning opportunities.

Grandparenting: Today more than 70 million Americans are grandparents and this will grow another 10 million by 2010;

grandparents spend an average of $500 a year on their grand-children.

Nutritionally focused restaurants: Salad bars, health restaurants, pur-veyors of organic foods, grocery stores dedicated to natural products and healthy food service at home

Generation-specific publications: Those who are searching for a foun-tain of youth need resources capable of providing details about the newest breakthroughs

Integrated medicine specialists: Baby Boomers will increasingly seek medical doctors and practices specializing in holistic approaches that integrate Eastern and Western medical tradi-tions

CHAPTER 11

Experiences over Possessions

A RE THERE any Baby Boomers who *do not* have garages or attics overflowing with unneeded possessions? Unused rooms and storage spaces become cluttered with inherited possessions from parents, an accumulation from years of child rearing, and abandoned hobbies.

In my basement, for example, sits a nearly new Tama Rockstar drum set—a somewhat impulsive purchase honoring my fiftieth birthday and one unrequited dream. I practiced for a year, but eventually realized that I was not becoming drumming legend Ginger Baker of Cream fame.

In several packing boxes, a black-and-white photography darkroom is stored, rendered useless by digital photography.

As they grow older, Boomers are more likely to crave experiences over belongings, and here is the irony: It often takes acquiring possessions to achieve experiences.

For example, Boomer adventure travel will recall those halcyon wanderlust years that so typified them as young adults. They will also seek personal growth experiences from walking tours and other educational programs.

To meet the generation's upcoming travel needs, expect Boomers to invest in high-end travel clothes, both lightweight and wrinkle resistant, digital cameras of all kinds, exotic rolling luggage, and ancillary travel education, such as foreign language training or cultural immersion.

National Geographic magazine has adapted to this aging pack with a compendium of Society sponsored adventure vacations called

National Geographic Expeditions. (Notice how this title captures more than your garden-variety European getaway.)

As a letter from the National Geographic Society president professes: "Our explorers and scientists often speak of the rush of adrenaline and the excitement of their discoveries, and their enthusiasm is contagious."

The letter then brings this sense of adventure, of expedition, to the would-be traveler: "There is something inspiring about the first sight of Machu Picchu rising above the mist, or discovering Oaxaca, Mexico, through the eyes of *National Geographic* photographer David Alan Harvey."

The expeditions cover the planet, from a primeval nature tour of the Galapagos Islands in Latin America, to an eleven-day whirlwind tour named "Spy Capitals of the World," which escorts the espionage buff from Washington, D.C., to Berlin and Moscow. Designed for the budgets of well-heeled travelers, an expedition costs from $2,400 for an excursion through the Antebellum South to an "epic journey" circumnavigating the globe on a private jet for $39,950.

By no means excluding other generations with this unusual menu of adventure options, the Society has addressed many of the "travel experience dimensions" sought by Leading-Edge Baby Boomers. These include:

- The illusion of high adventure without the physical risks,

- A sense of the exotic,

- The flexibility to include individualized side trips, and

- Turnkey experiences, neatly planned and packaged.

Unlike explorers made famous by the magazine, Expedition travelers can expect almost no inconvenience to their comfort, as well as compressed immersion into a place and time, with most adventures spanning just ten days. Tour guides are recognized experts in their fields, thus an additional benefit invites travelers to augment exotic travel with learning experiences. Because excellent *National Geographic* photographers are leading many of the Expeditions, guests can expect to bring home a catalogue of photos and enough nostalgic memories to feed warm moments of recollection for the remainder of life. [23]

The question that all marketers targeting Leading-Edge Boomers must answer is, "How can we enhance the experiential benefits of our product or service?"

The Broadmoor Hotel resort in Colorado Springs has spent in excess of $75 million dollars on renovations and upgrades during the last few years. Three golf courses are even more manicured and its restaurants are more tempting. Management has added a day spa, expanded exercise facilities, and, with the unveiling of a huge water slide, broadened the resort's appeal to children. These renovations are necessary and beneficial in the end, but they are not enough inducement to fill a hotel sporting checking-account-draining rates.

My recommendation to this hotel's executives would be to pump up the "e-factor." The resort needs to create many affinity faces that it can present to different groups, and then develop world-class experiences around the needs and wants of these segments.

For example, many Baby Boomers have developed a passion for gourmet cooking. Accordingly, the resort can create its own adventure travel events, similar to *National Geographic* Expeditions. The signature experiences can bring together aspiring gourmands and hotel chefs to explore the culinary arts. Gastronomic adventures could include experiential learning, cooking competitions, social events that might include food magazine editors, and, of course, lots of gourmet dining. Hotel management could schedule these cooking and eating events during a traditionally slow period for the hotel.

Suddenly, the comprehensive resort amenities take on a different dimension—even the workout facilities, where overstuffed guests shed the calories of over consumption.

What is the "e-factor" in your product or service? How can you foster peak experiences?

Baby Boomers love peak experiences.

Several years ago, my wife and I attended the first "Camp Jeep." Staged in the Rocky Mountains near Vail, Colorado, this three-day hullabaloo featured adventure experiences designed to transform

Jeep owners into fanatics. Marketing materials suggested images and metaphors that you might associate with a 1950's summer camp.

At sunup on the first day, nearly 1,500 Jeeps filed into an expansive valley that organizers had converted into a mystical city. Surrounded by stately mountain peaks, a modernistic white-tent village presented exhibits of Jeep concept cars and a surfeit of vendors offering everything from luxury accessories to logo clothing apparel.

"Camp counselors" provided expert-training experiences designed to help owners get the most from their four-wheel, off-road driving escapades. Food was always available in plentiful quantities. The organizers offered continuous fly-fishing lessons from Orvis experts, and kids could fish for trout in an overstocked pond.

After three days of multi-sensory stimulation and fraternizing with other Jeep owners, we attended one final event: an outdoor concert featuring Seventies' rock stars Kenny Loggins and Michael McDonald of Doobie Brothers fame. We were "rockin' down the highway" in our heads before sunset.

This elaborate experiential gathering worked beautifully. We bought our second Jeep Cherokee two years later.

Boomers Are Looking for New "Road Trip" Adventures

INDUSTRY PUNDITS credit surging recreational vehicle sales (RVs) to Boomers. The leading-edge members of the generation, born between 1946 and 1955, will all be between 50 and 60 in 2006, a life period most often associated with pricy RV purchases.

Obvious factors contributing to this trend include high disposable income and empty nesting. Since the terrorist attacks of September 11, 2001, anxiety about air travel has refocused many toward terrestrial excursions. A $50 million print, radio, TV, and internet ad campaign by the Go RVing Coalition has also raised awareness about RVs. [24]

But there are other forces at work. For one, Boomers have unrequited wanderlust and a yearning for greater freedom. During the late 1960s and 1970s when they were young adults, millions traveled overseas on European excursions. Even more crisscrossed the U.S. on road trips. The mega-successful Boomer movie, *Easy Rider*, chronicled two drug dealers as they thundered across the southwest on their Harleys in search of America.

Also influencing burgeoning RV sales is the Boomer passion for novel experiences. Like the wandering iconoclast in *On the Road*, the beat counterculture novel by Jack Kerouac, Boomers have always been experience seekers, and few activities offer more novelty than a wandering, slightly rebellious, loosely scripted RV trip.

Beyond the obvious force of life stage, Boomers are also considering RV purchases to satisfy deeply held "Bipolar Metavalues." Some of these values are *independence, community, spontaneity, transcendence* and *engagement*.

CHAPTER 12

Planet Downsize

OBSERVING my parents in their final years reinforced another lesson about aging. As we grow older, many material possessions lose their importance and value. With the exception of perhaps mementos and personal artifacts that represent cherished memories, many possessions stop fulfilling the needs that motivate younger consumers to acquire material goods. Belongings become albatrosses—objects just in the way, something else to give or throw away.

A consistent theme evolved in my dad's reaction to questions about what he might want for a birthday or holiday gift: "Give me a nice card. We don't need any more stuff!"

Downsizing does not imply that Baby Boomers will lose their material interests or their willingness to spend money on possessions. They will continue to buy things as long as they can. They will need consumables the rest of their lives, but another trend will become important: the drive to downsize. This means smaller homes, more utilitarian furniture, a functional wardrobe, and an overall need for greater convenience and simplicity.

Show the utilitarian value of your product.

Does your product enable, or will it just get in the way by adding debris to brimming garages and attics? Possibly this becomes a matter of perception. When you show the utilitarian value of your product, how it can contribute to convenience, then you enhance its appeal to those who are coming to believe that less is more.

Is your under-bed cabinet system a clever storage solution? Does your chaise lounge serve as a place to sit by day and then sleep at night? If someone plans to purchase just one more vehicle, has your engineering design team created an appropriate automobile? Is your high-technology parka the only coat someone will need in rain and snow, and will it travel well while protecting from wind?

In other words, downsizing means that Boomers will expect products to last while serving multiple functions. Space-saving attributes become a factor in the buying decision as many move from rambling three-story homes to small, condominium-style retirement communities.

Convenience will matter; so will product cleverness. As has been true since the generation's youthful period of material excess, Boomers will continue to be impressed with products employing new technologies.

When designing products for Baby Boomers, think smaller, think lighter, think multi-function, think high-quality construction, and think long-term value. Otherwise, they could interpret anything you might have to sell as just another unpleasant addition to an already overstuffed basement or attic.

What do Boomers Want for Special Occasion Gifts?

BOOMERS TODAY yearn for more than the extrinsic benefits of material possessions. Most have an abundance of stuff. Meaningful special occasion gifts involve experiences, connections, memories, and self-respect.

Boomers want respect.

Millions of Boomers have been struggling with decline of status. For some, this means premature disruption in careers due to layoffs and downsizing. Some face special occasions such as birthdays and the holidays without the normal sources of self-respect, including a flourishing career and current standing within a profession or business network. Other Boomers are watching their nests empty as children fly away to colleges and careers. For still another segment, health concerns, such as obesity, are eroding self-esteem and optimism.

Gift Strategies: Money can't buy respect; neither can traditional gifts such as clothing, electronics and jewelry. Respect springs from acknowledgement, appreciation, and attention. For the Boomer struggling with the unfair exigencies of mid-life, give gifts that say, "You matter." This could be as simple as a home-cooked dinner party for a few close friends, or a six-month membership to a fitness gym that offers rejuvenation programs such as circuit training and yoga. For the more ambitious gift giver, consider purchasing a video biography, now being offered by entrepreneurial television production companies, which will give the recipient a chance to put his or her life into a more positive context.

Boomers want communication.

Boomers grew up in a communal generation. They crowded elementary school classrooms and popularized the modern rock concert. They received interpersonal communications sensitivity training in college. They are nostalgic about long-term friendships, and many appreciate the networking power of today's communication technologies.

Gift Strategies: For someone who loves to chat over long distances with relatives and friends, give her a portable headset for her computer and point her to a free internet telephone subscription from Skype (*www.skype.com*). For the recently divorced, consider giving a membership to one of the online dating services such as *www.eharmony.com* or *www.match.com,* or to the more exclusive organizations that arrange fancy blind dates for groups of 3 or 4 couples. For the well-to-do, buy a high-end ticket package to one of the elite rock group events, such as Paul McCartney or the Rolling Stones, and include a few old friends from college days.

Boomers want a richer life.

In the hearts of mature adults, success does not mean more material possessions. Many feel a poverty of time and flexibility to embrace life's sublime experiences. Many are sandwiched between their aging GI Generation parents and their Twixter teens and young adults. Boomers lives are overflowing with duties and responsibilities and career demands. Recent consumer research corroborates the increasing significance of experiences over possessions; success today means stable marriages, fitness and opportunities to travel.

Gift Strategies: For time-impoverished Boomers, peak experiences provide welcome relief. For those with impossibly tight schedules, minievents include trips to day spas for rejuvenation, three-day vacations and an historical/cultural tour of a neighboring city. A rich one-day experience could begin on a Wednesday, include a leisurely breakfast at a favorite haunt, then a trip to an art museum and finally an afternoon movie and dinner. For those itching with wanderlust, a surprise reunion at a destination resort, including a few old friends, could become the keystone event of the year.

CHAPTER 13

Control versus Compromise

I T WAS a wrenching experience for me to watch my parents struggle with a progressive loss of independence. They had spent almost twenty-five years in retirement, living together peacefully in their single-story house, which as general contractor, Dad had designed to accommodate loss of mobility and the frailties of aging. They almost required me to drag them from their home, kicking and screaming. Although they understood the inevitable course of aging, they, nevertheless, fought the loss of independence as it became necessary for my mother to move to a nursing home and my father eventually to require assisted living care.

Those well-meaning people defined the word "stubborn" in their final years. It is not difficult to understand why.

They wanted to control their concluding years, and then the closing months of their lives. However, the established eldercare system gave them few options. They knew this, but they struggled for their freedom as ardently as Baby Boomers once fought for liberation from a political process dedicated to drafting young males and sending them to Vietnam during a most unpopular war.

Given Boomers' history of divisiveness, they may struggle even more vociferously than the GI Generation to guard freedom and remain in control of the course and quality of elder housing and late-stage care. A dormant coming-of-age rebellion could find renewed expression if society attempts to brush the generation aside as useless and irrelevant during their waning years. The more institutional—and therefore, impersonal—that eldercare institutions become, the more Boomers will fight back. They will demand control and will be reluctant to compromise tightly held values of independence, wanderlust, experimentation, and adventure.

They will lead this process and not follow policy wonks already established in the aging industry. It would be insightful for marketers to cast Boomers in the role of elder-revolutionaries. Although their motives may be as self-serving as my parents' were—to protect independence and freedom as long as possible— Boomers will seek long-term empowerment for people who are confronting a dependent status.

Boomers will undertake this challenge, not only for themselves, but also as a legacy: that no future generation experiences the hopelessness of old age so characteristic of the plight of elders during the second half of the 20th century.

Show them engaged. Show them defiant. Show them passionate about maintaining and augmenting the dignity of aging. Show them winning in the battle for control of the end-stage of their lives.

You will be reflecting many core values, and you will be embracing a higher mission to instill the aging process with greater dignity.

Mirroring your target audience is always the best way to insure loyalty.

CHAPTER 14

Institutions and Government

DURING the Vietnam War era, millions of Baby Boomers rebelled against almost all forms of authority: the federal government, politicians, multinational corporations, political parties, educational institutions, and traditional religious organizations.

Rebellion was high fashion.

Since this defining phase of the generation, the unruly spirit has become muted and diffused. Some of the generation, the conservative thread in particular, have denounced the generation's long-standing lack of respect for traditions, institutions, and the typical sources of authority in American society. These right-leaning Boomers have been highly critical of liberals, leftists, pacifists, and environmentalists.

There is an irony in this. The strident, outspoken criticisms by conservatives such as Rush Limbaugh and David Horowitz are another form of rebellion. Those in the generation who espouse conservative ideologies are in some ways among the most rebellious in their communication styles, their denunciations, and the extent to which they mobilize sympathizers.

Those among the Baby Boom Generation who have become "The Establishment" are also suspicious of, and hostile toward, institutions and government entities when the organizations are liberal, or when government policies may lead to greater intervention into the free-enterprise system.

Even outspoken conservatives demonstrate the generation's tendency toward confrontation and conflict with established power.

Whether you choose to perceive Baby Boomers and their collective prospects from a liberal or conservative political perspective or somewhere in between, you will discover a common tendency to challenge the status quo. You will uncover widespread and similar social dynamics, including a willingness to confront authority, act on principles, and mobilize visible protests.

This feisty attitude prevails as the generation faces its retirement years. It will find expression through heightened debate about aging and the role of social policy in the lives of America's oldest citizens.

Companies seeking mutually beneficial connections with Baby Boomers can build stronger ties by recognizing and revealing rebellious tendencies. Some humor may be appropriate, because most Boomers have gained perspective about their audacious fervency in youth, but humor in the form of implied ridicule will rarely fly.

Boomers recognize their youthful foolishness, but many refuse to let go of their need to cultivate higher principles of equality among people, to pursue the imperative of world peace, or to influence environmental conservation. Blame this on Martin Luther King or John Fitzgerald Kennedy, but many will face their final years with the same high-minded principles that molded them as adolescents. They want justice; they detest those who abuse power to satisfy self-serving purposes.

Marketers can build powerful marketing messages by being mindful of this psychology. Show Boomers as cynical of the status quo and passionate about positive change, and you will reach into the deepest crevices of the generation's collective motivations.

CHAPTER 15

Business and the Fairness Principle

AND-IN-HAND with many of the underlying motivations and values discussed in this book—from multiculturalism to empowerment—Baby Boomers will continue their lifelong quest for fair and inclusive corporate governance. This cannot be emphasized enough: the cohort came of age during a time of widespread distrust of authority.

Some Baby Boomers have left behind their more liberal sentiments spawned during the Vietnam War era and have become clamorous conservatives, angrily denouncing many of the excesses associated with that chaotic time in history.

Others have remained staunch liberals, retaining a belief that more government intervention, not less, is necessary to correct the wrongs of an inequitable economic and social-service system.

Although political and economic sentiments cover the widest possible range of viewpoints, the largest segment of the generation lives somewhere in the middle of these extremes. When asked, many Baby Boomers will claim to be socially liberal but economically conservative; in other words, they believe in providing government-directed programs to help less fortunate members of society, but they also believe that government should meddle as little as possible with the spontaneous functioning of the free-enterprise system.

> Baby Boomers claim to be socially liberal but economically conservative.

An overwhelming share of Baby Boomers believe they lived through a period when the government and its leaders deceived its citizens in many ways, and this engendered a distrust of unbridled corporate growth and multinational power. These sentiments live on today. The formative antiauthority generational zeitgeist has received substantive reinforcement in recent years with the emergence of pervasive corporate malfeasance.

Given that Baby Boomers learned early to distrust large government and market manipulation, most still prefer inclusive corporate leaders. Autocrats do not rank high.

Boomers gravitate more to companies and institutions that profess and demonstrate participatory leadership, egalitarian decision-making, and forthright corporate communications. They prefer to buy from those organizations that appear to approach change and corporate evolution with a commitment to decision making "of the people, by the people, and for the people."

The population of Baby Boomers who have substantial discretionary income is growing. Ironically, for these increasingly empowered consumers there is a corresponding reduction in the pressure to consume because they already own houses, furniture, clothing, and other goods. Eventually they will have more time to research their purchasing decisions, and Boomers will demonstrate a greater willingness to choose products and services based on corporate ethics. How companies behave as citizens will play a larger role in the buying process.

"The Golden Rule" will become fashionable again as a way to differentiate a company from its competitors. Companies targeting Boomers that receive negative publicity for corporate abuse may find it difficult to recover; Boomers just may be unforgiving.

Conversely, building a company or organization that holds ethical principles in high esteem, and demonstrates its ideology through good behavior, could be the one differentiating factor leading to market dominance, especially in a world where any product category fills quickly with parity products and services.

Thus, differentiate by demonstrating justice and fair play, by being inclusive in guiding corporate policy, and by continuing to build a company that serves its employees as well as its stockholders.

CHAPTER 16

Of Communal Instincts and Community

COMMUNAL living will reemerge.

For some Boomers, this will be a byproduct of economic necessity—the only way the less fortunate can survive a lack of financial resources for independent retirement. But for others, living in communal neighborhoods will satisfy deeper needs for connection, common causes, and caring. This is how peers will help each other deal with impersonal bureaucracies, abusive treatment, spurious care costs, the frustrations of diminished capacities, and loneliness.

Baby Boomers became accustomed to communal experiences at an early age with bulging elementary school classrooms. It was common for many to coexist in groups of 30 to 40 within classrooms built and designed for half as many. Boomers learned early in life to get along with each other, even under the pressures of overcrowding and loss of anonymity.

Another phenomenon most Boomers will recall is disproportionate numbers at public events. This generation may not have created the blockbuster movie, but it certainly added new dimension to this sought-after Hollywood showcase of cinematic success.

I vividly recall a ridiculous line of kids my age encircling a city block in hopeful anticipation of being admitted to a grade B Japanese monster movie called "Rodan." After waiting for an eternity in line, my best buddy and I were denied admittance because the theater sold out just as we reached the ticket window. We forlornly trudged home, unfulfilled, hours before our parents would have picked us up.

The crushing size of the generation forced its members to gather early, and helped us learn to be comfortable with enormous crowds of our peers.

During adolescence, the stadium-sized rock concert soon became the ultimate expression of group engagement. Elvis Presley set the stage, and a legion of Boomer rock bands followed.

Then came Woodstock, one of the largest gatherings of Americans to assemble in one place for a long weekend, sometimes under the worst weather and sanitary conditions. Many were willing to pay a large price to capture a vivid sense of the generation and its evolving culture by gathering together under a common cause, and as the sun begins to set, some will again.

Rock concerts featuring classic rock artists still fill to capacity in spite of inconveniences posed by large gatherings—staggering ticket prices, traffic jams near venues, less-than-ideal acoustics, and uncomfortable seats. As the generation creates new venues for group engagement, such as huge temporary RV cities in the middle of the Arizona desert, many will be drawn to congregate and connect.

There are two facets to communal experience: the gathering of tribes at cultural and artistic events, and the more intimate gathering of close friends seeking validation, safety, and harmony. This second communal motivation will become compelling as the generation reaches its final years.

Marketers can expect Boomers to adopt new living arrangements, such as independent patio homes built around a large community building where residents sleep in their homes but prepare food, socialize, and dine together. Traditional single-family homes will be converted for habitation by two, three, or more empty nesters and their single friends. One might even expect the emergence of a new genre of magazine focused on communal lifestyles, such as *Living Interdependently*.

Appealing to this sense of generational community can become a powerful motivator for marketers selling lifestyle housing communities, recreational facilities, entertainment events, and educational conferences.

CHAPTER 17

Social Causes and Volunteerism

A RECENT newspaper story distributed by the Associated Press captures the essence of Baby Boomers' predictable relationship to volunteerism:

> Having attained reasonable financial security, many are looking to get back in touch with long-shelved ideals from the 1960s as they change their focus from success to significance. This quest to do well by doing good might ultimately leads to career or lifestyle changes, but for millions, it is finding an outlet in volunteerism.[25]

My own spirit of volunteerism, which has manifested itself by thousands of hours donated to economic development organizations in Colorado, can be traced to my GI Generation parents.

My father volunteered his entire career and most of his retirement as a member of Kiwanis. Throughout my childhood, Dad would regularly attend Kiwanis meetings on Monday nights, leaving my mother and me free to dine with neighbors. He eventually became president of the local chapter in Topeka, Kansas. My mother was a lifelong volunteer for the Hospital Auxiliaries of Kansas, rising to the office of president-elect of the organization.

My family situation is typical. Many Baby Boomers recall their parents' active involvement in professional and philanthropic volunteer organizations such as Rotary, Junior League, Kiwanis, the Shriners, the Red Cross, and so forth. Part of our common upbringing included our membership in Boy Scouts, Girl Scouts, 4-H, and other organizations dedicated to teaching us the value of volunteering time and skills to help others.

Robert Putnum, once-upon-a-time an obscure academic, shocked many intellectuals and social observers when he published an article in the *Journal of Democracy* in 1995. The article postulated that Americans, and in particular, Baby Boomers, have become increasingly disconnected from community engagement, religious organizations, civic life, and even meaningful interpersonal networks. According to Putnum, this has led to an alarming reduction in Americans' collective social capital, or the critical network of informal and formal social relationships that have so typified the lives of GI Generation members.

The odd title for his follow-up book, *Bowling Alone: the Collapse and Revival of American Community,* originates from Putnum's empirical observations that more Americans than ever are bowling as a recreational activity, but there has been a 40 percent reduction in league memberships since 1980. This seemingly irrelevant observation stands as a metaphor for the alarming decline of broader group participation within civic, community, business, and social organizations.

Pundits and political leaders latched onto this book with grave trepidation because reduction in civic engagement can measurably affect the administration of social justice, public health and even economic prosperity. The "kinder and gentler" society envisioned by the first President Bush cannot happen in a democracy without true democratic engagement among its citizens. We cannot influence our own government if collectively we are isolated from each other and blithely ignorant of community issues.

Somewhat ironically, Putnum attributes at least 25 percent of this reduction in social and civic engagement to the "privatizing" impact of television viewing. Into a bubbling stew of national anomie, he also tosses two-career families, long commutes from distant suburbs, and the increasing demands on time from longer work schedules.

Since the mid-1970s, many Boomers have refocused time and energies on careers, child rearing, and the increasing demands of economic competitiveness, but I believe important lessons from childhood about group participation remain buried in the generation's collective psyche; many retain a spirit of social activism that took shape and found passionate direction in the Sixties and Seventies.

As retirement comes closer, many *are* changing their focus from "success to significance," where they hope to get back in touch with youthful idealism, and perhaps rekindle a belief that single human beings can positively change the world. Participation in philanthropic causes is destined to become fashionable again.

A 47-year-old California woman quoted in the article mentioned above observed accurately that Baby Boomers have been blessed in many ways that their GI Generation parents were not, with access to higher education, decades of economic growth, and a relatively stable upbringing.

Many left the Sixties and Seventies behind with a deluded confidence that they could influence positive change in the world, and now that they have more time and resources available for community projects, it is time for many to be constructive "with our gifts and giving of ourselves."

Most companies are not focused on philanthropy; they sell products and services to make a profit. So how can a company effectively take advantage of the predicted resurgence in Baby Boomer volunteerism?

The answer is marketing public relations.

The opportunity is always available for your company to embrace and support a worthwhile non-profit cause and then enlist your customers and stakeholders to participate in promotions that integrate advertising, sales promotion, and public relations.

Perhaps no high-profile company has done a better job than McDonald's Corporation has at executing marketing public relations strategies. One could argue that the corporation's signature Ronald McDonald House (RMH) program is unrivaled in concept and execution.

Throughout the country in major metropolitan areas, McDonald's has provided the leadership and resources to help build, remodel, and fund operations for large homes located near major hospitals. "The House that Love Built" provides shelter and sanctuary for parents with children who are receiving long-term medical treatment for such diseases as cancer and diabetes. The RMH provides a structured homelike setting, staffed by professional volunteers, where parents can stay indefinitely while a child is receiving chemotherapy, dialysis, or other long-term medical treatments. If parents are financially unable to pay a small daily rental fee, always substantially lower than neighboring motels and hotels, then they can stay at the RMH for as long as necessary without being charged.

In the fall of 2002, McDonald's reported that there are 212 Ronald McDonald Houses in twenty countries. Since 1974, RMH programs have helped more than ten million families with the assistance of 25,000 volunteers, donating one million hours of their time annually. More than 5,000 bedrooms worldwide provide a respite for families every night.[26]

McDonald's Corporation and local franchisees have made this fundraising challenge a keystone of their annual cause-related marketing programs. Customers embrace the worthwhile spirit of this cause by dropping pocket change in collection boxes throughout the year, and now and then by participating in more focused fundraising efforts to support major renovations and building additions.

Early in my marketing career, I was the account executive for an advertising agency that managed promotions and pubic relations for sixteen McDonald's stores in Southern Colorado. Children from our marketing territory who required prolonged medical treatment often traveled to *Children's Hospital* in Denver. The Denver franchisees asked the owners in my area to help raise money to support an ambitious renovation of the Denver house. The Denver RMH was running short of space because of increasing demand, so the company decided to expand space by renovating parts of the third floor and attic.

My agency team developed a unique fundraising idea, principally targeting Leading-Edge Baby Boomers.

An entrepreneurial company approached us, proposing to convert some of the nostalgia-laden 3D movies from the 1950s and rebroadcast them on television. This novel broadcast technology could preserve the 3D effects, thus bringing the visual excitement of 3D into viewers' homes. To watch a 3D movie on television, home viewers would still need 3D glasses, those weird sunglasses with one side of the frame covered by red plastic and the other side covered by blue plastic.

We embraced the nostalgia and fun of this idea and agreed to sell the required 3D glasses through all sixteen McDonald's restaurants in our marketing territory. The NBC affiliate agreed to broadcast the movie for a nominal advertising charge, which was well within the existing advertising budget. All proceeds from the sale of 3D glasses would be donated to the Denver Ronald McDonald House.

Our agency creative team proceeded to design promotional free-standing displays for each store. We also created television and radio commercials for mass marketing.

The second facet of the program involved building public awareness of the purpose and value of the Denver RMH for families living in Southern Colorado. To make this appeal vivid and emotional, we enlisted the help of a single Baby Boomer mother whose youngest daughter had been receiving cancer treatments at Children's Hospital.

Ten-year-old Laurel was the ideal child for our publicity campaign. She was energetic, gregarious, optimistic, and fun loving. We created a television news documentary about Laurel and her family, and we portrayed the many difficulties this family had encountered in managing cancer treatments far away from home and friends.

The RMH had served this family well by providing them sanctuary during Laurel's chemotherapy treatments. Katherine, Laurel's mother, was the true beneficiary because Katherine could not hold down a full-time job with Laurel being sick so often and periodically needing aggressive treatments over a protracted period. Katherine did not have adequate financial resources, and she discovered home and heart at the RMH. She also made critical connections with other parents who were experiencing similar ordeals.

The 3D movie premiere received substantial publicity and promotion from our media partners, including the NBC affiliate, a ratings-leading rock station, and the community newspaper. During the final days before the movie premiere, lines of customers often encircled the restaurants as people clamored to purchase their special 3D glasses. All major media covered the promotion as news stories, and we received hundreds of newspaper column inches and nearly an hour of cumulative broadcast news coverage. Our NBC partner even ran a five-part news series every night for five nights preceding the premiere.

Tiny Laurel became a local celebrity, with her story becoming the focus of an entire community. She accepted a proclamation from the mayor. She was the vivacious subject of dozens of news interviews. She embodied both the tragedy of childhood cancer and the hope restored by a special home far away from home.

McDonald's sold tens of thousands of the 3D glasses and eventually donated generously to the Denver Ronald McDonald House. The promotion received publicity valued at hundreds of thousands of dollars. Baby Boomer parents answered the fundraising call by donating time, resources, and support to the worthwhile cause. Every customer became a philanthropist by simply purchasing a pair of 3D glasses. Moreover, all sixteen stores in our marketing territory experienced substantial sales increases during the promotion because of incremental store traffic.

This marketing public relations program demonstrates that companies can successfully intertwine worthwhile causes with for-profit businesses. Programs like the one just described can attract customers to fundraising programs, while boosting sales and augmenting the relationship between a brand and its critical stakeholders.

Ultimately, marketers can satisfy nobler human motives by helping customers contribute their financial resources and time in support of programs designed to assist those who are less fortunate. We can rekindle the spirit of giving and present our communities with an outlet to express compassion and further demonstrate an essential humanity.

As a corporate brand development strategy, marketing public relations programs powerfully resonate with Baby Boomers. Although the overt motive is usually to promote sales by attaching an emotionally appealing fundraising component, your organization can stimulate deeper motivations of charity, group participation, and hope for a better tomorrow.

Marketing public relations is a powerful strategy to overcome negative perceptions and images connected to the recent troubling wave of corporate malfeasance.

Twixters Following Path Popularized by Boomers

SOCIAL PSYCHOLOGISTS are heralding the emergence of a distinct and separate life stage.[27] The period between 18 and 26 is now being repackaged as "youthhood" or "adultescence." Legally adults, but not quite grown up, they are being called "Twixters."

Twixters are in a transitional period between youthful frivolity and mature accountability. Many are delaying adult responsibilities such as commitment to careers and settling down. They hop jobs, forestall marriage, and extend education. For example, since 1970, the percentage of 26-year-olds living at home has swelled from 11 percent to 20 percent.

However, observers have failed to examine the innate psychic links between Twixters and their trailblazing Boomer parents. In fact, Boomers were the first generation to forestall adulthood.

When Boomers slammed into their early twenties, they confronted titanic political and cultural conflicts. The Vietnam War, numerous liberation movements, and a bellicose society convinced many to drop out of school and wait to have children. Further, generational size and competitiveness hindered rapid movement into adulthood. Beginning career jobs became more difficult to find as the 1970's unfolded. Spurious interest rates caused housing to become nearly unaffordable.

Moreover, Boomer parents are having influence on Twixters because of shared values, particularly passion and idealism. Like their fervent, protest-marching parents, Twixters want more from life than a paycheck. They are earnest about self-actualization. They yearn to make the right choices early in life and then change the world. Both cohorts value feminism, privacy, pluralism, tolerance, self-expression, environmental awareness, and egalitarian institutions.

CHAPTER 18

Holistic Solutions

HOLISTIC solutions look for connections and synergy between pieces and parts. It is an overarching view of everything—fragmentation seeking integration. Integrated health. Integrated marketing communications. Integrated curricula.

When a doctor examines a sore knee, we want him to consider our emotional health at the same time. When using our computers, we want a Windows-style operating system that pulls fragmented computer programs together into a system of interrelated solutions, with common keyboard shortcuts and a consistent user interface.

We do not want just to take Vitamin E; we want daily packets of nutriceuticals that integrate all trace nutrients known to maintain health.

This integrating paradigm has led to the formation of many intellectual trends focused on bringing together divergent views of the human experience into a common structure.

For example, in 1989, two national holistic health organizations met to create a new union, eventually called the American Holistic Health Association. AHHA "is dedicated to promoting holistic principles: honoring the whole person (mind, body and spirit) and encouraging people to actively participate in their own health and healthcare."[28]

Holistic health, as defined by the AHHA, is not just a synonym for alternative medical therapies; it is not, in effect, a turning away from singular reliance on traditional western medicine to embrace fringe modalities, perhaps scientifically untested approaches to medical treatment. Rather, the holistic concept is an approach to human health that embraces the whole person, bringing into focus the mind-body-spirit connection. It is an empowering view where people take active control of their own health by addressing all three sides of the human experience in a search for remedies that lead to cures. Empowerment is the fuel of the holistic health movement; this enabling paradigm has become part of a larger view of life, and it has found parallel expression throughout many intellectual disciplines.

In the field of marketing, the holistic health corollary finds expression through integrated marketing communications (IMC), whereby diverse media and messages become integrated. IMC is a customer-centric approach to marketing in the same vein that holistic medicine is a patient-centric approach to health.

Capitalizing on one-to-one communications, IMC stresses marketing to individuals by understanding and strategically reacting to customer motivations, values, lifestyle trends, attitudes, and behavior. The goal of this "holistic" marketing discipline is to integrate advertising, direct mail, e-commerce, public relations, sales promotions, and direct sales, all of which are data driven and guided by a thorough understanding of customers and stakeholders. IMC builds stronger brands because customers feel understood and appreciated. Company-sponsored messages consistently communicate common concepts with ideas derived from customer-driven insights.[29]

Show Baby Boomers the big picture. Help them understand how your products or services fit into more of a global view of things. Give Boomers options that allow them to express individuality, but give them a complete road map of all possibilities.

Empower them.

For example, many outdoor outfitters have developed high-tech clothing systems that begin with underwear and expand through layers to an external parka capable of withstanding gale-force winds and blizzard conditions. All the layers work independently but lead to an integrated whole, each part working together to achieve a common purpose: warmth, comfort, and dryness.

Do not just offer weight training as a way to preserve youth. Present aerobics and yoga in the same fitness package—maybe even meditation.

Do not just sell a stand-alone home computer. Include the digital camera, scanner, and printer so customers have a complete solution to create and manage their travel photographs.

This same philosophy must work within traditional marketing paradigms. Do not just sell customers a fast laptop; sell them the power to manage a company while sipping a café latte at Starbucks.

CHAPTER 19

Seeking Truth Though Simple Ideas

Ask not what your country can do for you; ask what you can do for your country.

Make love not war.

Sexism is racism.

With a little help from my friends.

The answer is blowin' in the wind.

Turn on, tune in, drop out.

Only the good die young.

Burn baby, burn.

Do you believe in magic?

You've come a long way, baby.

The thrill of victory, the agony of defeat

Come Monday, it will be all right.

I once was lost, but now I'm found.

BABY BOOMERS seek higher ideals and express their quest with distilled communication. They are the first TV generation to whom marketers and politicians have discovered how to bundle complex values and aspirations in ten-second sound bites and on seven-word billboards.

Baby Boomers' minds are busy with idealism and pragmatism, even today. They do not need complexity to understand complexity. They want intelligent ideas in minimalist packages. They respond to inspiring images and words, tersely communicated.

- Ask what they want, and then tell them what they need to get what they want.
- Make your communications crisp and concise.
- Be evocative, metaphorical, and direct.

Like a bridge over troubled water.

It don't come easy.

I'd like to teach the world to sing in perfect harmony.

Does anybody really know what time it is?

If it feels good, do it.

Offer them a complex Harley-Davidson motorcycle, full of powerful technology and the newest gadgets, but help customers understand why they want the machine beyond utility. Tell them simply that with this machine, they are "born to be wild."

Offer a new, complex computer operating system, but reduce its complexity to a simple metaphor: Start me up.

CHAPTER 20

Relevance and Legacies

NOTHING will alienate Baby Boomers more quickly than to simplify the later years as a quest for golf foursomes, ocean cruises, and puttering in gardens.

Boomers will embrace recreational experiences, and you can expect them to play hard, but for most, play cannot become the singular focus in life. Boomers need to be needed; they want to feel a sense of mission and a compelling humanitarian cause.

When the generation came of age, it fought for change on all social fronts. Some battles they won; others they lost. But the zeitgeist was to make the world a better place, hopefully before the end of the semester. As the body bags came home from Southeast Asia, most developed a sense of urgency. Changing the world became not only a search for relevance; for some, it became a life or death matter.

As Boomers reduce family and career responsibilities and have more time to reflect upon their lives, there will be an inevitable resurgence of idealism. However, this will not just be a quest for survival in a time of war. The common objective will not be the same nearly universal goal Boomers sought as young adults, when freedom and the opportunity to live safely became an overarching priority.

The underlying motivator in the future will be a reflection of looming mortality, the coming-to-terms challenges that all mature citizens must eventually try to address—the quest to leave the world a better place. When the end is near, concluding purposes matter. A priority becomes the heritage left behind.

Insightful marketers position their products and services as enabling. Home digital video studios become production facilities for time capsules or multimedia records of family history. Running shoes become foot comfort for marching gray activists. Adventure vacations become heroic odysseys to understand some of life's greater truths.

Relevancy reigns above all.

For many years, Baby Boomers have been accused of being self-absorbed, "the Me Generation." The media have convoluted some of the principled demonstrations and protests during the Vietnam era into self-serving outbursts of adolescent outrage, and somehow the larger messages of this confrontational mission are being lost in history.

Boomers will not tolerate denigration when time is short and the stakes for effective closure are high. They expect those who would sell them products and services to understand the underlying dynamic of the generation: a perpetual striving for connectivity—to each other, communities, the nation, and the planet.

This striving also seeks to leave something beneficial behind for future generations.

Make your product relevant, a way of bringing together communities and causes, and you will create a more loyal following from a generation willing to reward understanding of, and allegiance to, its ideals.

CHAPTER 21

It's Only Rock 'n' Roll

I F YOU'VE wondered how so many sane Baby Boomers can justify investing hundreds of dollars per concert ticket to see four middle-aged musicians play rock songs 30 years out of date, then you don't understand the influential allure of The Rolling Stones, nor perhaps do you appreciate the commanding appeal of rock music. Even though lead singer Mick Jagger is old enough to be a grandfather, his unparalleled power to fire up fans remains unassailable after almost four decades.

"It's only rock 'n' roll, but I like it."

Marketers have known about the special magnetism of classic rock music for at least a decade. Microsoft paid The Rolling Stones $12 million to license the song "Start Me Up." The soundtrack then became the theme song in the television advertisements introducing Windows 95. Some Baby Boomers cynically interpreted this "commercial sell-out" as another example of Microsoft's Bill Gates putting computer users "Under My Thumb," and many people who purchased the quirky operating system software felt "I Can't Get No Satisfaction."

In recent years, consumers have heard a succession of former hit rock songs become part of advertising history. Apple Computers began selling their rainbow colored iMacs with The Rolling Stones' "She's a Rainbow." Wrangler Jeans drafted "Fortunate Son," Creedence Clearwater Revival's powerful anti-Vietnam War anthem, a working class protest song that cuts deeper than any of the explicit Vietnam protest songs of the era.

The Who's Pete Townshend once sang: "The things they do look awful cold, (talking 'bout my generation), I hope I die before I get old."

And Boomers could only let out a collective gasp three decades after its brazen introduction when they heard "Won't Get Fooled Again" in Nissan commercials.

"Why don't you all just f-f-f-fade away?" indeed.

Rod Stewart sells Pampers. Music from the group Queen lures us to buy Aiwa stereos. And even John Lennon's "Instant Karma (We All Shine On)" has been procured to sell overpriced sneakers.

The point is this: Rock and roll is the unifying thread that ties together the complex tapestry of the Baby Boom generation. It presents the most common of shared experiences. You can drive from Tampa to Anchorage and find nearly universal recognition among Baby Boomers about the hit songs from three decades ago, and probably elicit positive nostalgic recall.

The generation will typically respond with reflective glad tidings and a sense of connectivity when marketers present these songs with up-to-date production techniques.

This music formula has punctuated and defined their lives.

At first it may seem ludicrous to think of people in their sixties, seventies, and eighties becoming excited about music honoring the anthems of youth and rebellion. But do not underestimate the Boomers.

Bring together the cutting edge of an electric guitar and the pounding urgency of drums with your product or service. Do this in a tasteful, non-exploitative way, and you will definitely attract attention and maybe get closer to earning economic goodwill.

CHAPTER 22

Case Study: Rock 'n' Roll Comes to a Conservative Art Museum

THE *Colorado Springs Fines Art Center* (FAC) presents a rich visual feast of Southwestern art, housed in an award-winning art deco edifice. Designed by John Gaw Meem, this soothing showcase was constructed in 1936 and is now listed on the National Register of Historic Places. The FAC's collection includes Native American and Hispanic art, 20th-century fine art, a tactile gallery collection, and a library collection with over 28,000 volumes, plus traveling exhibitions.

Given the limitations of its size and location, the FAC boasts impressive works by legendary artists such as Georgia O'Keefe, Charles Russell, and John James Audubon. Several times a year, the FAC conducts special exhibits covering such topical areas as early 20th-century photographers, southwestern artists, and great contemporary modern artists. The inviting building near the heart of Colorado Springs also hosts a Classic Film Series, Repertory Theater, and other special community events.

In the mid 1990s, the FAC had run into substantial difficulties with member recruitment and retention and its management became interested in developing a new membership campaign for the organization. Membership had continued to dwindle and skew older, with a large percentage of active members from the Silent Generation (people born between 1924 and 1945).

At the time, many members were attracted from similar highbrow membership organizations such as the symphony support group. Although the FAC board of trustees appreciated and honored its older membership base, there was nevertheless growing concern. Younger people, especially Baby Boomers, were not joining and participating in the organization.

Maybe Boomers did not feel welcome among the established social network, heavily represented by older community leaders. Maybe they did not appreciate the social and networking advantages of the organization. Just as importantly, perhaps they had not been invited with the right attitude to become members in a meaningful and memorable way.

Whatever the reasons, the Associate Executive Director asked my firm to help the membership committee develop an evocative new way to recruit members; he wanted a big idea that broke away from past ho-hum approaches; and our goal would be principally to attract Boomers.

I am sure that he did not anticipate my response.

My prior experiences with other membership development projects taught me a few important lessons about building momentum. One cliché continues to prove valid as a driving motivator throughout many different marketing situations: *Birds of a feather flock together*.

People often join community organizations to improve their chances of meeting and associating with others they admire and those whom they view as similar in economic status, values, and lifestyle choices. Prospective members want to be around people of influence or with whom they hope to develop business relationships. Sometimes aspiration drives their conscious or subconscious goals. They want to be near people who have achieved what they hope to achieve.

Second, many people do wish to give back to their communities and to make the world a better place. This is one classic way to achieve a form of perceived immortality.

Third, many people simply want to have fun with their playtime. Work in the form of community service can be entertaining, but demanding community service contributions must lead to engaging social experiences, leisure opportunities, an anticipated thrill of the unknown, or novelty.

Understanding the motivators that influence people to join social and membership organizations, and knowing a bit about my generation, I proposed a straightforward plan for the annual campaign. Several important insights led to my final recommendations:

1. The founder of Colorado Springs was an Eastern blueblood and Civil War hero by the name of William Jackson Palmer.

2. The goal of a membership campaign is to build a bandwagon effect, to make the possibility of joining the organization so compelling that it is almost irresistible. People want to jump aboard.

3. The most critically successful, imaginative rock album of all time, according to the conclusions of many critics, is The Beatles' 1967 record, Sgt. Pepper's Lonely Hearts Club Band.

Thus, I proposed a membership campaign with the appealing theme of *Sgt. Palmer's Fine Arts Club Band.*

With this idea, we conceptually constructed a bandwagon custom-tailored for Baby Boomers, literally and metaphorically.

Understanding that any promotional campaign needs to be driven by promotional offers and benefits, we agreed upon a basic package of new member benefits. Any new FAC member, including immediate family members, would receive free admission to the art galleries, special registration privileges in the art school, invitations to preview parties, discounts on the classic film series, discounts at the museum shop, a free subscription to the periodic news magazine, and free seminars about collecting, cooking, contemporary art, and creativity.

Just $52 per year delivered all these benefits. However, the value of each new member to the FAC, of course, far exceeds the nominal annual dues.

A typical benefits package was not enough to satisfy this Boomer strategist—not by a long shot. We added one other critical enticement: When a prospective member joined the FAC prior to a cut-off date about six weeks after the launch of the campaign, he or she would also receive two complimentary tickets to a very special event: a gala reminiscent of a Sixties "be-in." This atypical happening promised to include rock and roll, a special showing of art from the 1960s and 1970s, nostalgic food fare, and special guest celebrities.

The FAC board approved the idea with guarded enthusiasm.

A party themed around the Sixties?
Sex, drugs, and rock and roll?
Which guest celebrities . . . John, George?
How much?
How do you propose to market this ambitious idea?

But the cleverness of this marketing approach eventually disarmed even the most conservative critics, of which there were a few. It was the creative expression of this idea that became the most unifying and compelling.

Do you recall the concept for the famous Sgt. Peppers' album cover? The classic photographic montage portrays the "Four Lads" dressed in old-fashioned band outfits. Surrounding them are life-size photographic and artistic depictions of many famous people: Marilyn Monroe, Bob Dylan, Marlon Brando, Albert Einstein, Elvis Presley, Karl Marx, George Bernard Shaw, among other celebrities. The rather bizarre hodgepodge gathering also includes lots of curious props: a stone figure of a girl, a statue brought over from John Lennon's house, a water tobacco pipe, a garden gnome, a palm tree, a television set, a cloth figure of Shirley Temple, and so on.

I persuaded the FAC leadership that we could restage the same photograph using locally famous people, from news anchors to business leaders. The potential for this photograph to draw together a diverse but influential group of leaders, representing all facets of the community, was beguiling and ultimately motivating!

Four high-profile Baby Boomer community leaders portrayed The Beatles: the president of the Convention & Visitors Bureau, the president and CEO of a greeting card company, the vice-president and general manager of the CBS network affiliate, and, to be more inclusive of women represented in the target market, a high-profile member of the FAC board of trustees.

We surrounded our four rock musicians by other respected community leaders such as the head of a large philanthropic foundation, the president of the Chamber of Commerce, the owner of a major construction company, a bank chairman, the president of a large high technology manufacturing company, a TV anchorwoman, among many others. To spruce up the set with objects reminiscent of the original album cover, we added the FAC logo to

Sgt. Palmer's Fine Arts Club Band featuring Colorado Springs community leaders

the foreground, built from bright red flowers; included many objects similar to those found on the original album cover; and even threw in a rare and extremely valuable Georgia O'Keefe oil painting.

Then we gathered this bizarre assortment of people and objects for a photo shoot. What amazed me was the diversity of outlandish costumes chosen by some of these straight-laced, high profile people, reveling in their fifteen minutes of photographic fame.

I then worked with my art team to develop a direct mail package conceived to look like a compact disk. The influential photo emblazoned the cover of our CD; inside we placed a brochure with a complete description of the membership campaign and benefits.

Colorado Springs community leaders featured in direct mail legend

Staying metaphorically precise, the package copy evoked some famous song lyrics, including these introductory lyrics inspired by one of the album's most famous hits, "Lucy in the Sky with Diamonds:"

Picture yourself in a building on a parkway,
With glimmering oils and statues at sunrise,
Somebody helps you—you learn quite quickly,
From a docent with knowledgeable eyes.
O'Keefe's petals of pearl-gray and lime,
Coming to life in your head,
Look for friends with smiles in their eyes,
And you're home . . .[30]

Since many of the locally famous people are not recognizable to the public, except perhaps by name, title, and affiliation, we included, inside the package, a legend to help readers identify every person and important object. The address side of the self-mailer included another thematic headline from The Beatles: "a little help from our friends."

Coincidentally, the Sunday before we started the multi-stage direct mail campaign, the society columnist for the *Colorado Springs Gazette* led off her column with a highly supportive feature story about the FAC membership drive, and she included a black and white version of our cover photo. Thus, the community buzz started before the first self-mailer arrived in mailboxes. This favorable publicity did not happen by accident because the newspaper's society columnist also posed for the CD cover photo, along with the general managers of several local radio and TV stations, and a popular television anchorwoman.

We compiled lists of local organizations known to have heavy participation by Baby Boomers, such as the Colorado Springs chapter of the Junior League, a women's philanthropic group. Then we began a multi-stage direct marketing campaign by first dispatching our eye-catching CD self-mailers.

The second mailing about two weeks later featured a typical business letter, signed by the membership committee chair, a high-profile woman in the community. Her upbeat exhortation closing the cheerful letter said it all:

In the spirit of John Lennon and Paul McCartney's memorable words, the Colorado Springs Fine Arts Center will get by with a little help from our new friends. Come along; join the band!

Several weeks later, prospects received a follow-up self-mailer featuring the then famous cover photograph, and a gentle warning that time was running short for prospective new members to beat the cut-off date and receive two complimentary tickets to Sgt. Palmer's New Member Welcome Party.

We were not finished building our bandwagon.

The gala needed a celebrity or two to bring out the crowds. George, John, Paul, and Ringo were, unfortunately, not available, although Ringo eventually autographed several copies of the lead self-mailer as door prizes. However, one of our high-profile photo models is the vice-president and general manager of a successful local rock station, and he leveraged his music industry contacts to convince another rock legend to make a cameo appearance for no charge, other than travel expenses.

In 1970, *The Partridge Family* debuted on television co-starring a then 20-year-old David Cassidy. He quickly became the hottest teen idol of the time. He has been called "the ultimate teen idol," a cover boy on every teen magazine, and on the walls of almost every thirteen-year-old female's bedroom. After he convinced the producers of *The Partridge Family* to let him sing on the records, he became an international pop star. He filmed *The Partridge Family* on weekdays and spent his weekends performing concerts around the United States and Canada. In 1972, he conducted an infamous interview with *Rolling Stone* magazine where he posed nude. The article also exploded the myth that Cassidy was anything like his TV character he portrayed, Keith Partridge. David Cassidy was the perfect magnet to attract younger Boomer women and add star pizzazz to our gala.

The big event evolved to include a number of other surprises, including guest appearances from members of the Fifties' rock revival band Flash Cadillac, a group that became famous after its debut in the legendary Baby Boomer coming-of-age movie, *American Graffiti*. We also dressed up the evening with live remote broadcasts by local rock stations, Hollywood style spotlights piercing the winter night sky in front of the FAC, limousine service for VIPs, a state-of-the-art sound system donated by a local high-end audiophile equipment company, and a completely transformed building. Throughout the museum, guests encountered black lights, lava lamps, peace symbols, period artifacts, and Sixties'-era food. Many guests came to the gala dressed in bellbottom jeans, granny dresses, or mini-skirts.

You must be wondering by now: "How well did this brassy marketing program perform?"

The annual membership drive during the previous year attracted about 40 new members. (It is noteworthy to point out that our membership campaign offered almost identical benefits, except for the gala. Although I had attempted to sweeten the benefit package, the FAC board had declined most of my suggestions for budgetary reasons.) The Sgt. Palmer's campaign brought in over 400 new members initially—a 1000 percent increase in new members comparing year-to-year—and continued to influence membership growth from the Baby Boomer segment for several years thereafter.

We built a bandwagon themed around nostalgia with benefits important to Boomers, and hundreds jumped on in a groundswell that demographically changed the nature of the organization.

CHAPTER 23

Racial and Cultural Barriers

THE oldest Baby Boomers share common, indelible memories of the sad, successive assassinations of President John Kennedy, Martin Luther King, Jr., and Robert Kennedy. They have vivid recollections of the civil rights movement and the tentative first steps toward integration in American public schools.

As college-bound Caucasian teenagers from conservative Midwestern regions began their tumultuous college years, many forged their first intimate relationships with people of different racial, ethnic, and cultural backgrounds.

Ethnically diverse groups came together to organize protest marches against racial injustice and segregation or to combat the escalating U.S. commitment to the Vietnam War.

Those sent to Southeast Asia became immersed in other cultures and developed bonds with young Americans originating from very different neighborhoods and cultures. Caucasian Leading-Edge Boomers, more than any preceding 19th and 20th century American generation, embraced minorities and nontraditional cultures. The doctrine of "separate but equal" began to fade into history.

The counterculture movement, which began roughly in 1967 and continued through the end of the Vietnam War in 1974, blew open the doors to diversity. Boomers found personal expression through nontraditional spiritual explorations such as Transcendental Meditation and yoga. They enlarged their understanding of human nature through the Human Potential or Personal Growth Movement, leading many to sample sensitivity-group training, communal living, and musical influences ranging from East-Indian to African-American.

The leading edge of the Baby Boom carved up America's long-standing tradition of cultural and ethnic segregation, dissected alternative lifestyles, and adapted to diversity in their personal relationships, their preferences in music and art, and their political choices.

Multiculturalism became mainstream.

Having grown up in Topeka, Kansas, I had a profound and ironic connection to the nascent civil rights movement. Before 1954, which happened to be the year I started Kindergarten, racial segregation was common in American schools, as it was in Topeka. Public school administrators forced African-American children to attend schools many miles from their homes, although white-only schools existed in nearby neighborhoods. The black schools usually had substandard facilities and equipment.

Oliver Brown tried unsuccessfully to enroll his children in white schools, only to be shoved back by the prejudicial white juggernaut. On behalf of the Brown family, and many other families experiencing similar circumstances, The National Association for the Advancement of Colored People (NAACP) organized a class-action lawsuit to end discrimination in Topeka public schools.

The U.S. District Court of Kansas heard the case in June 1951. The NAACP made a clear-cut argument: segregation teaches black children that society considers them inferior, and black-only school facilities *are* substantially inferior to white schools. The Topeka Board of Education argued that segregation helps prepare black children for the social conditions they will encounter as adults. The district court ruled against Brown, citing an 1896 Supreme Court ruling, *Plessy vs. Ferguson,* that allowed for "separate but equal facilities."

The NAACP appealed to the U.S. Supreme Court in 1952, joining other existing lawsuits from around the country that similarly challenged school segregation. Known as *Oliver L. Brown et. al. v. The Board of Education of Topeka*, the galvanizing lawsuit caught a tidal wave of national headlines. A soon-to-be-famous attorney by the name of Thurgood Marshall, who later became the first black U.S.

Supreme Court Justice, argued the case on behalf of the suing families. Marshall's poignant claim was straightforward: children who do not *learn together* will never learn to *live together*. In May 1954, the Supreme Court ruled that separate educational facilities are inordinately unequal, and schools across the country must desegregate.

In his landmark opinion, Chief Justice Earl Warren wrote: "To separate (African-American children) from others of similar age and qualifications solely because of their race generates a feeling of inferiority as to their status in the community that may affect their hearts and minds in a way unlikely to ever be undone."

Buoyed by this ruling, African-Americans, in concert with a widening network of sympathizers from every race and culture, became inspired to fight for equality and justice throughout all facets of society. The *Civil Rights Act of 1964* and the *Voting Rights Act of 1965* followed this precedent-setting decision.

I had no awareness of this decision during my first few years in elementary school, and Southwest Elementary School (now Whitson Elementary) remained mostly white. There is not a single individual of color in any of my class photos from that time. However, as we started the 6th grade, my class anticipated a special teacher, someone who had developed a celebrity status in our school—Mr. Holland.

A kind and erudite African-American teacher, Mr. Holland stopped by our class three times weekly to teach science. Up to that point, I had been an average student, demonstrating little enthusiasm for learning, but Mr. Holland stimulated a dormant zeal for science; he set fire to my passion for learning about chemistry and biology. I remember rehearsing arcane and difficult biology terms, with atypical effort and repetition, to impress this extraordinary educator and to win his gentle encouragement. He commanded attention in the classroom, and his wit and clarity opened minds.

Growing up in a significant crucible of racial divisiveness, I nevertheless owe my lifelong passion for learning to a man who probably lived daily with veiled and obvious Jim Crow realities everywhere in Topeka but inside his magical classroom. I know from subsequent adult conversations with my classmates that Mr.

Holland was an influential early mentor to most of us in our long-term educational quest.

While perhaps shunning the most egregious expressions of a multicultural viewpoint, more common among their older brothers and sisters, younger Late Boomers easily accepted and adapted to a diverse, inclusive view of the American experience. As the youngest members of the generation reached college age in the late 1970s and early 1980s, America was dramatically transforming through immigration. Major cities and even the smallest Midwestern towns began to experience spectacular growth of Hispanic, Asian, and Middle-Eastern populations. Caucasian high school and college students began to forge close friendships with people of color.

Any business that seeks to win long-term patronage and customer loyalty today must recognize this affinity for cultural diversity. Boomers experiment, explore, and express themselves through a multiplicity of influences, and they respond best to companies willing to embrace this inclusive worldview.

This goes beyond using multiethnic models in print ads and television spots, as if a superficial display of inclusiveness. It means demonstrating a commitment to diversity through corporate hiring practices and sponsorship participation in multicultural community events.

It means giving back and meaning it.

CHAPTER 24

Eco-Friendly Perspective

AFTER former Wisconsin Senator Gaylord Nelson founded *Earth Day* in 1970, his protégé Denis Hayes left behind a promising graduate education at Harvard's Kennedy School of Government to organize the first national celebration of the planet—a seminal event credited with launching the modern American environmental movement.

Earth Day cherishes a philosophy that helped define an era of environmental activism: Ordinary people, acting together, can achieve something extraordinary—a healthy environment and a peaceful, just, sustainable world.

That heritage thrives today, especially among Baby Boomers who learned early in life that the fragile ecosystem had been under extreme assault by the Industrial Revolution during the last half of the 19th century and the first half of the 20th century. This was brought home to teenage and twenty-something Boomers most vividly with the revelations of the Love Canal controversy.

> Ordinary people, acting together, can achieve something extraordinary.

From the 1920s to 1954, various local firms including the Hooker Chemical Company had filled an abandoned, half-completed canal near Niagara Falls with tons of organic solvents, acids, and pesticides, as well as their by-products, many of them carcinogenic. The defiled water and land was Love Canal.

Subsequent epidemiological studies demonstrated that birth defects, miscarriages, low birth weight, cancers and respiratory disorders had been common among people whose homes were adjacent to or on the Love Canal landfill. The government tore down the houses and school and declared the area a disaster. These images galvanized Baby Boomers in collective denunciation of companies and governments that willfully pollute and mismanage the environment.The *Earth Day* ethos then implanted a message, clear and simple: We all have a stake in protecting the planet.

There is no shortage of environmental issues today: loss of biodiversity, global warming, industrial agribusiness, depleted and polluted water, vanishing forests, and polluting energy sources. Our fragile "Mother Ship" continues to show troubling signs of abuse. Many business and political leaders continue to demonstrate a fundamental failure to establish a global environmental consciousness.

Marketers hoping to build stronger ties with Baby Boomers (and sell more products and services) would be well advised to remember environmental concerns and a nearly universal desire to contribute to a more sustainable, healthier planet. This passion will become more relentless as the generation's time remaining on the planet becomes shorter.

Let the marketplace know of your environmental and planetary commitments.

So, if you build furniture, start buying lumber from forests certified by the Forest Stewardship Council. If you build cars, pledge to design and build eco-friendly cars. If you build anything labor intensive (clothes, circuit boards, cameras), stop using sweatshops, a human manifestation of global abuse. Encourage your stakeholders to become part of the solution.

Reduce. Reuse. Recycle.

Then let the marketplace know of your environmental and planetary commitments.

Environmental consciousness has become a mantra at Starbucks, the ubiquitous chain of gourmet coffee stores. Under the leadership of Howard Schultz, a Baby Boomer who joined the company in 1982 as director of retail operations and marketing, Starbucks Corporation grew from a single Seattle-based retail coffee bar in 1984 to 5,688 locations in 2002.

Displays in most stores tell of the firm's successful efforts to work with indigenous coffee growers in the tropical countries collaborating with the American caffeine monolith.

While enjoying a double-mocha latte, you can even pause between sips to read your paper cup and learn about the company's environmental consciousness. The company wisely tells about its corporate focus on selling sustainable, high-quality coffees. Starbucks has developed purchasing guidelines that embrace environmentally friendly products, and the company gives priority to vendors that share its concern for the environment. Some of the guidelines for paper products require suppliers to use post-consumer recycled materials, unbleached fiber content, and lead-free ink.

Starbucks is one of 500 companies to join *Climate Wise*, a program of the U.S. Environmental Protection Agency. This comprehensive national initiative works with companies to help them reduce greenhouse gas emissions, and ultimately mitigate global warming.

The coffee giant has also created a Green Team. The company's corporate website delineates the purpose of this grassroots internal organization:

"Since the early 1990s, Starbucks has relied on The Green Team, a group of partners throughout North America who serve as a link to our retail stores on environmental initiatives such as waste reduction, energy, and water conservation. Team members also provide critical feedback on measures that help us minimize our environmental impact."[31]

The Green Team has undertaken a number of beneficial initiatives, including waste reduction through introducing reusable tableware, recycling of store coffee grounds for use in home gardens and composts, and overall store energy conservation.

As Starbucks is demonstrating through its many comprehensive environmental programs, if you want to build a strong relationship with a generation that is revitalizing its commitment to a long-term legacy, start demonstrating your company commitment to conservation and restoring the long-term stability of a fragile ecosystem.

CHAPTER 25

The Medium Is the Message

THE Baby Boom generation became the first generation to grow up with television. From the moment post-World War II babies could peer between cribs rails, dynamic information inundated them daily from small phosphorescent tubes.

They cut their teeth on *Gunsmoke*, *Father Knows Best*, *Leave It to Beaver*, *My Three Sons*, *The Ed Sullivan Show*, and *Have Gun Will Travel*.

As the late Timothy Leary observed, television taught Boomers to be "reality consumers." They learned, at a very young age, to look at life as instructed by a Judy Collins' song: "from both sides now."

By the time Boomers became pre-teens, their young minds began processing more alternative realities in a single day than their grandparents processed in a year. Televisions brought vicarious experiences into their lives, giving them an ever-changing perspective of values, lifestyle options, human potential, and the process of change itself.

Things that were once a given were no longer immutable today. What was cool last week was not anymore.

Marshall McLuhan, the Canadian scholar and author of the seminal book *Understanding Media*, became the high priest of pop culture in the Sixties, in part because of his evolving perceptions of Baby Boomer college students, then populating his classes. He articulated and popularized several important concepts that have influenced understanding of media and presented refreshing new ideas about the best ways to influence others through media communications—in particular—Baby Boomers.

First, McLuhan introduced the idea of the "global village" long before technology fully realized worldwide satellite communications and the internet. A village is immediate, in the sense that something affecting one person in the village influences all other community members almost instantaneously. With the advent of worldwide connectivity through electronic communications, Americans can instantly know and experience what happens in any corner of the globe within minutes.

The fall 2002 terrorist bombing of a nightclub in far-off Bali and overnight worldwide revulsion illustrated again the power of global communications, the capability of media to gather together people from around the world. The technological realization of a global village has broadened consumer expectations for immediate and thorough information.

Second, McLuhan coined the concept leading this section: "The medium is the message." This simply means that the qualities of a communication medium have as much effect as the message itself. For example, reading a description of a scene from a Shakespearean play has a very different effect on someone than hearing it, or seeing a picture of a scene, or watching a black and white video, or experiencing a big-screen, Dolby surround-sound, digital extravaganza at a movie theater. The level of mental engagement that a medium fosters influences the way receivers perceive and process the message.

Finally, and related to his famous aphorism, McLuhan introduced the idea of "hot" versus "cool" media. A hot medium is one that requires active engagement on the part of the receiver to lend interpretation and meaning to the message. A political cartoon is hotter than a written political manifesto because the former requires active engagement of imagination, complex thinking, and the availability of experience. The manifesto requires engagement to a lesser degree because the manifesto author carefully provides details for his arguments, and the receiver has to bring less personal experience, knowledge, and insight to the medium to receive the message.

On the other hand, a cool medium is one requiring less active mental engagement on the part of the receiver. A televised political documentary is cool in the sense that viewers can watch the show without necessarily activating the higher cognitive powers of critical thinking, analysis, and judgment. Viewers simply take in the flowing narrative and video images.[38]

The challenge confronting those who hope to market success-fully to Baby Boomers is to integrate understanding of the target audience with the influence any marketing medium might have on awareness, motivation, and ultimate purchase behaviors.

Since Boomers are rapid consumers of new realities, the first task is to assemble a new reality. The broadcast media have wired Boomer brains since childhood to be responsive to these rapid paradigm shifts.

Marketers have accomplished reality modification repeatedly, as Boomers' public image, and therefore self-image, has evolved to embrace new identifying reality constructs, from teenyboppers, to hippies, to yuppies, to liberated empty nesters.

As the generation marched through the final decades of the 20th century, marketers developed new realities that have been the fodder of pop culture. From "Where's the Beef?" to "Just do it," Boomers have learned more about themselves from the package of values, or realities, that have been built around consumer products.

The greatest difference in the future is that you will need to be more sophisticated about building new product and service realities. The major question to answer: What will be the best plausible reality for Boomers in the context of your product or service?

The challenge is to integrate understanding of the target audience with the influence any marketing medium might have on awareness.

Are you building houses or a lifestyle community dedicated to bringing neighbors together through front porches and a community center? Does your upscale kitchen appliance serve some utilitarian cooking purpose, or does it warm up the center of a home? Is your day spa a place for relaxation or rejuvenation? Does your new magazine promise information or insights? Is your new ski lodge a bundle of amenities, or a complete escape experience?

As you consider the reality of your product, search elsewhere within this book for ideas about what form your product reality might take within the context of this generation and the fundamental drivers of their spending behavior.

Next, you need to decide which advertising media best communicate with Boomers, not only with consideration of the media chosen, but also the messages communicated. Boomers are known to be better readers than younger, more video-centric generations, so can your marketing story be better told through a sixteen-page special advertising supplement in a national magazine than via the flitting, fleeting imagery of national television advertising?

A November 2002 issue of *Time* magazine demonstrated the power of the weekly magazine as a persuasive medium for communicating an updated product reality for a Blue Chip company.

Following its heated merger with Compaq Computer, widespread employee layoffs, and substantial internal reorganization, Hewlett Packard Company reintroduced itself with a sixteen-page advertising supplement. The ambitious corporate manifesto sported gorgeous graphics and photography, and connected the revitalized company brand with "the world's great companies, thinkers and doers." HP then provided proof of this claim by showing dramatic two-page spreads representing its technology solutions for NASA, Amazon, Federal Express, the BMW Williams Formula 1 Team, the Hong Kong government, BirdLife Finland, and DreamWorks.

Many people whom HP hopes to influence positively are Baby Boomer readers who are in important positions of authority within the business and public sectors. The HP message isn't limited just to advertising copy, graphics and photography, but also to the supplement's context: sixteen sturdy pages of quality paper bound into the center of a widely distributed weekly newsmagazine.

As a medium, the magazine brings topical relevance and authority into homes and offices. In this instance, the magazine delivered to HP management a loyal consumer franchise characterized by news junkies. Suddenly, an advertising medium takes on the authority of a news medium.

Always consider the medium as the message. Does your marketing message need the influence of news reporting, thus the imperative of stimulating news coverage through publicity? Alternatively, do you need to build a "buyer village" around your product, and therefore have an opportunity to create an internet community?

Hot media guarantee deeper emotional and time investments because consumers must actively engage in the exploration and learning process. Hot media assure better assimilation and responsiveness to marketing messages. Thus, many marketers have employed the extensive reach and interactivity of the internet to engage prospective customers with webinars, on-line PowerPoint demonstrations, and instant customer support.

Roaring Pine company has developed a software technology that enables prospective internet customers to click a button and chat online with a customer service specialist or technical expert.[32] If you are searching the internet for holiday gifts on an enabled web site, you can click a button and immediately have live human discourse in the form of text-based questions and answers. You type your questions in a text box, and an agent replies within seconds. The agent can clarify and resolve your concerns, show you how to complete orders, and cross-sell or up-sell your product selection by sending other web pages featuring similar products to your computer screen.

The internet provides a format to deliver deep content, networked communities of like-minded people, and self-directed learning. No communication medium in our lifetime has promised more potential to change the way we conduct business and consume—a hot medium with limitless engagement potential.

Television implies brief, high-impact messages designed to communicate perhaps a single, emotionally charged idea, such as protecting your family through adequate life insurance coverage.

Newsmagazines bring the context of highly topical news and investigative reports to your product advertisement.

Radio can deliver an immediate message and reach decision makers during their morning and evening commutes.

The medium is always the message, so consider it too.

CHAPTER 26

Multi-Disciplinary Contributions

ALTHOUGH this generation's impact has been significant in the entertainment world, Baby Boomers do not want their legacy to rely solely on the great work of rock musicians and Hollywood actors. They are certainly proud of the accomplishments of two famous Bruce's—Bruce Springsteen and Bruce Willis—but the people they admire in their everyday lives include thousands of heroes who never achieve mass-market celebrity. These unsung superstars may be famous for their accomplishments in only a single quiet industry—and many prefer anonymity to celebrity—but they are nevertheless as important to the Boomer legacy as its Tinsel Town celebrities.

For example, have you heard of James Thomson, born 1958? The once obscure University of Wisconsin developmental biologist is one of the leading scientists to advance stem cell research and help discover miraculous new cures to diseases that have plagued humanity for millennia. His most significant breakthrough was to learn how to prevent embryonic cells from morphing into specialized cells and thus to keep multiplying indefinitely, achieving a form of cellular immortality. Undifferentiated stem cells have the potential to grow under scientific guidance into one of the 200 types of cells that make up a human being. This releases the potential for physicians to direct the growth of stem cells and then to replace damaged cells in malfunctioning livers or injured spinal cords.

Or how about Dr. Wise Young, born 1950? Head of the W.M. Keck Center for Collaborative Neuroscience at Rutgers University,

Young has demonstrated that when high doses of a steroid known as methyl-prednisolone are administered within eight hours of a spinal chord injury, 20 percent of nerve function can be saved. This can be the difference between breathing unassisted or relying on a respirator, and walking or spending one's life in a wheelchair. Thousands of people owe him a hearty handshake (which they may not have. been able to accomplish before his discovery) for the mobility and independence his research has preserved for them.

How about Ben Carson, born 1951? The Johns Hopkins surgeon is world-renowned for his skills, undertaking operations that once were only the providence of science fiction. He has developed a successful procedure to remove half of a child's brain to give children suffering from severe, uncontrollable seizures a successful shot at normal living. He is one of the foremost surgeons in the world recognized for mastering the delicate task of separating conjoined Siamese twins with attached heads. What makes Carson even more praiseworthy, however, is his heroic journey from the ghettos of Detroit.

He grew up poor in the 1950s. His parents divorced, and he nearly failed the fifth grade. His courageous mother swiftly intervened. She restricted television viewing and required Carson and his older brother to read books and write weekly reports. Carson fought a boiling temper that nearly led him to kill a neighborhood boy. Nevertheless, through intense spiritual soul-searching, he found a more enlightened viewpoint that ushered him to the top of his class and a lifelong commitment to breakthrough surgery, medical research, and youth education.

Dr. Robert Langer has greeted his fellow Americans from a full-page photo in *Time* magazine in honor of his impressive achievements. A professor of chemical and biomedical engineering at Massachusetts Institute of Technology, Langer created a dime-sized synthetic wafer that ushers chemotherapy to the brain to fight brain tumors. When physicians confronted the decreasing and depressing availability of transplanted organs, he engineered three-dimensional frameworks to grow cells for organ transplants. Collaborating with another scientist from Harvard, he discovered how to use polymers to build tiny scaffolds that can then be seeded with skin, cartilage, or even liver cells. He has also discovered a "pharmacy on a chip," which can deliver medication to the right place at the right dose at the right time. Born in 1948, Langer is thought of in academic circles as a "mission impossible" scientist. He holds over 300 patents and has won numerous scientific awards.

Dr. Eric Nestler, 49, of the University of Texas Southwestern Medical Center in Dallas, understands better than most how addiction ruins lives. A psychiatrist and neuroscientist, he discovered that the most popular psychoactive drugs of abuse—alcohol, cocaine, and heroin—have the same effect. They all corrupt the "feel-good" pathways within the brain, leading first to dependence and then addiction. His research has revealed that an addicted person is not the same individual that friends and relatives might remember; an addicted person has changed in fundamental personality traits. Addiction weakens will, making it difficult to impossible for the addicted person to stop the cycle. Nestler is discovering new pharmaceutical compounds that mimic the action of euphoric drugs, without the addictive side effects, and block cravings while disrupting the addictive cycle.

Consider also Tim White, born in 1950, who, as a boy growing up near Lake Arrowhead, California, collected pottery shards from ancient Native American campsites located in the San Bernardino Mountains. High school counselors advised him sternly about the impracticality of a career pursuing knowledge about dinosaurs. He refused to let go of his childhood absorption with fossils and proceeded to become one of the world's leading collectors of hominid fossils. After years of study in Ethiopia, he pushed back the narrative of human evolution by 2 million years to the instant when human beings took a different evolutionary path from our closest mammal relatives, the chimpanzees.

Does the name Coleen Rowley ring a bell? A staff attorney with the FBI, just a few years short of retirement, she has confronted the angst and alienation that are often the plight of whistleblowers. In May 2002, Rowley chastised her employer in a 13-page memorandum. This mid-level lawyer identified many of the Bureau's shortcomings in analyzing the case of Zacarias Moussaoui, a French-Moroccan who had signed up for a local flight school and had shown a questionable keenness to operate a 747, allegedly with the intent of becoming the twentieth highjacker during the terrorist attacks of September 11. Time magazine honored Rowley as one of its three Persons of the Year for 2002.

Last, how about Elisabeth Spelke, born 1949? The Harvard psychologist studied how babies interact with the world and dispelled a myth that they see the world as "one great blooming, buzzing confusion" until about the age of two. She has confirmed that babies as young as three months expect objects in the world to obey physical laws, such as not being able to pass through physical barriers. Babies can connect what they see with what they hear. These insights have led to greater understanding about healthy infant care and early childhood education.[33]

The point for marketers is this: As Boomers grow older and enter their retirement years, they will come to appreciate companies' products and services, when marketing communications portray this generation's role in advancing all areas of human thought and exploration.

Their entertainment industry accomplishments provide only a single, limited view of how they have lived their lives during the last five decades.

A new kind of hero-worship, featuring real people who have given significantly to their professions and communities, will demonstrate your organization's commitment to balance and fairness. Balance and fairness are primary motivators of Boomer's social and political views. Balance and fairness will win their loyalty; its absence may drive them away.

CHAPTER 27

Childhood over Adolescent Nostalgia

PUNDITS often assume that Leading-Edge Baby Boomers are emotionally entrenched in the years when media referred to them as "Flower Children," roughly 1967 through 1974. If someone wants to play the nostalgia card, he or she will usually pull out the beads and peace symbols. A recent slew of television commercials rely on classic rock music from that era to appeal to an apparent Sixties' imprinting.

I cannot prove this empirically, but I believe powerful nostalgic feelings also subconsciously resonate around the period from the late Fifties through the mid-Sixties. For older Boomers, this was a time of relative innocence.

The Fifties remind Boomers of huge product fads, from Hula Hoops to Barbie Dolls, and from Silly Putty to Slinkies. It was a time of innocent television programming, from *Father Knows Best* to *Lassie*. Most Boomers born between 1946 and 1955 can recall powerful marketing images from this childlike chapter of American history. The American economy was experiencing significant expansion; dads worked and moms stayed at home to care for children; and corporations had unrivaled latitude to create and promote their mass-produced products.

In the early Sixties, the war in Vietnam was still being covered in back-page blurbs; musical lyrics focused on love, cars, and surfing. Young people were concerned mostly with school, social events with peers, and cruising Main Street.

Yes, the assassination of President John Kennedy sadly and intractably interrupted these young lives, but this enormous blow to innocence did not break the optimistic spirit of an up-and-coming generation of teenagers. Within months after JFK's death, most had heard about Four Lads from Liverpool, and The Beatles once again captured a collective imagination and buoyant view of the future. "The British Invasion" gave Boomers new music to celebrate being young, falling in love, and reaching independence.

Ah, *those* were the good times.

Although the sex, drugs, and rock and roll that came later had their pleasurable influences, these diversions, as most Boomers will attest, exacted a large price. A price that included our peers returning from Vietnam in body bags, violent confrontations with the so-called "Establishment," derision by the "Moral Majority," and a lingering sense of unease. The pleasure triumvirate became an escape mechanism from all the disorder; it did not correct the underlying problems.

Moreover, many went slightly crazy for a while.

Which scenario would you choose to answer the call of nostalgia: warm summer nights on the beach with your girlfriend or the boy of your dreams and nothing much to worry about but how to finance another tank of gas, or a whacked out acid trip with a bunch of reprobates disconnecting you from reality?

If you want to reach Baby Boomers by appealing to major developmental influences that recall comfortable memories, then I recommend focusing also on the cultural phenomena that punctuated early childhood and adolescence: the late 1950s through the mid-1960s.

That is when Boomer teenagers worried the least and expected the most from life experiences.

CHAPTER 28

Monologue versus Dialogue

FOR many Leading-Edge Baby Boomers, their earliest communication growth experiences occurred during the Human Potential Movement of the late-Sixties and Seventies. This was the era of sensitivity training when many tried to understand others and discover how others understand them. Most often, these revelations occurred through a guided group setting.

Many discovered a timeless truth in interpersonal relationships: to be self-disclosing and genuine in communications with others is to earn their trust and positive regard.

Some learned this through what was then called "T-Groups" or college classes focused on interpersonal communications. Others discovered the value of honest self-disclosure through team-building programs offered by employers. Pop psychology books, such as *I'm OK—You're OK*, and mainstream magazine articles began to examine the subject of authentic interpersonal communications and relationships.

> To be self-disclosing and genuine in communications with others is to earn their trust and positive regard.

Still other Baby Boomers learned the art of effective interpersonal communications through such executive training courses as those offered by the Dale Carnegie organization.

Few escaped at least one experience that required them to take a hard look at their ways of communicating with others. Boomers learned the true meaning of dialogue.

This underlying principle remains today, although many have

forgotten some of the beneficial lessons of honest, genuine communication with others. Modern American corporate culture does not often reward truly honest people who freely reveal their true feelings and needs.

The most important lesson remains indelible, and this is the premise that mutually beneficial, long-term relationships exist on the foundation of give and take. Marketers need to understand the power of this dynamic force and to apply it in marketing strategies.

Most marketing communication programs are monologues. The advertiser talks through a broadcast commercial or print ad about a unique product benefit, ostensibly one that meets customers' needs, and customers simply purchase the solution. The advertiser has not created and nurtured a feedback loop.

One often wonders if Microsoft has ever asked customers for feedback on its ubiquitous Word program. Probably it does not matter to Microsoft what you think of its software because it essentially has a monopoly. Many marketers without a monopoly act as if they do have one. They do not understand their customers, ask for feedback, and then react to the feedback with self-correcting improvements and upgrades.

Every touch-point with a customer is an opportunity to receive feedback, from mail-in surveys (rewarded, of course) to on-line chat rooms and toll-free customer support. The more you encourage and share customer feedback, the more likely you will be to create a sense of community around your product or service.

As Christopher Locke points out in his business book *Gonzo Marketing*, today's buyers are more likely to become loyal, enthusiastic customers to the extent they are allowed to participate in a community of like-minded people. The key to success is to allow these communities to form, primarily through the internet and well-designed websites, and then give them the freedom to act and react independently of the marketer.

In other words, you control the source and initial content of the community (a company website), but you allow the ensuing content created by customers (via live chats, FAQs, and posted customer stories) to follow its own, spontaneous evolution. Yes, you have to monitor this process to weed out lunatics, but you can allow most of your customers and stakeholders the freedom of self-expression.

Amazon.com is beautifully demonstrating this concept by encouraging customers to write reviews of books and other products. As an occasional *Amazon.com* customer, I place greater faith in a compendium of customer reviews than I do in the professional book reviews supplied mostly by publishers and authors. The interactivity of this site continues beyond initial posting of a review because lay reviewers can rate the helpfulness of other reviews, and the two-way communication builds a new culture around the book or item under scrutiny.

On your own company website, you will recognize success when stories, myths, and anecdotes about positive company and product experiences begin to appear. Common, real, and personal stories bring meaning and context to products and services, and anecdotes demonstrate an evolution of your customer base from people who just receive your communications to advocates who participate in the evolution of your company by adding to its mythology.

You will be successful with Baby Boomers, and for that matter, all age groups, to the extent that you create meaningful dialogue.

This may seem self-evident, if not pedantic, because the mantra of two-way communications has been a part of business culture for a long time. However, I am referring to a different level of communication, beyond polite criticism and contrived company responses to negative customer feedback. I am envisioning a corporate connectivity that evolves beyond a Pollyannaish belief in the inherent goodness of the company.

I am suggesting that the most enlightened companies of the near future will provide safe havens for their customers to share their human experiences in an environment of mutual trust and positive focus. These companies will develop true communities, and both companies and customers will continue to thrive because they embrace candor.

CHAPTER 29

Living Creatively in the Later Years

W HEN Baby Boomers came of age during the Sixties and Seventies, they became enmeshed in a highly creative time in the 20th century. The Beatles and the rest of the "British Invasion" sparked new creativity in rock music, which led to the formation and subsequent popularity of such American super-groups as Crosby, Stills & Nash, The Eagles, and Fleetwood Mac. The rapid success of sophisticated rock groups led to more experimental and avant-garde forms of musical expression, such as the rock opera *Tommy* by The Who and the Broadway musicals *Jesus Christ Superstar* and *Hair*.

English critic Lawrence Alloway first coined the term "Pop Art" in a 1958 edition of *Architectural Digest* magazine to represent "the paintings that celebrate post-war consumerism, defy the psychology of Abstract Expressionism, and worship the god of materialism." Pop Art attracted a larger mass audience to visual communications than perhaps at any other time in American history. This celebration of consumer society became a dynamic movement honoring creativity and nurturing the extraordinary breakaway successes of commanding artists such as Peter Max, Andy Warhol, Jim Dine, David Hockney, Jasper Johns, Robert Rauschenberg, and Roy Lichtenstein. These artists evolved quickly beyond the stage of starvation to become popular among intelligencia, and then to become household names and eventually icons.

Wherever Boomers turned, the arts had become the fire and ferment of a cultural revolution.

Wherever Boomers turned, the arts had become the fire and ferment of a cultural revolution.

Album covers—in past times, just glamour photographs of the artists featured within—became social statements as well as exciting new forms of artistic expression. Musical lyrics evolved beyond trite clichés about love, automobiles, and teenage angst, to take on grave social issues such as war, revolution, and racial justice.

An upheaval in the literary arts led to breakaway magazines such as *Rolling Stone* and the eventual prominence of such contributing writers as Hunter Thompson and Tom Wolfe. The generation adopted renowned new fiction authors such as Kurt Vonnegut, Jr. and Ken Kesey, who explored contemporary Boomer themes in their writing.

In addition, popular clothing fashion evolved to become an entirely fresh departure from the norms and traditions of society in the previous stultifying years. Boomers expressed this garment creativity by wearing wild prints and patterns, beads and baubles, bell-bottoms and granny dresses. Some began to appear as if characters from the Victorian era; others embraced the washed denim and leather fabrics of the working class.

Creativity became the fuel of the cultural engine, propelling many rapid changes in the social contract. Many would-be Boomer artisans adopted a creative outlet to help discover a more authentic and meaningful way of living.

Some became bluegrass and rock musicians, others took up 35 mm photography with the passion of *Rolling Stone* photographer Annie Leibowitz. Still others dabbled in sculpture, dance, silkscreen printing, candle making, and leather clothing design.

Creativity and art are in the Baby Boomer DNA. For those who have maintained a creative outlet through the years, avocations and hobbies may become predominant preoccupations as new retirees embrace working calendars with fewer restrictions and greater freedom. These hobbies may even evolve from avocations to new forms of modest income and a way to supplement under-funded retirement assets.

For those who have forsaken their creative passions during the last thirty years, there could be a renaissance of creative exploration through continuing education and vocational-technical schools. Many will seek ways to add depth and texture to their retirement years with hobbies that actually produce something tangible, from screenplays to decoupage.

The passionate quest for creative immortality is likely to become a powerful trend during the next few years, and this driving fervor will open new doors of opportunity for marketers.

The most important question you can ask is this: How can our product or service be adapted to meet the needs of a market that is becoming zealous about self-expression and invention?

As an example, let us examine financial planning, an important task during the final adult years but also creatively mundane. How could a smart company offering financial planning for wealth preservation and inheritance better serve the needs of people seeking meaningful self-expression through creativity?

Well, this powerful underlying motivation could be tapped through a number of novel strategies. The financial planning company could host a weekend retreat, and selected clients could begin the workshop by writing and reading to the group a one-page vision statement to answer this question: How do you want to pass along your financial legacy to your children?

Alternatively, the financial planning company could invite its A-list guests to bring family photos and mementos to the retreat, and each person or couple could assemble a legacy montage, supplemented by photos cut from popular magazines that illustrate the desired outcomes and enduring benefits of a more creative, visionary financial plan.

Each participant could create, and then share a story about the years following his or her death. Imagine the power and empowerment that might evolve from stories that convey, in richer details, the ultimate benefits to successors of a carefully developed plan for wealth preservation and inheritance.

While this illustration may appear somewhat out in left field, I propose it to encourage your own thinking about how you can build creative expression into the bundle of values surrounding your product or service. The extent to which you empower customers to use imagination to produce positive expressions of self is the degree to which you will effectively involve Boomers and stimulate an innate, creative passion.

Changing Workforce Dynamics — Forestalling the Boomer Exodus

RETIREMENT AGE looms on the horizon for a generation, and employers are rightfully becoming apprehensive. Of greatest concern is how companies and government can preserve Boomers' experience, acumen and relationships. Of additional importance is how business can accommodate an aging and shrinking workforce.

According to research by the AARP, 68 million workers will be older than 45 by 2012 and will then represent over 40 percent of the nation's work force. At the same time, one in three Americans will be over 50.

A Merrill Lynch survey in 2004 predicted that over 75 percent of Boomers plan to work in some capacity in retirement. Over 10 percent intend to start new businesses.[34] AARP's research further confirms that nearly 8 in 10 Boomers are planning to work at least part time. Classic retirement is not in the cards for most aging Boomers or their employers.

The dilemma for companies to address, sooner than later, is how to create a business environment that reenergizes long-term Boomer employees while attracting new talent from the same generational labor pool.

It's understandable why Boomers are restless. Many are retiring early to pursue unanswered dreams. Some are fed up with job stagnation. Some fear the implications of recent layoffs and corporate downsizing, preferring to act rather than react. Boomers are also seekers, and many are confronting the dissonance between their youthful dreams and present-day realities.

Companies committed to mitigating a Boomer exodus are developing new ways for their Boomer employees to rejuvenate and recommit. Hardened HR practices are gaining flexibility, such as job sharing, flex scheduling, and intermittent sabbatical-style breaks. New businesses are appearing to help companies and Boomers actualize phased retirement, capturing the Boomer legacy with "knowledge sharing," "social network analysis," and "cultural change management."

Marketplace advantages will accrue for companies that create aging-friendly brand strategies. This means redefining the organizational understanding of its workforce composition, determining how older workers are treated and valued, identifying what older workers will be doing to further company interests, and creating intrinsic and extrinsic rewards for older workers.

Companies can then market an age-friendly image through advertising, recruitment marketing, and internal employee communications. In addition to retaining and attracting older workers more effectively, companies with Boomer-friendly images can also expect to increase share of market and build a stronger franchise with older customers.

CHAPTER 30

Discovering the Anthems of Boomer Aging

SOME marketers are already ahead of the curve in understanding the business potential of the 50 and older crowd. Bright people in storied offices above Madison Avenue are now engaged in a search for the Boomer "Holy Grail," the defining symbols, messages or icons that will open the collective checkbooks. They want to discover our late-life anthems before we write them ourselves.

For example, Sony Electronics launched an aggressive advertising campaign in November 2002, and directed its message at Baby Boomers who are just beginning to taste the liberating temptations of empty nests and disposable income. The giant consumer electronics manufacturer and marketer decided to aim its newest product messages at "Zoomers," another term for Baby Boomers allegedly coined by *U.S. News & World Report*.

The lead spot tells the story of a 50-ish man who cashes in his assets, sells his business, and answers a longstanding dream of traveling in outer space. Joe Pytka, the legendary television commercial director, filmed the spot at the Star City Cosmonaut Training Facility outside Moscow.

The Boomer hero travels to Russia to prepare for his extraterrestrial voyage, and of course, he documents the escapade on his Sony Handycam. The commercial ends with the hero blissfully floating in a space capsule miles above earth's surface, Handycam in hand, and then the ultimate "screw the world" character-generated message: "When your kids ask where the money went, show them the tape."

For the music bed, the creative team added the rock song "Carry On," a Crosby, Stills, Nash & Young anthem from the 1970s, covered by Alana Davis. The finished spot became a near-perfect portrayal of Boomer nostalgia justifying present and future consumption behavior.

Based on what you have read in this book, what's right and what's wrong with this television commercial?

On the one hand, the idea is clever, and the hero fulfills his ultimate fantasy, cost and practicality be damned. He makes bold changes in his humdrum life, and maybe he finally embraces some well-deserved time away from his spouse, children, and other adult responsibilities.

Okay, he handsomely rewards Number One, something all adults have thought about doing on one occasion or another, but when push comes to the shove, few to none actually take such a deep plunge.

The commercial has all the production panache of an exquisite movie, with the warm hues of 35 mm film, and the broad landscapes of a movie theater epic.

Clearly, the agency and its client have the best intentions. This is what makes the spot such an interesting object lesson about packaging and conveying marketing messages to Boomers. On the one hand, the spot seeks to communicate with a generation's sense of maverick independence and willingness to "go for it."

On the other hand, this Boomer hero takes everything to the extreme. Even if Sony intends viewers to interpret their spot as a humorous, over-dramatized portrayal of real fantasies, other messages come through the fast cuts and fun visuals.

Sony and its creative team at WPP Group's Y&R Advertising prey on tired Boomer stereotypes to give their creative idea more impact (probably unintentionally). The intended message is uplifting, empowering; the hidden message is potentially one of derision and denouncement.

On the underside of this commercial, what viewers see is one Boomer's total rejection of responsibility for others, except for that beautiful videotape the protagonist will leave behind for his kids—and nothing else.

Thanks for the memories, Dad.

Is there any image more self-absorbed than a man cashing in his lifetime earnings, forsaking financial responsibility for his children after his death, and dumping everything into a single fantasy trip to circle the globe a few times?

This portrayal of Baby Boomer yearning looks characteristically egotistic, conceited, and thoughtless, right in step with the stereotypes that continue to follow Boomers as they travel through life's stages.When you think about it, the spot is another metaphor for mind expansion by self-medication, in this case an intoxicating voyage around the planet.

Y&R evokes Boomer's alleged maverick mindset, but in this portrayal, there is little honor or dignity. It is hardly about giving back, but is, rather, just another form of taking. And this is not smart marketing in the long run.

My role model is not someone who would disinherit his children, fritter away his assets on an expensive orbital trip, and, in fact, give up everything for his own short-term gratification. That does not mean "Carry On," it means "Cash In."

Quoted in an *Advertising Age* article about this campaign, Ken Dice, Sony senior vice-president of consumer segment marketing said, "When we started to think about talking to and engaging Zoomers, we realized that no one created an anthem for this generation."[35]

Mr. Dice and others in powerful marketing positions need to understand that the true anthem of the retiring generation will not be, "Sock it to me because it's all about me." Dice and many of his peers may be missing uplifting opportunities. Boomer anthems will be more about generosity, public service, social justice, and humanitarian causes. Self-indulgence without service or substance will not fly in the future as a motivating sequence.

How much more amazing and congruent would have been a campaign built around true Baby Boomer heroes, the men and women who daily sacrifice and give back in some incredible ways, as described elsewhere in this book?

The same Handycam could have been brought into these powerful mini-docudramas depicting real life and real people—giving back and making a difference. It happens every day, and the Sony Handycam could be there.

If a Sony Handycam can help me better realize my beneficent goals of service, relevancy, and creative expression, then I need one.

CHAPTER 31

ED and Getting to the Point

PURSUING innovation is at the heart of the corporate culture for Pfizer, Inc. The pharmaceutical giant's website trumpets this mantra with its marketing slogan, "The Champions of Innovation."

Innovation has led this company to create a recognizable lexicon of pharmaceutical brands: Bengay for muscle soreness, Benadryl to relieve allergic reactions, Cortizone for itching and rashes, and Visine for eye irritation.

Innovation has also guided research and development toward the discovery of newer stand-apart prescription brands such as Lipitor for high cholesterol, Zoloft for depression, and perhaps the firm's most remarkable recent success story, Viagra, the "little blue pill" for erectile dysfunction (ED).

Pfizer's chairman, Hank McKinnell, Ph.D., heartily acknowledges the role of his multinational firm in the phenomenon of an aging population:

> Ultimately, our goal is your healthy aging. That means being a true partner with you and your physicians in extending the length and vigor of your life, while keeping you and your loved one out of hospitals, operating rooms, and nursing homes.[36]

Viagra has enjoyed an uncontested playing field in the industry of middle-aged romantic conquest since the firm's introduction of its ubiquitous impotence medication in 1998. All good things must pass.

In 2003, federal regulators approved Levitra, an impotence treatment from GlaxoSmithKline and Bayer AG, and Cialis, a drug developed by Eli Lilly & Co.

Clearly, the pharmaceutical giants are anticipating the needs of the Boomer Generation.

The marketing and media clash among three galactic-sized pharmaceutical conglomerates spells relief for some battle-weary advertising agencies on the rebound from several years of recessionary ad spending. As observed on the online version of *Forbes* magazine: "The tug-of-war between the three pharmaceutical groupings is already under the spotlight, given the hype and sensitivity surrounding the treatments and their growing place in the consciousness of America's 'Baby Boomer' generation."[37]

This tug-of-war means potent advertising budgets to announce relief of impotency. And have those announcements been prevalent!

Pfizer spent an estimated $50 million on its little blue pill in 2003.[38] All three pharmaceutical titans spent heavily on the Super Bowl in January 2004, with the average spot costing $2.3 million.

Before this watershed media event claiming 58 million viewers and a commercial line-up dominated by impotence messages, it was customary to suggest the benefits of ED medication by using wink-heavy allusions without actually mentioning "erectile dysfunction." For example, Levitra made the point by showing a middle-aged Boomer

Pharmaceutical giants are anticipating the needs of the Boomer Generation.

throwing a football at a tire swing suspended by a rope from a large backyard tree. After several near-misses, he finally nails it with a bulls-eye toss; watching nearby, his wife smiles knowingly and appreciatively.

Another strategy has been to hire middle-aged celebrities associated with strength and virility to speak frankly about their own shameless quest to overcome ED. Bob Dole, the former senator from Kansas and Senate Majority Leader, made his out-of-the-bedroom debut for Viagra. Then Chicago Bears coach Mike Ditka admitted his own ED challenges and the macho solution called Levitra.

Viagra was poised to become a brand name that defined the

genre, as Kleenex and Q-Tips did. The early buzz it created propelled it straight to late-night TV monologues by David Letterman and Jay Leno. The drug went from snickering gossip to prime time. Then competition arose.

Reeling from a stinging loss of 14.4 percent market share of the $1.74 billion male impotency drug market to its new rival Levitra, Pfizer decided to break creative boundaries with a new television commercial for Viagra introduced in March 2004.

The big idea is quite simple. The setting is a typical middle-class neighborhood somewhere in middle-class America. Baby Boomers of every ethnicity are spinning and twirling in slow motion with joy in their hearts.

The viewer sees high-fives and back slaps. Background rock music embellishes the exuberant mood. As if a flashback to 1977, the viewer hears "We Are the Champions" sung with shrill clarity by the late Freddie Mercury.

It's not until the final few seconds of the spot that Viagra makes itself known as the sponsor of such optimism and satisfaction. Viagra users are champions, and their female counterparts share the joy of their victory.

Two public relations critics aptly label much of pharmaceutical marketing as "disease mongering." While the public might still think of drug companies with the preferred image of dedicated scientists in white lab coats working diligently to save humanity from diseases, the reality is that marketing absorbs more than twice the money these companies invest in research and development.[39]

As the authors observe, "Conventional wisdom says that drugs are developed in response to disease. Often, however, the power of pharmaceutical PR creates the reverse phenomenon, in which new diseases are defined by companies seeking to create a market to match their drug."

The late Lynn Payer wrote a book entitled *Disease Mongering*, in which she observed the phenomenon of pharmaceutical economic interests exaggerating the severity of illnesses and the potential for drugs to eradicate these maladies. She concluded, aptly: "Since disease is such a fluid and political concept, the providers can essentially create their own demand by broadening the definitions of diseases in such a way as to include the greatest number of people, and by spinning out new diseases."

The absurdly exaggerated creative strategy unveiled by Pfizer to promote its temporary cure for impotence, undertaken by an increasingly desperate pharmaceutical company, reveals yet another example of Boomer stereotypes (hedonism, narcissism, superficiality) driving a brand message and attempting to over amplify a problem.

The rock music by Queen is certainly a trumpet call and powerful recognition signal, especially among younger Boomers, who were in their late teens in 1977 when Queen popularized this anthem of determination and optimism.

But the interplay between a soulful rock ballad and the stresses imposed by impotency stretches the point to near absurdity. The creative solution makes a parody of middle-age and suggests that Boomers are so absorbed in sexual performance that they will literally dance in the streets when presented with a psychosexual ticket to ecstasy and release from the shame of impotence.

This ad has all the characteristics of an idea created by people who view their target audience with mild distaste, as if Boomers are so shallow as to elevate release from impotency to the very pinnacle of their hierarchy of needs.

As Freddie Mercury lamented before he died on November 21, 1991, "But it's been no bed of roses, no pleasure cruise. I consider it a challenge before the whole human race, and I ain't gonna lose, and I need to go on and on and on and on."

The creators of Viagra's "We Are the Champions" television advertisement undoubtedly overlooked the irony of selecting a powerful signature song by an artist who died of a sexually-transmitted disease to promote its remedy for sexual dysfunction.

If Pfizer is a company of people who are truly "Champions of Innovation," perhaps their market focus would be better approached with advertising messages that champion Boomers instead of implying subtle derision of their age-related diseases. This would be innovative as the rival ED drug companies turn up the volume on the need for and benefits of medication for this problem.

Television commercials can treat this problem with sensitivity and an eye on intimacy. Imagine how much more resonant an ad would be if it portrayed the purpose of its potency medication to be a way to strengthen relationships that have stood the test of time.

Sexual dysfunction is, in spite of Pfizer's massive advertising investments, a private matter and needs to be treated with sensitivity, if not for the benefit of Boomers, then certainly for the millions of innocent children exposed to these ads. It is not a funny disease to sufferers, nor is a temporary amelioration of erectile dysfunction a public triumph to be celebrated on the streets of Hometown, U.S.A.

Boomers possess a vast economic treasure chest from which pharmaceutical companies will withdraw huge monetary rewards for drug innovations. Maybe this symbiotic relationship deserves true empathy on the part of those who plan to reel in the riches. Sexual potency is not the central preoccupation of life among middle-aged adults; empathy and love are.

CHAPTER 32

Products that Empower

AS Baby Boomers have marched through the decades, our relationships to the products we purchase have changed, and will continue to do so for the remainder of our lives.

When we were teens, products serving purposes beyond mere necessity solidified personal identity. Bell-bottom jeans signaled to others that we were at least sympathetic to, if not part of, the counterculture movement. Go-Go boots identified a hip woman. A leather jacket with lots of fringe suggested a deeper commitment to be "one with nature" and opposition to everything plastic or saccharine.

In our twenties, we purchased fuel-efficient cars such as Toyotas, Datsuns, Subarus, and Volkswagens to reflect a growing urge to be more environmentally responsible, and, given the dramatic increase in gasoline prices, to save a few bucks. Many purchased tools and learned the techniques of organic gardening to stay more connected with earth, while cultivating less toxic fruits and vegetables.

When we reached our thirties and forties, we embraced luxury products as yuppies to demonstrate our success in business and life. BMWs, European vacations, and gourmet cookware became emblematic of the good life for which many were striving.

As Baby Boomers live through their final decades—when many pay more attention to religion and spirituality—marketers can expect them to seek products and services that empower.

Purchasing products will no longer be just a matter of acquisition for the sake of necessity or social status. Discretionary purchasing will also be motivated by deeper needs to express human potential and achieve both spiritual and religious congruency.

Boomers will embrace communication tools that connect them with others, from high-speed internet access, to motivational weekends in experiential programs designed to enhance "mindfulness." They will invest in educational travel that helps them better understand the messages and meaning sent through cultural artifacts by past civilizations. They will choose living arrangements that simultaneously foster independence, while creating communities that encourage interdependence among like-minded peers—places where people can continue to be stimulated, to learn, and to grow. They will travel the country as "silver birds," but always the wanderers in search of meaning.

Does your product empower Baby Boomers? If so, how? If not, how can you redesign the product to help your customers achieve a purpose beyond mere utility? How can your product help Baby Boomers contribute to their personal legacies, uncover fundamental truths, or get in touch with a Higher Power? Does your product have hidden magic, majesty and mystery? How can you bring these ideals forward in your marketing communications?

As Boomers pass through their final years, each will need to answer lingering questions and resolve conflicts. Each will hope that when the final grades arrive, he or she has mattered. Each will wish to have served a useful purpose, and to have realized his or her dreams. Each will find an entirely personal way to resolve these life-long questions and to put life into perspective.

Nevertheless, as a generation sometimes reviled for its self-absorption, Boomers, as a cohort, will prefer to use the products and services of society to make at least one final statement: their profound gratitude for having grown up in the greatest country on earth at an advantageous time in history.

CHAPTER 33

Experimentation for Life

AND-IN-HAND with the widespread motivation shared by Baby Boomers to explore creativity is a correlating need to experiment. Old age is often associated with the values of comfort, predictability, and routine, but healthy Baby Boomers will defy these generalizations during the final years of their lives. Many will head in the opposite direction and embrace unabashed experimentation as a concluding lifestyle.

Experimental behavior could manifest itself in a number of ways. As mentioned earlier, the adventure travel trend is gaining momentum in the early years of the new century.

The tour offerings coming forward by the National Geographic Society and other companies are not your grandfather's idea of a group tour. Although they retain some of the comfort features that Boomers will continue to favor, the new travel adventures highlight exploration, flexibly planned excursions, and periodic days without planned agendas. Many of the trips follow byways outside the traditional tour bus routes, with cultural engagement as a priority. Even some of the more traditional routes include intellectual and emotional immersion into the people and history of exotic locations.

Additionally, Baby Boomers can be expected to experiment with alternative approaches to cohabitation. Pundits, such as the noted gerontologist Dr. Ken Dychtwald, are predicting the emergence of new lifestyle communities, with people choosing to live among peers who share the same passions. For example, can you envision a retirement community where the common social glue is the residents' passion for motorcycles, and even more specifically, Harley-Davidson motorcycles?

"Saddling Up," a recent *Time* magazine article, documented an emerging motorcycle-loving trend among a burgeoning segment of the Boomer population. In fact, the article observes: "Baby Boomers are the fastest growing segment of America's million-member motorcycling population; their numbers are increasing 10 percent a year. Nearly a third of Harley-Davidson riders are now 50 or older."[40]

The allure of motorcycles and the open road also supports a tendency for many group rides to have philanthropic purposes, thus meeting another emerging need within this generation: to give back. According to the American Motorcycle Association, roughly 3,000 local, regional and national group rides with a fundraising purpose take place annually; and AMA chartered clubs and associations raised almost $6 million for charity in 2001.

As middle-aged Boomers become truly elderly, of course the numbers who can tolerate the physical challenges, and who possess the psychomotor skills to operate a motorcycle safely, will be mitigated. However, is it too much of a stretch of the imagination to conceive of a retirement community, perhaps even located near the Harley-Davidson corporate headquarters in Milwaukee, Wisconsin?

Here, retired enthusiasts could still share their passions for black leather vests, mechanical puttering around with their motorcycles, and the maverick, iconoclastic culture that has evolved around these American machines representing power and freedom.[50]

Seekers of quiet and solitude can live elsewhere.

Companies in the next twenty years that have earned a special relationship with their loyal customers may be able to develop lifestyle communities with their products as the centerpiece—and at a profit.

A major bookstore chain could build a literary community devoted to Boomers who love literature. An adventure travel company, such as National Geographic Expeditions, could build a community dedicated to those who love exploration and travel to exotic, far-away places. A computer software company such as Microsoft could build a community around the interests of computer geeks. This community could include futuristic home management and monitoring technologies that help aging residents handle the activities of daily living.

My speculation here is not without real-life examples. A far-sighted senior housing project in Santa Fe, New Mexico, embraces the "conscious aging" movement. Proponents of the movement seek spiritual growth and authentic discussions about aging and death.

Artist Geoffrey Landis and psychologist and educator Stefan Dobuszynski are leading a group of people committed to building "Jubilados" (retirement in Spanish). Landis and Dobuszynski expect to build 128 units on thirteen acres outside Santa Fe. The facility will include a health care unit, a hospice, a meditation hall, and enough space to house 160 people. The entrepreneurial pair intends to lure those who have devoted their lives to pursuing social causes and spiritual development.

Vivian Gornick, a New York-based writer, is leading an aggressive development program to build the House of Elder Artists in New York City. The 100-apartment building will become a residence for women who have spent their careers in the arts. The concept includes private apartments and public rooms where residents can dine together, give lectures and seminars, conduct art shows, and keep mentally active until the end of life.[41]

Even smaller companies without substantial resources could potentially create lifestyle communities. A Canadian company that specializes in van conversions for middle-aged road warriors is another example that comes to mind.

Beginning with a Chevy or Dodge van chassis, a converted van is then rebuilt from the wheels up, with the addition of a new fiber-glass body, homelike fixtures, and luxury appointments sufficient to create "a motorhome that drives like a van." These exceptionally well-built, aerodynamic van homes come complete with kitchens, galleys, a queen-size bed, and bathrooms with showers, thus creating the motorhome experience without the boxy, inefficient appearance of the traditional "silver bird" rolling chateau. RoadTrek Motorhomes have been designed and built with Baby Boomers in mind.

Rather than pursue the investment and risk of a permanent RoadTrek lifestyle community, this company could organize and host temporary winter communities, logically located in the desert southwest. Here, roving Boomers could gather to celebrate the winter holidays, while enjoying rock concerts, fellowship with peers, and a common passion for open road travel.

Experimentation means adventure travel, sampling new lifestyles, and undertaking uncommon challenges. Businesses can expect Baby Boomers from every socioeconomic stratum to try new ways of experiencing and sharing life. The more effectively companies anticipate and guide this basic need, the more likely they will be to integrate their products and services into the lives of the people they would like to reward and keep as customers.

How Boomers Are Transforming Travel & Tourism

TRAVEL AND TOURISM is already a $1.3 trillion industry in the United States, generating $100 billion in tax revenue for local, state, and federal governments.[42] With Boomers entering a life stage typified by extensive travel and immersive learning, they are bringing new opportunities to an industry already responsible for over seven million domestic jobs and the nation's number one service export.

Throughout their wandering lives, Boomers have contributed to the growth of many new forms of travel entertainment, from European excursions to backcountry trekking. As the generation prioritizes more time for travel and learning—so-called edutainment—tourism industries will continue to realize substantial growth and evolution.

For example, two up-and-coming trends being fueled by Boomers include heritage and cultural tourism.

Heritage tourism is tied to a geographic location and connected to neighboring history, customs, historical figures, traditions, and mythic stories. This form of travel presents underdeveloped opportunities for smaller communities and off-the-beaten path destinations. In concert with the period of life when history takes on added significance, Boomers will progressively seek out locales that showcase fascinating, transforming journeys into the past.

Locales that amplify Boomers' own nostalgic coming-of-age experiences will become breakaway top-sellers. For example, London tourists can enjoy one of several all-day walking tours of The Beatles' most famous landmarks, including Abby Road Studios and The Palladium Theater, birthplace of Beatlemania.

Equally compelling as a travel industry growth prospect, cultural tourism involves immersive experiences with less emphasis on a specific locale. For example, Boomers are rushing into regional art museums to see rock icon photographs by Linda McCartney (Paul's late wife). Ronnie Wood, guitarist for The Rolling Stones, is luring hip crowds into hip galleries to view his striking sketches of the band that made him famous.

For culture-thirsty Boomer travelers, a trip to Milwaukee must include a tour of the Harley-Davidson motorcycle factory. In Cleveland, the Rock and Roll Hall of Fame has become a Woodstock generation must-visit destination.

National Geographic has responded to these trends by developing its travel product called Expeditions, in line with changing Boomer tastes. Expeditions include out-of-the-ordinary journeys, education from preeminent tour guides, and access to off-the-beaten path experiences (such as a private tour of the Sistine Chapel after hours). Emphasis is on learning, cultural immersion and peak experiences.

Finally, hotels and resorts will continue to create new travel experiences that appeal to Boomers, offering gourmet cooking, wellness education, skill improvement in leisure sports, and room/event packages tied to neighboring festivals and special attractions.

CHAPTER 34

It's about Time

BEGINNING in pre-school, children learn about the meaning of time and its inexorable passage. As they grow up, they gain increasing intimacy with clocks, calendars, and seasonal events. This is critical preparation for life and ensuing adult responsibilities.

Americans govern their daily affairs with scrupulous time management. Our lives become overscheduled with homework assignments, final exams, job interviews, client appointments, project deadlines, recurring holidays, tax deadlines, vacations, and social events.

A phenomenon of the aging process to which most people attest an experiential understanding is that time seems to speed up as we age. There is never enough time in a day to check off everything on the list. We return from a long July 4th weekend and suddenly it is Thanksgiving. New Year's Eve transforms into Labor Day within the blink of an eye.

Measuring, monitoring, and meeting the obligations of time consume our adult lives, and suddenly we retire, or at least slow down the pace.

During the counterculture movement in the 1970s, some experimented with laidback, time-insensitive lifestyles by taking up residence on farms and in communes.

One of the cinematic and iconographic images of the era occurred in a 1969 movie called *Easy Rider*. As Captain America, a cocaine-dealing, Harley-riding misfit, Peter Fonda starts a cross-country odyssey in search of the real America with Billy, his co-star, Dennis Hopper. When Fonda and Hopper rev up their Hogs to begin a trip east from California through the American southwest, Fonda tears off his watch and tosses it blithely onto the roadside.

When Captain America casts his wristwatch to the ground, the literal and symbolic flourish demonstrates his newfound freedom and rejection of obsessive time constraints in modern society. For these vagabond anti-heroes, time will no longer be of consequence. They will follow their whims and let spontaneity guide their days. Along the way, they encounter many faces of America: big cities, small towns, bigoted local townspeople, hippie communes, red-necks, back-road diners, and whorehouses.

As they take to the open road, cross the Colorado River, and pass through unspoiled buttes and sand-colored deserts, the lyrics of "Born to Be Wild" sung by Steppenwolf, reinforces the theme of timeless abandon:

Get your motor runnin'
Head out on the highway
Lookin' for adventure
And whatever comes our way
Yeah Darlin' go make it happen
Take the world in a love embrace
Fire all of your guns at once
And explode into space

I like smoke and lightning
Heavy metal thunder
Racin' with the wind
And the feelin' that I'm under
Yeah Darlin' go make it happen
Take the world in a love embrace
Fire all of your guns at once
And explode into space

Like a true nature's child
We were born, born to be wild
We can climb so high
I never wanna die

Born to be wild
Born to be wild [43]

Emblazoned in the collective generational memory by the showcase of this breakaway movie and years of repetition on Classic Rock radio stations, the powerful rock anthem evokes the complementary images of riding Harleys, an old-west tableau, adventure travel, spontaneous love, and the power of mind expansion. The brassy lead singer speaks to an "Age-of-Aquarius" sensibility by inviting Boomers to embrace nature, freedom, wildness and psychological nirvana. The song proposes the immortality granted by unstructured rowdiness and lack of discipline, an essential freedom unfettered by final exams, conference calls, staff meetings, project due dates, and planning sessions.

Captain America and Billy stop at a horse ranch to repair Captain America's flat tire in symbolic, parallel juxtaposition to a rancher who is shoeing his horse nearby. Their odd appearance does not intimidate the rancher, and he admires Captain America's "good-looking machine." The vagabonds join the rancher's family for an outdoor meal, and Captain America compliments the rancher on his simple life of hard work, reinforcing an attraction to the man's commitment to building a life that is the timeless embodiment of freedom:

> You've got a nice place. It's not every man that can live off the land, you know. You do your own thing in your own time. You should be proud. [44]

This symbolic rejection of society's time chokehold remains in the heart of many Boomers. Although few literally identified with the sociopathic characters portrayed in the movie, many did connect with a lifestyle unburdened by economic competition and calendars controlled by others. The independence to shape each day by personal agendas sparked optimism and youthful fantasies of freedom.

Nevertheless, most Boomers began their demanding careers, adding more and more time constraints, with pressures accelerating as they climbed corporate ladders. Since their full entry into the workplace, Boomers have progressively struggled with the ever-increasing strain of time—usually not having enough of it.

The media have often characterized the 1980s as the yuppie era when the leading edge of the generation became obsessed with career achievement and material acquisition. Many routinely worked 60, 70 or even 100 hours a week. Children also became a factor as delayed Boomer families presented a new time-crushing reality.

Then, quite ironically, Boomers played a significant role in changing the very nature of business time, leaving behind the years of anti-establishment, do-your-own-thing lifestyles.

Bill Gates and his neophyte team of former hippies at fledgling Microsoft developed the first computer operating system in tandem with IBM's rollout of the PC, or personal microcomputer. Gates and his many Baby Boomer peers rapidly designed and deployed micro-computer software that distributed power to, and then took time away from individuals. Seemingly, the more personal computing power executives received, the faster their business expectations increased for greater productivity—accomplish more in less time.

Never stop working.

Then Steven Jobs introduced the Apple desktop computer, the first microcomputer for "the rest of us," offering an amazingly simple computing interface for non-technical people who wanted to command the muscle of computing without paying the price of learning obtuse software languages such as DOS. The freewheeling members of society, particularly those employed in advertising and the graphic arts, embraced Apple's vision of "the power to be your best."

The genie had escaped the bottle, and Americans began embracing microcomputers and computer networks as their preferred way to achieve greater empowerment and business productivity. Every business and creative function could be accomplished faster, and often better, than through the former interface of large, centrally controlled mainframe computers.

At the end of the same decade, another Baby Boomer ushered in the internet era. Tim Berners-Lee founded the World Wide Web initiative in 1989, which he had developed for his own use as a researcher at the European Laboratory for Particle Physics in Switzerland.

A graduate of Oxford University, Berners-Lee has a background in text processing, real-time software, and communications. Soon after conceiving the worldwide web, he specified hypertext markup language (HTML) as part of the WWW initiative to facilitate better communication among high-energy physicists.

A thought-leading Baby Boomer, Berners-Lee then developed three computing standards that made the web such a powerful communication tool, and changed everything. First, URLs (uniform resource locators) are the standard for pointing to documents on any computer connected anywhere on the network. Second, HTML is the standard that tells the browser how to display and interact with the words and images. Third, hypertext transfer protocol (HTTP) is the standard for transferring hyperlinked documents.

This unprecedented communication medium continued to evolve with logarithmic speed to meet the mushrooming requirements of the academic community, which was then becoming accustomed to cross-country networking and email conversations among peers and colleagues through private electronic pipelines.

What began as an electronic library system for a group of physicists, transformed into the international information and marketing bazaar we know today as the internet.

While writing this section, I searched the internet for more information about Berners-Lee by typing an inquiry into Google, the popular search engine that reaches into the depths of all the servers and computers linked by the internet. Google searched 3,083,324,652 web pages and found about 113,000 matches in less than a second.

Imagine trying to communicate this research capability to someone just ten years ago. The idea that anyone with a home computer hooked to a telephone line could take command of so much information in such a short period would have seemed like a script from a science fiction movie.

Because of these technological and commercial paradigm shifts, Boomers have helped to accelerate and remold the meaning of time, particularly business time.

For example, before personal computing and internet connectivity, in the direct-mail field, it might have taken eight to ten weeks to conceive, design, produce, print, and distribute a direct-mail campaign. It was virtually impossible to accelerate the time sched-ule for such a complex integration of mechanical production steps and vendors, ranging from printers, to list brokers and mail houses.

Today, marketers can execute an ambitious direct-mail cam-paign in two weeks. The price for this accelerated timetable is time. When handed such a task, team members will work extraordinar-ily long hours, and cajole cooperation from multiple vendors, who, to remain competitive, will accommodate ridiculous schedule demands.

Thanks to accelerated computing technology and the internet, Boomers have helped create a world where there are no longer boundaries between weekdays and weekends, or days and nights. We have learned to work 24 hours a day, seven days a week, and 365 days a year. More always needs to be accomplished in less time—now at internet speed.

This continuing source of pressure in our lives has a predictable consequence as Boomers begin to retire, or at least reduce their business and child-rearing commitments. We are ready to slow down, to escape the daily struggle with time, to metaphorically cast away our watches.

Slowing down in this context does not necessarily mean that we will become inactive or sedentary. Quite the opposite, Boomers will embrace adventure travel and physically demanding hobbies for many years. We will seek novel experiences. We will volunteer to help nonprofit causes.

Slowing down means that we will adopt slower-paced lifestyles and living arrangements that recall the earliest years of our lives, the *Leave It to Beaver* years, when people took time just to commis-erate over the backyard fence and putter in the garden.

Consider what is beginning to happen with those already in early retirement, or actively planning retirement in the near future. Boomers are changing retirement migration patterns, answering the call of an inner need to show down from the hectic habits of the last three decades.

Instead of flooding such former retirement hotspots as Florida in the footsteps of their parents' generation, Boomers are moving to smaller and medium-sized communities in the "New West" and "New South."

One of my business colleagues provides a contemporaneous example of this phenomenon. Based primarily in Los Angeles, he spent his career in the broadcasting industry. John often lamented to me about the pressures and pace of his frenzied life, which included multiple news-reporting assignments for various Los Angeles radio stations and nationally syndicated news services. He was always rushing between clients and projects, and he often traveled across the country to provide corporate training and produce long-format television commercials. His accomplishments fill a ten-page resume, but in the fall of 2002, he finally reached a stage when he could afford to slow the pace.

Slowing down means that we will adopt slower-paced lifestyles.

John purchased a condominium near Park City, Utah, where he manages his home-based consulting business part-time. Nevertheless, his new priority is to take time every day to enjoy the comforting tableau of the Rocky Mountains and a low-key, neighborhood community. His typical workweek will soon diminish to 20 or 30 hours versus his former lifestyle of 60- or 70-hour workweeks.

In addition to Park City as a new retirement Mecca, experts on retiree migration are observing exploding Boomer population increases in such areas as Henderson, Nevada; Prescott, Arizona; and Georgetown, Texas.[45] It should not come as a surprise if many Boomers start relocating to the same small rural communities that attracted middle-class college students who were then transforming into hippies and starting communes.

Some Boomers are choosing to remain in the larger cities where they've spent their careers, but they are seeking gated and protected communities where houses have been downsized, streets are wider, front porches are larger, lawn caretaking responsibilities are minimal, and community centers attract neighbors for periodic social events.

Companies engaged in marketing travel, leisure, and lifestyle products should demonstrate the pace-slowing attributes of their products and services. Like Captain America casting away his watch,

> This generation seeks both extremes: high-adventure leisure and travel experiences balanced by low-key lifestyles.

how can you demolish the slavish connotations of time? How can your product or service help Boomers find liberation from the constraining limitations of incessant deadlines and appointments?

Show Boomers taking leisurely walks around the neighborhood, or gathering in groups to commiserate over café lattes, or enjoying peaceful time with nature. This is not to contradict recommendations elsewhere in this book suggesting that Boomers should be depicted as active and engaged. This generation seeks both extremes: high-adventure leisure and travel experiences balanced by low-key lifestyles, where their homes and neighboring communities become havens for relaxation, contemplation, and easygoing socialization.

CHAPTER 35

Icons and Images

Peanut butter sandwiches with strawberry jam
Alfalfa sprouts in salads
Patchouli stick incense
Hand-made, multi-colored candles
Peace symbols as necklaces
Stained glass lamps
Indian bedspreads
Faded, worn blue jeans and old cowboy boots

THESE are the tastes, smells, sights, and textures of Baby Boomer coming-of-age memories.

These were not just objects extracted from the montage of their everyday lives back then; these were their icons, suggesting more transcendental purposes.

Natural living. Higher consciousness. Abundant health. Artistic expression. Heightened sensuality. Spirituality. Sexual healing. Laid-back comfort. Anti-authoritarian sentiments.

These material objects came to represent a more integrated life, greater focus, higher awareness, and spiritual well being.

Boomers intentionally added meaning beyond mere utilitarian purpose to the tastes, sounds, smells, and textures of their daily lives. Some journeyed to alternative realities through drug trips to discover extraordinary meaning in mundane, everyday objects and experiences. Some of these experiences became punctuation marks by virtue of novelty. Boomers were young then, and the world was still fresh.

When Boomers reach the final stages of life, these powerful images and experiences from youth will gain renewed power if employed wisely. They will choose to reconnect with these icons and their mythology to re-experience the freshness of those discoveries, at once simple in idea but complex in meaning and interpretation. If you know the triggers to best achieve a heightened experience of your product or service, employ them.

Don't just display your new bagel toaster; set the stage of experience. Show your machine with a freshly toasted sandwich, brimming with chunky peanut butter and lusty strawberry jam.

Don't just show a new home for sale, vacuous and void of furniture. Rather, before the next tour with empty nesters, light some glowing candles and a stick of sandalwood incense to add warmth to its rooms.

Don't just gather political supporters in the name of world peace. Bring out yellow daisies, white doves, and peace symbols.

This is not to suggest that you should trot out sensual experiences from the Sixties and Seventies as blatant and obvious attempts to manipulate. Those who can talk the talk but did not walk the walk have done this too many times, and rather badly.

This iconographic dance is along a fine line. Marketers often make the mistake of thinking that an advertisement should offer literal, and therefore, stereotypical reference objects about the group it is targeting. This can lead to a message that speaks down to rather than includes the target audience. Playing the icons with the wrong tone or in the wrong context can suggest manipulation or condescension, somewhat with the same result as when an adult tries to use teenage slang and then fails to understand the subtleties of an expression.

Creative integration of those youthful icons into the experience of your product or service, in a way that does not summon conscious attention or suggest imprecise understanding, can reach into both the deepest wells of collective experience and many cherished remembrances.

Certainly, you are playing the nostalgia card by evoking these icons, as others have done with every generation's peculiar cultural lexicon of foods, fashion, entertainment, and values. But the key to doing it well is the art with which you show—rather than tell—the story.

The objects of Boomer youth are the embodiment of stories about discovery, relationships, values and dreams—icons. Understand the objects contextually, and you will be closer to understanding Boomers' hearts.

Once you crack this code, your product will become the priority, not just another discretionary choice.

CHAPTER 36

Muhammad Ali: from Paladin to Pariah to Pitchman

ASSIUS CLAY was Superman. The poetic boxer stood for everything a young Boomer male wanted to become: self-confident, physically powerful, intelligent, fearless, wealthy, and famous —a 20th century gladiator.

He was also a Black man, which communicated volumes to teenagers wanting to see the promise of Civil Rights fully manifested with the installation of African-American heroes in the mythology of the growing counterculture. He represented the best and brightest of a new breed of transracial heroes beginning to emerge in sports, business, cinematic arts, and politics.

He was Black and belligerent; Black and beneficent; Black and bold, and he quickly became and remained one of the most recognized and admired athletes worldwide. In December 1999 *Sports Illustrated* named him "Sportsman of the 20th Century."

Born January 17, 1942, Cassius Marcellus Clay won the light heavyweight gold medal at the 1960 Rome Olympics. He soon captured media attention with his smooth-talking self-confidence and wit. In his own self-assessment: "Cassius Clay is a boxer who can throw the jive better than anybody."

Clay helped catapult boxing to the forefront of spectator sporting events when he fought Sonny Liston in Miami for the world heavyweight boxing title. While promoting this match, he coined his famous rhythmic chant, "float like a butterfly, sting like a bee." At the age of 22, he became the pretty prince of boxing.

Inspired during this time of rampant racism by the bellicose black activist Malcolm X, Clay decided to join the Nation of Islam and adopt the name Muhammad Ali: "beloved of Allah" in Arabic.

When Cassius Clay became a Black Muslim in 1963, he also became a symbol of all that tradition-bound America was beginning to fear and hate: Black Muslims, Black Power, and Black Panthers. In so doing, he turned his back on mainstream America by rejecting the "slave name" upon which rested his early fame.

Defying the white establishment, this once powerful symbol of Olympic triumph and The American Dream picked up another torch that inspired the downtrodden, disfranchised, and dispossessed worldwide. Ali was, as Eldridge Cleaver observed, "the black Fidel Castro of boxing."

In 1967, he refused the military draft on religious grounds, and the World Boxing Federation stripped him of his title and boxing license. The U.S. government charged him for violating the Selective Service Act. He told the media, "I ain't got no quarrel with them Viet-Cong. No Viet-Cong ever called me nigger."

In spite of his moral and religious objections, the get-Cassius faction across America condemned him as a traitor, and the courts sentenced him to five years in prison. Quickly released on appeal, his conviction was overturned in 1970.

It is not without irony that Muhammad Ali became a favored celebrity pitchman forty years later, plugging products for America's mainstream, blue-chip brands.

During the 2004 Super Bowl broadcast, for example, Ali appeared as himself in television commercials not once, but three times, for IBM, Gillette, and as part of a CBS network promotion to encourage Americans to vote. Around that same time, he also appeared in advertising campaigns for Apple Computer and Coca-Cola. Adidas athletic shoes hired him as spokesman to help solidify its new message in a print, television, and internet advertising campaign dedicated to the theme, "Impossible is nothing."

David Schwab, director for marketing and media at Octagon, a sports agency owned by the Interpublic Group of Companies, observed that Muhammad Ali could not be thought of as just a celebrity. "He's an iconic brand. He himself *is* an IBM or Gillette."[46]

The IBM campaign was particularly noteworthy for adopting impressions of Ali most fondly remembered, while unselfconsciously skirting issues raised by his civil disobedience and alignment with revolutionary factions during the Sixties.

In this TV commercial, Ali sits before a quixotic, curious boy who represents Linux, IBM's open source computer operating system, an "underdog, upstart software technology." Ali exhorts the boy to "Shake things up, shake up the world," hearkening back to the time when the great fighter rattled the boxing world while shaking up the Moral Majority's deeply held beliefs in the duty of all citizens to support unflinchingly their government during times of war. Ali, the African American, gave added poignancy to this message with his advice, delivered affectionately to the blond, wide-eyed child.

Icons are eternal, no matter their flaws and foibles—even despite the ravages of a debilitating condition like Parkinson's.

But those who Boomers once loved, and sometimes loved to hate, have changed the texture of modern marketing communications. Those who wrote history rise above the mundane and banality. When timeless icons such as Ali are used with intelligence and respect, yesterday's heroes become today's goodwill ambassadors.

Through this process, advertisers also connect powerfully to Boomers' coming-of-age zeitgeist, adding force and personification to a brand. Even transgressive image residuals from the Sixties—such as in Ali's situation—can boost a brand, making it appear more iconoclastic, individualistic, and unconventional—a valuable position in a world of parity products and services. The "road less traveled" remains today a mythic Western value that continues to define the American experience; the celebrity man or woman who has taken that road, equally so.

With a unique combination of skill, style and character, "The Greatest" became a three-time heavyweight champion and the world's most acclaimed athlete. He became a symbol of conquest, and he became the object of racial derision.

But this superstar athlete and defiant radical transformed into something more. Through the magic of modern branding, he rose again as a powerful symbol of achievement in the face of adversity. That's also why he became the go-to retired athlete for companies revitalizing brand images of courage, character, and charisma.

Ali's career was, in the end, ironic and iconic.

CHAPTER 37

Anger over Fear

ANGER and fear land on the negative side of the spectrum of human emotions, and are mostly associated with undesirable emotional states—especially among members of the "peace and love" generation. Under the right circumstances, both emotions serve as mechanisms of survival.

Fear, while under the most extreme conditions can be immobilizing, causes humans to avoid the source of fear, perhaps even to take flight and run in the other direction.

Anger focuses attention and mobilizes people to take action against threats.

Marketers have always considered these emotions in developing their selling arguments. Insurance companies remind us of our mortality and life's uncertainties as an essential part of their marketing communications, thus tapping the deep reservoir of fear. Politicians often call upon human anger to mobilize the electorate against opponents for such abusive acts as favoritism, cronyism, and nepotism.

Negative emotions can become powerful motivators in the right hands.

However, of these choices, Baby Boomers respond most effectively to anger. They grew up in a time of unprecedented rage. The leading edge of the generation has vivid memories of the civil rights movement and the violence it spawned, from the assassination of Medgar Evers and Martin Luther King, to race riots in Los Angeles and Detroit.

Baby Boomers respond most effectively to anger.

Then came the Vietnam War, a "police action" that eventually claimed the lives of 58,169 American soldiers and injured more than 304,000, out of 2.59 million who served. Although the percent fatally wounded is similar to other wars, amputations and crippling wounds were 300 percent higher in Vietnam than in World War II. One out of every ten Americans who served in Vietnam was a casualty. Over 75,000 Vietnam veterans are severely disabled.[47]

Anyone who lived through the period from 1967 to 1974 remembers collective social anger in its most extreme, civil disobedient form: protest marches and college lockouts; confrontation with all forms of authority, from university administrators to construction workers; and escape behavior, from drug abuse to nomadic, hitchhiking wanderlust.

The Vietnam War made almost every young person angry, no matter how he or she viewed the moral issues and the human cost.

The rock music of the time reflected and incited fury. Barry McGuire sang about "The Eve of Destruction." "The I-Feel-Like-I'm-Fixin'-To-Die Rag" from Country Joe and Fish became one of the most popular indictments of military conscription. Bob Dylan sang "Rainy Day Woman #12." Dion sang "Abraham, Martin and John." Eric Burdon and the Animals sang "Sky Pilot." Janice Ian sang "Society's Child." And, as if a presage about things to come, Buffalo Springfield implored greater sanity with "For What It's Worth."

After the murder of four Kent State students by members of the Ohio National Guard on May 4, 1970, rock super group Crosby, Stills, Nash & Young recorded a searing ballad entitled "Ohio." The song enflamed emotions with a rallying musical call to action.

The lyrics also evoked the villainous images of Richard Millhouse Nixon and robotic "tin soldiers" summarily gunning down unarmed students without clear-cut provocation. The pounding battle cry asked student sympathizers to recall the powerful, Pulitzer-Prize-winning photograph taken by yearbook photographer John Filo, who had borrowed a camera shortly before the fatal confrontation. The photo shows young Mary Vecchio as she kneels screaming over the body of slain 19-year-old student Jeff Miller.

Anger manifested itself throughout Baby Boomer culture, from rock music to surplus military camouflage as a fashion statement. Arguments spilled from classrooms to family rooms.

Anger remains in the soul of the generation, although this powerful emotion's collective manifestations became dormant during the last three decades of the 20th century. The public does not often witness streets filling with angry, middle-aged Boomers marching arm-in-arm against political and social injustice. But, under the right circumstances, anger can be called up for duty once again, and can motivate Baby Boomers to make choices about certain categories of products and services.

From a fundraising perspective, organizations such as People for the Ethical Treatment of Animals (PETA), the National Rifle Association (NRA), and the National Association for the Advancement of Colored People (NAACP) have shown that anger against injustice lives on. Anger motivates.

Having experienced first-hand my parents' declining health and increasing old-age dependency on the social service system and corporate caregivers, I can suggest with some authority that Baby Boomers will one day face many challenges worthy of their anger.

The generation that spawned the youth culture in America will not placidly accept the humiliations and affronts to dignity that typify many of today's eldercare services and facilities. They will not passively allow themselves to become marginalized by society or the government, and even during the final few years of their lives, those who can speak out raucously, will.

Many economic opportunities await smart companies as they retool and refocus their products and services for an aging population. And a lot of what they offer to the elderly will be directed at maintaining independence, facilitating personal freedom, and preserving health as long as possible.

When you think about it, these products and services will play a role in assuaging anger, a normal human reaction to confinement, condemnation, alienation, segregation, and rejection.

This is not to suggest that a marketer necessarily needs to make a one-to-one correlation between the product and mitigation of anger.

For example, one would not need to write this headline to make a point: "With Acme's Electronic Health Sensors in Your Home, You'll Never Face the Humiliation of a Military School-Style Nursing Home."

Rather, the same company could communicate a subtler message and allow prospective customers to draw their own conclusions: "Stay at Home Longer with Acme Electronic Health Sensors. Don't Let Strangers Control Your Retirement Days."

The first message is a blatant call for anger; the second taps it without bludgeoning the reader.

Behind either of these messages is a motivational trigger: dormant anger about losing independence and being forced to submit to impersonal, daily care by strangers. Perhaps such headlines as these in the future will recall today's angry confrontations between Boomers and the social service system. This is our parents' time of declining health and growing dependency, and those who encounter today's eldercare system can expect a substantial dose of righteous indignation.

CHAPTER 38

Seeking Spiritual Answers

N 1971, John Lennon asked the world to imagine that there is no heaven through his influential song, "Imagine."

The legendary poet-musician bid us to withdraw from the over-burdened promises of immortality, embodied and embellished by formal religions; rather, he challenged us to embrace secular spirituality, to honor peace and brotherhood in the present, and not be drawn in by the unrealized promise of salvation in a hypothetical afterlife.

His song struck a responsive chord in the hearts of millions, and though to some it is a rebuke of formal religion, to others it is a powerful call for religiosity: the gathering and honoring of timeless principals embodied in the great religious traditions.

This anthem spoke to seekers of higher spiritual truths, and its simple lyrics resonated with a generation. The timeless ballad from a cultural icon has been etched into the spiritual glossary of Baby Boomers.

When I hear this song, I reflect back to a campfire conversation about ten years ago, with a woman named Jane, a cousin of a long-term business associate. We had gathered at a campsite near the foot of Pikes Peak to enjoy crisp fall air and blazing aspens in golden transformation. The camping area filled with the odors of fresh food cooking over a fire, and spiritual connections emanated from this primitive gathering.

John Lennon's enigmatic entreaty beckoned from a nearby radio. After dinner we gathered with friends around a large campfire. I spoke intimately without qualification or pretense.

"Our generation needs another spiritual leader," I suggested, almost as a test. "We need someone who will pinpoint our collective feelings and better articulate our quest for the remaining years of our lives."

Jane sat quietly on the other side of the fire and listened without challenging. Yet, I saw disagreement in her eyes. Her head cocked as if to listen to another, more distant voice.

"This leader needs to be a veteran of the time when we came of age," I continued. "I believe this may come to pass. He or she may rise during a crisis such as economic upheaval, a war, or an environmental calamity. But whatever the precipitating event or events, this person will come forward at a time when Boomers will be most receptive to a reexamination of our deep-seated spiritual quest. Think of this person as our generation's Billy Graham."

Jane looked at me curiously. "I'm not sure that we need a leader. I am trying to break from a commune right now. They've controlled my life and wasted twenty years . . ."

"This leader will not take away our free will," I argued, "but he will articulate our common feelings as have the poet-singers of our time."

She looked at me with further suspicion, so I pressed my argument. "Consider Mahatma Gandhi, for example. He did not tell the Indian people how to act or feel. He simply modeled and articulated a doctrine of peaceful resistance and ethnic pride. This is the type of leader that I'm referring to."

"Why do we need any more leaders? JFK, RFK, and Martin Luther King have been dead a long time."

I paused and studied Jane's distant gaze but persisted. "Because we have become fragmented as a generation. We need a collective spiritual purpose. We often lack a sense of community."

Jane asked, "Isn't it possible that there is a collective force, perhaps a consciousness, with whom we are all in touch? And whatever is happening to this generation is happening around campfires like these . . . where people are turning to each other and talking?"

I sensed her fragility, the lost years spent following a charismatic leader who turned out to be a false profit.

"I remember how free we felt," she confessed. "I mean, I would grab a backpack and just stick my thumb out . . . travel anywhere. People weren't as they are now. It isn't even safe for me to lie beside a stream in the forest, where I feel closest to God. You can't do that anymore. It's often not safe to be honest."

Suddenly I saw a delicate soul sitting in the plastic lawn chair— someone fragile and still innocent in some ways; someone disillusioned and bitter in other ways. She was so much in need of safety and comfort—call it a yearning for soul petting.

Brad, her husband, pulled her close, and he stared at me through the dancing flames as if I was speaking words that he and she needed to hear.

"That's what I feel," I whispered. "We need a spiritual leader to awaken meaning for a sleeping generation."

Jane squinted through the dancing flames. "Maybe it's all of us finally reaching inside and manifesting only what matters."

Jane's cautious revelations about her deepest feelings, imparted to an argumentative stranger, pointed backward to a time of spiritual starvation when Baby Boomers feasted at an international buffet for alternative spiritual quests: Transcendental Mediation, Gestalt Psychology, Scientology, the Human Potential Movement, Existential Psychology, and the New Age Movement. This cornucopia of spirituality provided a diverse array of choices upon which to carve a meaningful and relevant life. Nevertheless, excesses sometimes overwhelmed revelations.

> The affirmation of a worthwhile life in the face of alienation—this is the unfinished business of a generation.

For those who succumbed to the excesses of psychoactive substances and only found emptiness, there came the 12-step programs for alcohol, cocaine, and barbiturate addicts.

The creation of community, driven by the yearning for meaning, the affirmation of a worthwhile life in the face of alienation— this is the unfinished business of a generation. The quest is inherently spiritual, and it is becoming a pressing priority.

As freedom from work pressures fill days with time for greater soul-searching, an elder culture reflecting some of the Sixties spiritual culture will likely flow into the void. Jane's uncertainty, and that shared by her fellow Baby Boomers, will find new sources for enlightenment and significance. Boomers are seekers, and their search will intensify during the next ten years.

In his book, a *Generation of Seekers*, a seminal exposé on the spiritual quest of Baby Boomers, Professor Wade Clark Root analyzes many underlying, spiritually-rooted motivations: the importance of experience over beliefs, distrust of institutions and leaders, the universal urge for personal fulfillment, and a yearning for intergenerational community.

Professor Clark also underscores how core values set up a distinctive brand of spirituality that typifies a wide segment of the generation. These values include many traits discussed elsewhere in this book:

- Acceptance of different lifestyles and cultural traditions;

- A sense of personal responsibility for life experiences and results;

- An enduring belief that strength comes from within, and dogmatic adherence to traditional religious prescriptions will not bestow emotional potency;

- A revealing attraction to self-disclosure, the willingness to share feelings openly in the face of reprisal.

A growing percentage of the generation seems to be following John Lennon's enjoinder by casting aside traditional religion in favor of spirituality, a spirituality grounded in temporal meaning and a life-value perspective.

This has created a new spiritual lexicon dominated by such words as quest, journey, growth, searching, choice, exploration, mindfulness, and integration. Of their spiritual searching, Boomers ask for answers to enduring existential questions, insights rooted in direct experience, integration of body and mind, an egalitarian view of religious expression, and emotional ascendance through strengthening community.

Many in the generation are relativistic in their quest, willing to reach into the realm of many divine resources, from ancient

Buddhism to cutting-edge cosmology, from crosses to quarks.

This searching culture has generated a marketplace of new spiritual resources, including books, videotapes, audiotapes, weekend retreats, newsletters, institutes, and digital networks. Spiritual leaders enter this fray, espousing eclectic paths to transcendence, drawing upon timeworn religious traditions and New Age psychobabble.

First, marketers of spiritual products and those who wish to influence Leading-Edge Baby Boomers through spiritual messages must take for granted a dominant religious and spiritual pluralism. For many in this cohort—all but the most religiously dogmatic—the path to salvation has few conceptual barriers.

Second, spiritual concerns have, at their roots, a collective desire for community, abundant health, brightening horizons, and, ultimately, life satisfaction. As mentioned previously, there is an underlying search for holistic solutions, those modalities that join together body, mind, and spirit.

Finally, spirituality is the wellspring of character and an integrated awareness of the inner self.

The questions your marketing messages must help answer are of temporal proportion, nonetheless as wrenching as what happens after the end of life:

Who will care for me?
Will I be able to provide for my family?
Who am I?
Where am I going?
Could there be more to life than this?

Answer these questions within a spiritual context, and this generation will listen. However, do not foist counterfeit witness, embellished with promises of happiness, or cast down aggressive appeals to belief authority.

Jane, a Sixties and Seventies veteran of false spiritual control, will not listen, and neither will most of her generation.

CHAPTER 39

Six Forces Destroying Retirement for Boomers

ABY BOOMERS once flaunted young-at-heart mantras proclaiming reverence for spontaneity and a quick-fix perspective:

If it feels good, do it.
Do your own thing.
Live for today.

Fast-forward thirty years and these aphorisms are becoming niggling stereotypes ushering them into retirement.

From the perspective of their vociferous critics, Boomers have become the furry costar of *The Tortoise and the Hare* fable, heedlessly hopping ahead of the plodding reptile with a want-it-all-now mentality. As children learn long before they can spell catastrophe, the careless rabbit runs out of gas before the finish line. Moral: "Winners are purposeful and persistent rather than rash and reckless."

Cynics blame Boomers for their excesses, their self-absorption and failure to plan wisely for the inevitable consequences of aging. As accusers censure, this country has too many overleveraged people in middle age, racking up credit-card debt and at the threshold of insolvency, representing a massive retirement planning malfunction.

Some dire warnings estimate that at least one-third of the generation may be financially unprepared for retirement as the oldest Boomers begin crossing the "golden years" threshold in 2011.

According to AARP's analysis of Federal Reserve data, Leading-Edge Boomers—those born between 1946 and 1955—have a median net worth of just $146,000, including home equity.[48]

Considering over three decades of employment history, this is a gloomy average performance and hardly an adequate nest egg.

However, closer examination of sociological and demographic factors reveals other issues contributing to why many Boomers may be inadequately prepared for retirement.

1. A history of generational overcrowding

In the short span of 20 years, from 1946 to 1964, America grew by 76 million Boomers. The country was not equipped for this population explosion.

Boomers share overcrowding nightmares such as snaking lines encircling movie theaters. They recall public school classes convening in temporary manufactured houses erected to compensate for lack of space inside old school buildings. They remember competing against peers at every turn, from getting into a good university to winning a promotion.

It has always been a buyer's market when it comes to tapping the Boomer human resources aquifer. Overcrowding has limited the careers and opportunities for many. Doors have not opened; promotions have not happened; salaries have not steadily increased.

2. Corporate downsizing

In 1996, *The New York Times* ran a series of articles about job erosion across America, leading eventually to a book entitled *The Downsizing of America*. As the editors observed, between 1979 and 1995, 43 million jobs vanished. "And while many more have been created, increasingly, the jobs that are disappearing are those of higher-paid, white-collar workers, and many of the new jobs pay much less than those they replaced."

Boomers were often the first to endure sacrificial "resource reallocations" because they populated the middle-management jobs of greatest vulnerability. A new language emerged to describe their plight: downsized, separated, severed, unassigned, or surplused. The situation for Boomers today is more tenuous than it was in the mid-90s—and they are older and more vulnerable. Too many vie for too few jobs.

The Economic Policy Institute in Washington corroborated this view with a recent revelation during a time of alleged recovery: "Since the business cycle expansion began in November 2001, payrolls have contracted by 1 million (1.2 million in the private sector), making this the weakest recovery in terms of employment since the Bureau of Labor Statistics began tracking monthly data in 1939."[49]

Downsizing means job losses, but often it means more. As *The New York Times* concluded: "For two decades, most people had also seen their wages level off or decline, and now dispossessed workers were frequently finding that the replacement jobs available to them paid appreciably less than their lost positions. Everywhere, people were working longer hours and feeling expendable."[50]

3. Exportation of blue collar, then white collar jobs

Academy Award–winning documentary director Michael Moore has built a reputation as an irascible filmmaker. He first became nationally prominent when his contemptuous lens exposed General Motors for exporting manufacturing jobs from Flint, Michigan—a decision that decimated Flint, thrusting both the city and its workers into poverty.

Roger and Me was more than a feisty documentary; the film became a metaphor for the breakdown in loyalty between large corporations and workers. It warned those who hang on to the belief that a job well attended is a career entitlement.

The downsizing virus afflicting American blue-collar jobs has now become a contagious trend for white-collar sectors.

Massachusetts General Hospital transmits CAT scans for examination by Bombay radiologists. Information technology workers in Connecticut watch their jobs drift to Bermuda. Computer techs in Ghana sort New York City's parking tickets. General Electric's investment-credit arm, G.E. Capital, has added 15,000 stock researchers—in India.

It is depressing that nobody warned blue-collar Boomers who, when displaced from manufacturing jobs a decade ago, hustled off to community colleges to learn information technology and other exportable white-collar occupations.

Who could have imagined that high-tech workers in India

would someday take over Boomers' white-collar jobs for a fraction of Boomers' annual salaries?

4. Shift from defined benefit to defined contribution retirement plans

Once upon a time, employers wanted to buy and reward loyalty. They accomplished this in part with guaranteed or "defined benefit" retirement plans. That was the governing view for most of the 20th century.

Then along came "defined contribution" plans, the ubiquitous 401(k). In a growing economy, this type of plan could accumulate significant wealth in a shorter time, irrespective of length of tenure—an investment approach preferred by younger investors.

The number of employees covered by employer-paid defined benefit plans has fallen precipitously in the last two decades. *U.S. News* estimates that guaranteed retirement programs cover a third fewer workers today than two decades ago.

Furthermore, many Boomers will outlive their companies, and then what happens to their retirement accounts? Just ask former employees of Enron, Arthur Anderson, Global Crossing, or dozens of other dot-bomb era companies.

5. A market crash beginning in March 2000 that decimated market investments

As implied above, The Employee Retirement Income Security Act (ERISA), signed into law in 1974, made it possible for the traditional security of a long-term retirement plan to become a market shell game. This legislation allowed companies to throw the risk of funding retirement programs squarely on the shoulders of employees. And risk it has been.

On April 3, 2000, the U.S. NASDAQ exchange recorded its largest one-day fall, 26 years after ERISA became law. Thus began the process of evaporating retirement savings.

Since the stock market collapse began, corporate pension funds have lost $630 billion—a 14 percent decline. Lost in this staggering number is a full accounting of the number of people whose private retirement accounts and long-term personal savings are in jeopardy or who have already suffered financial ruin.

For example, a high-profile video production executive in Denver watched his retirement nest egg shrivel from over three million to under $30,000 in eighteen months.

6. Generational discrimination or genism

Baby Boomers have been catching bad vibes since they arrived at the threshold of adulthood. They became the frequent topics of derision during the Vietnam War era, with President Richard Nixon dismissing them as bums. Vice President Spiro Agnew called them "an effete corps of impudent snobs."

During the 1980s, Boomers ushered in the "greed-is-good-era", and their collective image morphed into the narcissistic, materialistic yuppie—a characterization as demeaning as Sixties' monikers such as *flower child* or *hippie*. These old stereotypes are resurfacing in new ways.

A 28-year-old webmaster for The Cato Institute, writing recently for *Fox News Online*, begins his op-ed harangue with an unsupported but pervasive observation: Baby Boomers are "the most self-aware, self-congratulatory, and self-destructive generation in American history." He then dwells on the implications of this image as it pertains to Boomers in retirement:

> Boomers I think suffer from a natural inferiority complex. The generation just before them—the World War II generation — saved the world, after all. And when your parents saved the world, what, really, can you do to better them?
>
> So when Boomers aren't busy voting themselves entitlements to prolong their lives, they're striving for immortality— if not for Greatest Generation status, which is taken, then at least for The "Damn the Results, At Least We Tried" Generation.[51]

A photographer from Canada has recently taken on a crusade to elucidate all the evils wrought on society by Boomers, as he sees them. His ever-expanding blog can be found on the internet under the heading, "Boomer Deathwatch."

He apparently stumbled across some of my comments in a news report on *CBS Marketwatch.com*, where I had observed, "Generational prejudice is the last area where we can openly be prejudicial and stereotypical and comfortably get away with it in mixed social situations."

My point exceeded the boundaries of a single generation, but was an observation of the psychological tendency of xenophobes to lump people together by the accident of birth date and then assign negative images to the group, thereby denigrating the image of individuals within the group. We have called this tendency of group exclusion by many names throughout history such as racism, sexism, and a few other "isms." Frankly, no generation today escapes negative stereotyping, and generational divisiveness seems to be the last frontier for those who wish to lump people together based on broad, ill-defined generalities, the proclivity to define the society in terms of *us* and *them*.

This zealous Canadian levied his self-righteous interpretation of my comments with the following assessment:

> There's something fantastic, perhaps even a little obscene, about a member of a demography that's reaped a lifelong social and economic cornucopia deciding late in life that they're being discriminated against, purely because they aren't being marketed to as sympathetically or as assiduously as they think they deserve. Be assured, though, that it won't last—their voice is loud, their gravitational pull immense, and in some office somewhere a harried group of young men and women are wracking their brains figuring out how to make adult incontinence sexy and dignified.[52]

Generational stereotypes are not limited to younger people; some of the nastiest Boomer critics are Boomers. Steve Chapman, a columnist for the *Chicago Tribune*, waxed philosophic about the horrific implications of political dominance by America's elderly in an article posted on MSNBC's *Slate* online magazine, entitled, "Meet the Greedy Grandparents. Why America's Elderly Are So Spoiled." Chapman rails against America's elderly and their apparent self-serving devotion to a mushrooming Social Security debt, as well as the recently enacted federal legislation providing prescription drug benefits under Medicare. He finds his fellow Boomers guilty of mismanagement, by commission, if not overt acts of greed, and their culpability inexcusable:

> Boomers have gotten our way ever since we arrived in this world, and the onset of gray hair, bifocals, and arthritis is not going to moderate our unswerving self-indulgence. We are the same people, after all, who forced the lowering of the drinking age when we were young, so we could drink, and forced it back up when we got older, so our kids couldn't. On top of that, we're used to the best of everything, and plenty of it. We weren't dubbed the Me Generation because we neglect our own needs, Junior. If politicians think the current geezers are greedy, they ain't seen nothin' yet.[53]

Does all this negativity foreshadow a difficult time in retirement for Boomers? As society has learned from decades of racism and sexism, individuals who are part of a group, detested by some and disliked by many others, often experience discrimination. Although sometimes restrained and difficult to measure, discrimination is nevertheless limiting with long-term economic consequences.

Age discrimination filings with the EEOC under the *Age Discrimination in Employment Act* have increased rapidly during the last few years. In 2001, there were more than 17,000 filings; in 2002, more than 20,000 filings. Most of us know someone who is convinced that a statistically disguised layoff was in reality due to age-related factors.

It is also true that displaced workers face different odds of maintaining the same or higher salary if reemployed, depending on age. In today's fractured corporate environment, workers aged 25 to 54 have a better than 70 percent chance of reemployment in equivalent jobs. People aged 55 to 64 have a less impressive 51 percent rate of reemployment, and in January 2002, 29 percent reported reemployed earnings losses of 20 percent or more.[54]

Why has the retirement opportunity horizon clouded for so many unemployed or underemployed older workers?

Connect the dots, and it is easy to see that discrimination today against Boomers and those slightly older may have something to do with how employers perceive them: as over-the-hill workers, too expensive, not as productive, and expendable.

Forestalled or thwarted retirement savings bode ill for Boomers. Both the affluent minority and the struggling majority must recognize that the coming retirement funding crisis is a reflection of many complex demographic and sociological issues. It is rarely a consequence of failed moral rectitude.

The upsetting political and social ramifications of aging Boomers, on the threshold of retirement in an unsympathetic nation, captured the attention of the *Harvard Generations Policy Journal*. The report presents a sweeping assessment of the extraordinary transformations guaranteed by an aging nation, with or without conscientiously guided public policy. Paul Hodge, director of the Generations Policy Initiative, warns that the aging of America is the most pressing issue of this century. Political leaders must address this crisis now through a new paradigm of public policy that is "comprehensive, intergenerational, and interdisciplinary."[55]

Former Vice President Spiro Agnew denounced Boomers when they were young and arrogantly naïve. One unwarranted criticism thirty-five years ago may actually hold shades of truth for the future. Given the gloomy retirement and healthcare outlook for so many aging Boomers, would it be any surprise if they do become "nattering nabobs of negativism?"

From a business perspective, greater public awareness about the looming, widespread retirement crisis creates new opportunities.

Forward-thinking companies build their brands by projecting empathy in marketing communications. Socially responsible corporations convey messages that reveal the real-life pressures unique to their markets. Leading companies create plausible avenues of escape from human failings and financial shortcomings. Industries have been built around personal tragedies with services addressing a win-win outcome.

Leadership is always bold, as reflected by those companies that have shown high-profile social responsibility for diseases often associated with aging such as breast and prostate cancer, arthritis, and Alzheimer's disease.

Assuming there will be a large majority of Boomers who have some retirement benefits but not enough to pay all the costs of daily living, many companies can provide supplemental income through a variety of part-time work solutions. Middle-class Boomers can effectively provide services reflecting their former careers, such as a lawyer in retirement providing law clerk and research services for his former firm. A former school teacher can become a substitute teacher. A former nurse can work part-time in a geriatric practice. Companies friendly to former leaders will in fact lead.

A smaller group of Boomers will not have any retirement benefits other than those provided through Social Security programs. Struggling elderly will also provide new avenues for the farsighted.

Consider for a moment the emergence of companies that buy back houses in foreclosure and then rent the same houses to their original owners. Although this can be Darwinian when down-and-out people are manipulated to give up too much to pay for help, honest companies can nevertheless profit from the tragedies of failed home ownership while helping people stay in their homes as tenants.

Consider the companies that have profited with integrity from new government programs that help the downtrodden. In the near future, we may become accustomed to companies that provide cooperative networking solutions, such as cooperative housing, food cooperatives, and work-share solutions for people needing work but who are unable to fulfill fulltime job responsibilities.

In a nation dominated by customers over the age of 40, new business services will also appear that answer the call of too many, too old.

For example, financial services companies can develop products that liquidate nontraditional assets to help those struggling in retirement. Imagine the business benefits that could be derived from creatively converting assets into retirement benefits. These services could include reverse mortgages, loans against anticipated inheritances, and tangible asset valuations that are then converted to annuities. Imagine the untapped wealth to be found in Boomer family heirlooms, antiques, and undeveloped land.

Facing 60: Changing Boomer Priorities

ON JANUARY 1, 2006, the oldest Baby Boomer turned 60. For the following 19 years, one Boomer turns 60 about every 7.5 seconds. Boomers are confronting a demanding life stage, fraught with unique developmental challenges. Representing 26 percent of the U.S. population, this demographic tidal wave will continue to refocus businesses on how best to capitalize on a distinctive set of new priorities. Here are a few examples:

Take better care of Mom and Dad.

Over 13 million Boomers care for aging parents and, according to a survey by Campbell-Ewald Health, one-fourth have live-in parents.[56] Taking care of parents is an emotional rollercoaster. Caregivers can feel profoundly grateful for a chance to give back, yet hopelessly constrained by the demands of doctor appointments, insurance hassles, shopping, and so forth. An enduring metaphor for a fresh beginning, entering a new life stage, such as turning 60, encourages overwhelmed Boomers to renew dedication to constructive parental caregiving.

Business opportunities: Senior support organizations, assisted care facilities, in-home medical and support services, adult day care, caregiver education and training, "mother-in-law" detached cottages offered by housing developers

Keep the weight off.

Obesity is an intensifying health nemesis for Boomers, with more than 30 percent already packing too many pounds. But those who are svelte in middle age also have reasons for caution. In a comprehensive study under the auspices of the National Heart, Lung, and Blood Institute, researchers discovered that 20 percent of the women and 25 percent of the men in the study grew from optimal weight to obesity in four years.[57] Obesity increases the incidence of high blood pressure, heart disease, stroke, arthritis, and asthma. Obesity is a precursor of early death. As they cross the threshold of 60, Boomers will progressively confront the medical dangers of growing girth

Business opportunities: Fitness facilities, marketing dietary supplements, online weight management portals, psychological services for compulsive eaters, support networks, fitness franchises such as Body Pump

Find more love.

Almost 13 percent of the Boomers never married and over 14 percent are now divorced. At least a quarter of the generation is searching for romantic connections. Nielsen Net Ratings discovered that Boomers are the most avid users of personal ads posted on the internet.[58] The Web resource of choice is Yahoo! personals, and the typical user is male, 45, earning between $50,000 and $75,000 in annual income. The astonishing growth of internet dating services, such as *eHarmony.com* and *Match.com*, provides further confirmation that middle-aged men and women are using online dating services to help them cross the lonely-hearts chasm.

Business opportunities: On-line dating services, companies marketing personal expression cards and gifts, community-based dating services, personal advertising services.

Save more for retirement.

Although the vanguard of the leading-edge of the Boomer generation can theoretically start receiving Social Security checks in 2008, the prospect for a long and comfy retirement is looking more dismal every year. Speaking at a gathering of bankers, then Federal Reserve Chairman Alan Greenspan said, "We may have already committed more physical resources to the Baby Boom generation in its retirement years than our economy has the capacity to deliver."[59] Since roughly one-third of the generation is financially insolvent, with net assets of $10,000 or less, Boomers are recognizing the coming calamity of miniscule retirement savings and an insolvent Social Security system.

Business opportunities: Financial planning, online financial analysis services, mutual fund companies, long-term care insurance, financial self-help books and seminars, annuities, debt consolidation services, adult education, employment agencies and services.

PART 3

PRACTCES

Occasionally in life there are those moments of unutter-
able fulfillment which cannot be completely explained by
those symbols called words. Their meanings can only be
articulated by the inaudible language of the heart.

—Martin Luther King, Jr.

A musician must make music, an artist must paint, a poet
must write, if they are to be ultimately at peace with
themselves.

—Abraham H. Maslow

We can tell our values by looking at our checkbook stubs.

—Gloria Steinem

CHAPTER 40

LOHAS: Genesis of a New Market Segment

ARK JOYOUS is athletic, personable, unfaltering and deeply committed to the natural environment. A former naval officer and national park ranger stationed in the Redwood Forest, he understands and appreciates pristine wilderness and responsible land development better than most. He has made his living during the last twenty years as a Colorado real estate broker specializing in mountain properties, with an underpinning ethos of environmental responsibility, team collaboration, and community development.

Mark's primary mission in life is to help as many people as possible become aware of human interconnectivity across boundaries and around this precious planet and our blue orb's fragility, as well as the looming threat to stability should humanity fail to evolve beyond self-serving boundaries and short-sighted natural resource exploitation. Like so many of his Boomer peers, he is deeply concerned about the ability of the planet to provide sufficient and sustainable natural resources for his grandchildren and their grandchildren.

He discovered his purpose while working with children in the Redwood Forest, becoming entranced by their innate awe of nature and thirst to learn about its mysteries.

His goal today is to help more people, children and adults alike, embrace a whole-planet perspective. One way he's approaching this is through his philanthropic cause, EarthSeeds Project, a Johnny Appleseed-like approach for the new millennium. Several educational programs involve spreading "seeds" of a "healthy, harmonious, and sustainable living Earth." He is developing fun, celebratory, positive approaches to environmental awareness instead of the Sixties' countercultural approach that served to polarize as many people as it converted.[60]

As co-founder and executive director of Global View Foundation, a nonprofit organization which has grown quickly to become an international grassroots movement, Mark is dedicated to high-impact education and empowerment by disseminating photographic representations of Earth as depicted on posters, flags and other printed media. He believes that "to change the world, we must first change humanity's global view."

His team has created several globes: one that is beach-ball size and others that are human size and as large as twenty-feet in diameter. These globes present the most accurate view of Earth ever created. They lack geopolitical boundaries and depict an authentic reproduction of the planet—an orbital view from an astronaut's perspective. The globes were painstakingly designed by assembling thousands of photos taken by satellites and numerous orbital missions. The Astronaut's Globe presents a true, awe-inspiring view of our home from outer space, Spaceship Earth.

The stated goal of Mark's foundation is to place these powerful reproductions of the planet in schools, churches, and at community events around the world. His website *EarthSeeds.net* elaborates:

> The view of Earth, as astronauts see it, is a powerful vision for all humanity. Regardless of people's politics, religion, age, or any other demographic, it has been proven that Earth's image invokes a sense of awe, wonder and positive feelings among all who see it. Truly, it is the one thing we all share in common. The astronaut's view of Earth allows people, especially children, to see the Earth as a living Spaceship.[61]

Mark, an impassioned environmentalist, personifies a powerful marketing segment in the United States uncovered just since the beginning of the new millennium. This consumer segment has been christened LOHAS, an acronym that stands for Lifestyles of Health and Sustainability.[62]

Although few people fully express and actively demonstrate Mark's unquenchable passion for our planet, the LOHAS consumer is represented by an eyebrow-raising 27 percent of the U.S. population. This group includes people who are ardently concerned about personal health and emotional wellbeing plus protection of the environment.

These are not citizens simply possessed by idealistic, ethereal values; they are consumers who make purchasing decisions based on how effectively companies approach product manufacturing and distribution with a view toward responsible resource utilization and long-term planetary accountability. Many are also committed to broader social issues such as protecting women's, children's and worker's rights.

LOHAS consumers shop for energy efficient electronics; green household products; organic and natural personal-care products; organic and natural foods; hybrid automobiles; green building products; socially responsible investments; and alternative healthcare services.

Collectively, they purchase nearly $350 billion in goods and services annually, preferring products that meet their value-driven expectations for wellbeing, social justice, self-development and sustainable living. They are dedicated to the environment, systemic human health, spirituality, and personal growth. They believe in the interconnectivity of all humankind on a macro scale and the integration of mind, body and spirit within the individual. Many envision themselves similar to a manifesto presented by Mark's website: "as unique, independent Crewmembers of a Global Family united by the responsibility to care for the planet and all living things."

The Natural Marketing Institute (NMI) originally quantified this important new segment through pioneering research in 2001, initially by distributing a comprehensive survey to a statistically random and representative sample of Americans and then by analyzing survey data using sophisticated cluster analysis.

The firm's discovery process analyzed 16 variables with a multiple regression model to identify the LOHAS segmentation. In addition to the LOHAS segment, NMI researchers discovered three other broadly defined, tangentially related consumer segments called "Nomadics," "Centrists," and "Indifferents." Although these three additional consumer groups reveal specific business opportunities and marketing insights, especially the Nomadics, further discussion about segments other than the LOHAS consumer lies outside the focus of this chapter.

NMI completed the third annual update of its wide-ranging research program in March 2004, based on a survey completed by 2,060 U.S. adults, a representative sample from a consumer panel of 7 million Americans. The conclusions of this survey meet the most discerning standards of statistical predictability and can be projected to the U.S. adult population, with a 95 percent confidence level and a standard deviation of plus or minus 2 percent.

Discovery and description of the LOHAS market, and its surprising magnitude, has quickly led to a business revolution among proponents of responsible businesses across many industries. The LOHAS segmentation demonstrates the interconnectedness of a wide cross section of U.S. adult consumers, bound by similar values, and spanning an extensive range of product and service categories. Exemplary companies targeting this segment sell resource-efficient and healthful products such as organic foods, personal care products, green cleaning products and eco-tourism—among others.

Moreover, this segment includes 55 million American consumers, 47 percent of whom are between the ages of 45 and 64. It therefore doesn't come as a surprise that many Americans who were still young adults during the inauguration of Earth Day in April 1970, and the modern environmental consciousness it propelled, correlate highly with the LOHAS segment. In raw numbers, over 26 million members of the LOHAS segment are also Boomers, born between 1946 and 1959, or members of the Silent Generation, born between 1940 and 1945.

Steve French, executive vice president and managing partner of NMI, emphasizes the sizable correlation between values identified in the LOHAS segmentation and those possessed by Americans aged 45 or older: "Our research findings substantiate what some companies and policy makers have assumed to be true for a long time. Many Americans reached adulthood in the 1960s and 1970s during the emergence of a global environmental awareness and greater focus on personal health, and they maintain those same values today, although they've become more sophisticated as consumers with the passage of time. The major difference today is that they have considerable financial resources and commitment to search for and buy products and services that serve their long-term environmental and health goals."

This research project further demonstrates that members of the LOHAS segment possess strong opinions, and they have a greater influence on the direction of the marketplace than average consumers.

Marketers can also take comfort learning that these consumers are fervently committed to their beliefs for the long run, and most product development and marketing strategies will stand the test of time. How they feel today reflects how they'll feel tomorrow. Considering all four broad segments identified by NMI, LOHAS consumers are the most brand loyal and the least price sensitive.

Interestingly, of the 16 factors used to describe the LOHAS consumer segmentation, those willing to spend 20 percent or more for sustainably-made products earned a mean score of 4.1 on a five-point scale, with five being the strongest possible agreement level. This factor ranked third in importance of identifying the LOHAS consumer, led only by "choosing environmentally friendly products" and "teaching family/friends the benefits of environmentally friendly products." An astounding 85 percent of LOHAS consumers are willing to spend 20 percent more for products that are manufactured using environmentally sensitive and sustainable methodologies.

LOHAS consumers are behaviorally driven. As mentioned earlier, they are not just typified by expressed attitudes; they transform their attitudes into action. They pay more for products meeting their criteria; influence friends and family members to do the same; and choose products from sustainable and environmentally friendly sources. Products must appeal to more than beliefs; products must appeal to LOHAS lifestyles. Members of this segment seek companies that truly align corporate values with their own values, and they are quick to spot "green washers"—companies that create facades and make feeble but insincere attempts to line up with environmental values.

NMI's data analysis contradicts the widely accepted belief that younger people are more idealistic and therefore more likely to make consumption choices based on core values. Younger people are much more likely to choose products based on the lowest price.

The research once again dispels the myth that brand choices solidify with age. Clearly, older consumers are amenable to marketing communication approaches that address core values; strategically sound business approaches can and do influence brand switching.

NMI's LOHAS research amplifies an important theme presented throughout this book: as consumers grow older, they become more connected with values related to relevance, self-actualization, and legacies. Furthermore, as consumers age beyond 50, they tend to choose products and service providers that are environmentally responsible and committed to human health; they buy from companies that share the same long-term values; and they choose products manufactured from sustainable resources.

> As consumers grow older, they become more connected with values related to relevance, self-actualization, and legacies.

The conclusion: businesses interested in developing products and services to target adults age 45 and older have a significant business opportunity when targeting the Boomer/LOHAS consumer. Product development, marketing communication strategies, and corporate goals can be aligned with values held by this vital lifestyle and attitudinal cluster, embracing its bedrock standards of health, self-development, environmental sustainability and social responsibility.

In its ongoing research program, the Natural Marketing Institute has also developed a series of proprietary consumer research studies called *Understanding the LOHAS Consumer Report*.™ These reports provide detailed evaluations of products and services described by the broad categories of greatest interest to this influential consumer, including:

Understanding the LOHAS Consumer™
A Focus on Consumer Packaged Goods

This report reveals consumer attitudes, purchase drivers, usage rates, and sources of influence for multiple consumer packaged goods industries, including food, beverage, household cleaning products, personal care, and dietary supplements.

Understanding the LOHAS Consumer™
A Focus on Durable Goods

This report contains consumer attitudes, purchase drivers, usage rates, and sources of influence for multiple durable goods, including electronic appliances, automotive, and green building products.

Understanding the LOHAS Consumer™
A Focus on Media and Sources of Influence

This report examines the various sources of information consumers rely on when making purchase decisions, their readership of over 40 different magazine titles, and their watching/listening of over 15 different stations, channels, and programs.

Specific categories covered by the NMI LOHAS research, reflecting the impressive variety of products and services important to these consumers, include:

- **Green Household and Cleaning**

  Recycled paper goods, non-toxic cleansers, rechargeable batteries, non-toxic dish detergents, natural household cleaning products, compact fluorescent light bulbs, water purifiers, environmentally friendly lawn and garden products, natural pet-care products, air purifiers, natural-spectrum light bulbs.

- **Natural and Organic Personal Care**

  Aromatherapy, beauty supplements, natural bodycare products, natural cosmetic products, natural haircare products, natural skincare products, natural and organic oral-care products, organic haircare products, organic skincare products, personal-care products for a specific health issue, spa treatments and massage, and vitamin-fortified personal-care products.

- **Healthy Foods**
  Foods or beverages with specific health claims, fortified foods or beverages, natural foods or beverages, organic foods or beverages, soy foods, soy milk and soy beverages.

- **Socially Responsible Investments**
  Stocks or mutual funds which avoid issues that are insensitive to a host of social concerns, such as the environment or child labor, or that sell unhealthful products such as tobacco.

- **Renewable Power**
  Renewable power from a consumer's current electric company or use of solar panels.

- **Dietary Supplements**
  Herbal supplements, homeopathic remedies, weight-loss supplements, calcium supplements, multi-vitamins.

- **Alternative Healthcare**
  Acupuncture and acupressure, biofeedback, chelation therapy, chiropractic, enzyme therapy, homeopathy, nutrition therapy, magnetism, massage therapy, naturopathic medicine, reflexology, and Tai Chi.

- **Hybrid Vehicles**
  Vehicles (cars and SUVs) with engines that use a combination of gasoline and batteries.

- **Green Building Products**
  Products that improve the environmental and health impacts of the materials used in either renovation or new construction of homes, office buildings, and stores.

According to NMI researchers, LOHAS consumers are compelled by values to seek products and services that are health promoting, environmentally friendly and demonstrate a global social consciousness. A significant segment of Leading-Edge Boomers are equally compelled, having acquired and nurtured a sophisticated view of the planet: the panoramic view of Mark Joyous—an "astronaut's view of the Earth"—a global family portrait.

CHAPTER 41

How the Mature Mind Meets Messages

RARELY do advertisements communicate the same messages universally. Different cohorts can and do interpret the same message differently, based on sociological, cultural, sexual, and age differences. In the fields of sociology and aging, experts like to refer to this phenomenon as the *age-period-cohort effect*. Some of the television commercials presented during the February 2004 Super Bowl provided a good demonstration of these differences.

Bud Light brand of beer unveiled several TV commercials that principally targeted heavy beer drinkers, young males aged 21 to 28. One commercial began with a young couple in a sleigh. They were surrounded by all the elements of an impending romantic encounter, a snowy winter night, isolation and solitude. The young man offers his partner a candle so she can see him in the warm glow, and then he leaves the carriage momentarily to get a couple of beers from a cooler. The horse pulling this sleigh lifts his tale and issues loud, methane-charged flatulence. In the next moment, we see the young woman charred and stunned, an image recalling Wile E. Coyote in a *Road Runner* cartoon.

This commercial obviously tested well with the target audience; Budweiser and its advertising agencies pretest commercials with focus groups to make sure they meet all the basic criteria of aware-ness advertising: attention getting, memorable, and positive brand associations. On the other hand, even though this commercial would elicit a chuckle from all but the most prudish of any age group, older adults with whom I'm acquainted viewed this style of humor as sophomoric, a throwback to junior high school locker room absurdity favored by adolescent boys.

Somewhere buried in this commercial there must have been a selling message about the benefits of Bud Light beer, but the positive associations between a farting horse and the beer were elusive to this armchair critic and many of his contemporaries.

By December 31, 2004, all Baby Boomers became officially older than 40, meaning that this entire cohort has arrived at some stage of middle age. Older consumers do interpret the condensed communication found in advertising differently than younger consumers. Following are some of the major differences:

Emotional responsiveness

Once people arrive at the middle years of their lives, they have amassed a backlog of experience. Most, if not all, of the powerful life experiences we remember have emotional overtones. A memory includes what we recall objectively about the experience, coupled with the emotions associated with the recollection. The more life experiences we have, the more we can provide our own emotionally-driven interpretations of what we see and hear in the context of the present.

Best Western hotel chain developed a magazine advertisement with a photo of a middle-aged couple on a motorcycle. The couple appears elated. A six-word headline brings home the point: "Because you promised yourself you would."

The headline leads to ambiguous but equally effective interpretations among members of the targeted Boomer audience. From one perspective, the ad reminds Boomers of their youth and typical wanderlust urges when they were in their twenties, the yearning for simplicity, the open road and a partner with whom to share the novel experiences promised by travel. The ad reminds readers of their yearning to experience life in the fullest way possible. Health and opportunities for travel can be fleeting, especially with impending careers and families on the horizon.

Another interpretation considers the same promise, but not as an unrealized dream of youth; rather, the ad calls for a middle-aged awakening. Now that the kids have been educated and career ladders have been climbed, it's time to enjoy the benefits of planning and saving for retirement. It's time for a renaissance of freed calendars and open roads.

Either interpretation is correct. The older consumer addresses the ambiguity of this ad with personal values and experiences. The well-crafted message successfully allows each reader to complete the story because, almost universally, most of us promise ourselves to smell the roses—someday.

Best Western could have chosen to be more specific and literal when constructing this magazine advertisement, but it was not necessary. Any positive interpretation leads to the same conclusion: It's time to head out on the highway, and to stay at Best Western hotels along the way.

Recent scientific breakthroughs in neural imaging technologies corroborate the role of experiences and emotions in the decision-making process. An article in *Newsweek* magazine disclosed how the brain processes advertising:

> When the possibility of buying something first occurs to a person, the visual cortex, in the back of the head, springs into action. A few fractions of a second later the mind begins to turn the product over, as though it were looking at it from all sides, which triggers memory circuits in the left inferotemporal cortex, just above and forward of the left ear. Finally, when a product registers as a "strongly preferred choice"—the goal of every advertiser—the action switches to the right parietal cortex, above and slightly behind the right ear. [63]

Again, when an ad triggers positive associations with remembered experiences, the featured product passes the first critical obstacle to a purchase decision.

Metaphorical sophistication

As most of us learned in high school, a metaphor is a comparison, often relying on juxtaposition between two dissimilar ideas, one thing conceived as representing another. When one idea reinforces and embellishes the other concept, adding new texture to meaning, then we have a powerful metaphor. A powerful metaphor can ele-vate a product or brand. A recent advertising campaign for Volkswa-gen illustrates the potent force of metaphor extremely well.

First, a little background.

A once-obscure German manufacturer entered the U.S. market back in the Sixties by enlisting help from a legendary New York copywriter by the name of William Bernbach and his respected advertising agency, Doyle Dane & Bernbach. Recognizing some of the obvious deficiencies of the little car, the agency brilliantly posi-tioned the vehicle as an antiauthoritarian statement. They gave the VW its image as the brand of choice for those who: a) wanted to treat the environment more responsibly by shunning Detroit's big gas guzzlers; b) could only afford an economically-priced car; and, c) saw all the contradictions in this car when compared with the prevailing products of GM and Ford. This ugly little car broke the mold of conformity. The agency tapped into emerging Boomer val-ues, including environmental awareness, rejection of traditional symbols of power, such as the chrome-laden, fin-sporting U.S. cars of the time, and function over form. Ugly became beautiful.

My G.I. Generation father gave me one of the most appreciated gifts of my young life when, upon graduation from high school, he handed me the keys to a blue Volkswagen Beetle. Never has my emotional attachment been greater to a vehicle than to my VW, which I started calling the Blue Badoinke. My friends further per-sonified the car when referring to it by its given pet name.

This make of car and its minivan companion helped define the Sixties. A common symbol of the era, or metaphor, is a VW bus brightly repainted with flowers, peace signs, and other beatific images of love and utopia.

Then the Age of Aquarius ended.

Volkswagen became stagnant during the 1980s and early 1990s, seemingly unable to compete with the Japanese manufacturers such as Toyota, Subaru, Honda, and Nissan. After struggling to redefine its image around newer, more sophisticated car designs, and performing poorly, the company decided to return to its roots by reintroducing the Beetle with sleeker lines and state-of-the-art automotive technologies.

The company unveiled its resurrected car with advertising that harkened back to the days I joyfully cruised the back roads of northeast Kansas in the Blue Badoinke. The ad depicted its new Beetle simply with a side view, surrounded by white space. The headline communicates everything: "Less flower. More power."

The ad succeeds so well in communicating so much with so few words because of its metaphorical appeal to Boomer nostalgia, a sense of shared history, and lingering warm feelings about those halcyon days of *Flower Power*.

Cultural independence

Although Boomers share a unique and powerful history, what I have referred to as a "coming-of-age zeitgeist," now, as middle-aged adults, they are less dependent on appeals to a universal culture. In their book, *Ageless Marketing*, coauthors David B. Wolfe and Robert Snyder successfully defend a powerful idea: older adults are more "introspective, individuated, and autonomous" than younger people. This is intuitively reasonable.

Younger markets can be characterized by wide adoption of styles and fads. Marketers of mega-brands such as carbonated beverages count on this. Younger American adults tend to be more homogeneous in their views of culture. This isn't to conclude that there are not different views and attitudes within youth cohorts; rather, it's a cross-generational observation that younger people tend to follow a deeper call to develop their social maturity as they reach adulthood. Social maturity evolves with our understanding of shared group values and then adopting these values as our own.

> Almost every adult can recall fads and styles zealously adopted in youth without much questioning or resistance.

Almost every adult can recall fads and styles zealously adopted in youth without much questioning or resistance. In the Fifties, teenage boys flocked around fast hot rods and the James Dean approach to fashion such as white t-shirts, black leather jackets, and blue jeans. In the Sixties, Boomers typically dressed in bell-bottom jeans and leather regalia. In the Seventies, teens became enchanted with leisure suits and platform shoes. In the Eighties, MTV and the

"Madonna" look became popular. In the Nineties, grunge, body piercing and tattoos became the rage.

As people mature, they withdraw from the pack instinct that characterizes young people. Styles become more fluid. Group-think, more common in youth, dissipates.

Marketers can address this hallmark of aging by appealing to a middle-aged sense of individuality. People at this stage of life are much more comfortable with images of aloneness and contemplation. A developmental hallmark of middle age includes the desire for an identity apart from the pack, as opposed to being viewed as part of the pack.

Hard-sell imperviousness

One ramification of group autonomy is resistance to obvious sales manipulation. By the time adults reach the fall season of their lives, most have accumulated many unsatisfying consumer experiences. These never-forgotten memories could include a hard-selling car dealer who promised a deal but left the buyer wanting. Or it could have been the sour taste left by an impulsive value-purchase of cheaply constructed furniture. Most of us eventually learn how long-term memories of poor quality overshadow the short-term satisfaction of a bargain price.

While we progress through life as consumers, we learn to suspect those who press us too hard to buy. We grow disgusted with the local automobile dealership and a "celebrity spokesman" who delights in loudly proclaiming every Thursday during the late news that the coming weekend is the last chance for "unbeatable, close-out prices."

Mature consumers have greater reverence for marketers who respect their intelligence, who honor their maturity by creating marketing dialogues rather than monologues. A mature relationship is one that embraces reciprocity, with both parties giving and taking. The one-sided sales argument is never a reciprocal interaction; it is rarely a show of respect by the marketer for her customer.

Successful businesses targeting Boomers recognize that relationships should precede selling. Trust precedes commitment.

Information consumption

Marketers build brands by fostering emotional linkages with customers.

Recognizing its much diminished image during a public fight with federal regulators and antitrust litigators, Microsoft Corporation decided to rebuild its nefarious image by doing a better job of honoring customers. The company responded in part by unveiling a new marketing communication theme: "Your potential. Our passion." The giant company became focused on building new emotional ties with customers by exonerating customers' creative and achievement potential. The underlying sales message: Use Microsoft software and create great things. This is how the company described its new approach:

> Our mission is not just to unlock the potential of today's new technologies. It is to help unleash the potential in every person, family, and business. We want to help you do the things you do every day—express your ideas, manage your finances, build your business—faster, easier, and better. At Microsoft, we see the world not as it is, but as it might someday become.[64]

Once the emotional tie has been fostered, however, Boomers tend to become information junkies. Many want to know everything possible about their purchases, especially for products requiring a large capital investment such as automobiles and high-end computer technology. Again, because they are less reliant on pack mentality, Boomers seek lots of information to mitigate the financial risk of a large purchase or to justify further an emotionally-driven decision. They are less enamored of brand appeals without the availability of substance or logical support.

This means that marketing appeals need to be multilayered. Imagine a marketing pyramid dissected into horizontal sections. At the apex of this pyramid is the emotional building block. The information in this segment is superficial, but the selling message presents a powerful metaphor or concept that resonates with Boomer values. Each successive block proceeding to the base of the pyramid provides more details about the product, from benefits and features, to customer success stories and technical specifications.

The worldwide web has become an important component of contemporary marketing. Brand advertising through mass media can reveal the brand's unique sell-

Once the emotional tie has been fostered, Boomers tend to become information junkies.

ing message and instill emotional context for the brand. The company website provides deeper layers of information, from customer success stories and product anecdotes to manufacturing specifications. Information-hungry customers can discover all the knowledge necessary to support a buying decision before it is consummated, or to mollify post-purchase anxiety once the product has been purchased.

Marketing theory requires making generalizations about target groups. Marketing practice requires acting on these generalizations.

One-to-one marketing is an idealized vision of marketing that merges the power of database technologies with digital media so that, for example, printed brochures for a lifestyle retirement community can be customized for each recipient.

A retiring Boomer known to be interested in fitness receives a brochure emphasizing the athletic facilities. Another Boomer craving social connections receives a brochure emphasizing the many hosted annual social events. Thus, a mailing campaign of 10,000 brochures consists potentially of 10,000 slightly different brochures, each uniquely adapted to address individual buying motivations.

In the science fiction movie *Minority Report*, starring Tom Cruise, public billboards in the not-too-distant future "talk" to each passerby with a personal communication. The imaginary technology identifies the passerby, accesses a central database to assemble critical personality and lifestyle attributes, and then speaks to the person as if an inquiring friend. "Are you still having trouble with constipation, Tom? You know a daily bowl of high-fiber Bran Flakes will help you stay regular! Our newest variety has less sugar and is perfect for your lower carbohydrate diet."

This vision has not been fully realized, nor, in the opinion of this author and most privacy advocates, should it be. However, with a better understanding of Boomer and middle-aged values, marketers can do a better job of speaking to their customers with empathy, clarity, and relevance.

CHAPTER 42

A Primer: Crafting Marketing Copy
to Win Boomers as Customers

COPYWRITING is one of the most powerful crafts of all modern art forms. It is forceful in the sense that more people are behaviorally influenced by advertising copy than through almost any other form of media communication.

Think about it. In what other art form can a message as lean as a few words sell millions of products, create thousands of jobs, and change the way we live?

Take Lee Clow's work for example, a legendary creative director with Chait/Day Advertising in Los Angeles. You may remember his signature television commercial. It helped propel the personal computing revolution as we practice it today.

In this sixty-second TV spot, a series of vignettes depict robot-like humans, all of whom look identical in gray uniforms, a bleak and depressing setting inspired by George Orwell's novel, *1984*. The automatons are sitting in a theater and listening trance-like to Big Brother, who is droning on about parasites, disinformation and an Information Purification Directive. Then a young woman dressed in bright Olympic running clothes dashes into the theater. She is being chased by storm troopers, and she is charging ahead defiantly toward the somnambulating screen. When in throwing range she flings a sledgehammer at the screen, breaking a collective trance and nullifying mind control by the totalitarian leader. Light pours from a hole in the massive screen and the robotic servants of the state change their expressions from zombie-like to awed, enlightened awareness.

Just seventeen words culminate this inspired idea: "On January 24, Apple Computer will introduce Macintosh. And you'll see why 1984 won't be like *1984*."

Even if you work with a Windows-compatible computer today, the graphical user interface governing your work—and the ethos that led us to today's era of ubiquitous Windows-based PCs—was born that fateful day: January 24, 1984.

Powerful ideas embellished by powerful words change the world. As Apple Computer announced on that historical date, Macintosh gives you "The Power to Be Your Best." The same company today exhorts you to "Think Different."

Copywriting changes behavior, influences human perceptions, and defines and reflects our common culture. Copywriting is the place we begin a mind-altering dialogue with Boomers.

Why is copywriting the foundation of all marketing that targets Boomers?

We begin this discussion by better defining the role of copy in marketing.

Copywriting is the challenge of turning ideas into sales, the burden of grabbing attention from over-stimulated consumers, and the responsibility of building new perceptions of reality. Copy, in this sense, must compel people to take action; it must jerk them from self-centered preoccupations; and it must sometimes convince them to change deeply held views.

Copywriting is the craft of translating carefully digested demographic and psychographic data into precisely targeted words. Copywriting is an aftermath; it is the consequence that follows an analytical thinker's attempt to understand customers almost better than customers understand themselves. It is the byway where survey research, focus group narrative, and physiological testing intersect into a logical composite. It is statistics translated into words.

But copywriting is also an art. This begins with the choices a writer makes between words and their connotations. Must you "prove," "corroborate," or "verify" value to clinch a sale? Which word is more precise, more believable? A "blood-red sunset" communicates something different than "carmine alpenglow."

It is this artful manipulation of ideas that has caused Boomers to give up piles of treasured LP records and purchase a newer form of musical plastic called Compact Discs. It is an art to make undecided minds become advocates of an underdog political candidate because of a strident half-minute criticism about his deceitful opponent.

But constructing words with impact implies understanding of communication, and to communicate means to know how words will be received in their relative context by your prospective customers.

A nail means something different to a carpenter than to a podiatrist.

Thus, you must understand for whom you are writing—at many different levels—and this requires information. Some of it may come from intuitive understanding, but the best copywriters always study research and digest industry wisdom. They learn a great deal about a particular group of customers, their wants and needs.

Powerful copywriting evolves beyond measurement and analysis. Successful execution implies empathy. A marketing thinker reaches into the human psyche, sometimes at a level beyond conscious awareness.

Copywriting, then, is the artful use of words and ideas that have been constructed in a precise way to affect an understood group of people. The words are compelling and purposeful, and that's always relative to whom they are aimed.

But more than causing necks to jerk or hearts to quicken, brilliant copy is enduring. Great words linger. They tap into our myths, our dreams, our aspirations, and live beyond exposure to a few ads. Great copy is iconographic and becomes part of common language, and as mentioned, both defines and reflects popular culture.

Since the emergence of copywriting as a fundamental part of economic interchange, the craft has changed how we understand and express reality. It is a bridge connecting an over-educated electronics engineer with a grandmother who needs a device capable of calling for help should she fall. It is a looking glass into character that so many of us view when forming our judgments about the veracity of a senatorial candidate. It is the wellspring from which pours our charitable benevolence to the less fortunate, as well as the bulkhead protecting us from a mind-controlling cult leader.

Imagine a magazine advertisement for Michelob Ultra, Budweiser's new brand addressing the sweeping craze for low-carbohydrate diets. The photo shows a healthy-looking middle-aged man. As he is climbing out of a swimming pool, his expression is intense, his body, sinewy. The punchy headline makes a psychological connection between this vigorous man and the beer: 'If this is your fountain of youth [referring to the pool and implying vigorous exercise], this is your beer."

Advertising copy in its simplest form is one path to commercial success. In another sense, it can become a way to change the world.

Every writer or marketing thinker who wishes to build a powerful, enduring brand relationship with Boomers must first check out his own perceptions, memories, associations, and expectations. If he likes Boomers, then the advertising message will reflect this. If disdain lingers in the background, then this too will sometimes become manifest in the ultimate selling message.

What do you REALLY need to understand to become a more effective, Boomer-focused copywriter?

A surgeon could not perform surgery without hands as a copywriter cannot write without language. You do not, however, need to become a sophisticated writer. As you will discover, copywriting begs for simplicity: short words, short paragraphs, lean language.

Copywriting is a unique writing form in which words mesh with other visual and auditory elements such as photographs, illustrations, jingles, voice-over announcements, and video. Copywriters need a basic understanding of the communication medium for which they are writing.

For example, if you are writing an advertisement for the newspaper, you must be aware of the size of an ad and in which section it will appear. In concert with a graphic designer, you must decide if the ad will appear in black and white or if you will spend extra for color.

How will you convey your message? Will the ad stand alone with copy? Or will you include a photograph to attract attention? If the ad demands a photograph, how will your words and the photo work together?

Cohort marketing encourages the use of age-appropriate photographs and other visual elements that can evoke nostalgic memories and knowing reminders. When we see our peers, we see a reflection in a mirror. When we recall earlier times in our lives, we connect with powerful building blocks of who we are today.

But, again, research can guide critical advertising choices. For example, studies show that many Boomers prefer to see peers in advertising who are slightly younger—in other words, an aspirational reflection in the mirror. For example, healthy Boomers around the age of 55 tend to see themselves as much as 12 years younger, or around the age of 43. Thus, it would make sense to select models that are in their early- to mid-forties in advertising targeting Boomers in their mid-fifties.

The point is that you need to understand the copywriting context for each medium you employ to disseminate your commercial message. This information is easily accessible.

Elements of culture, psychology, sociology, selling, merchandising, marketing, and consumer behavior

Copywriters make it their business to understand human motivation and behavior. They are usually experts at understanding current cultural trends. The ultimate goal of an ad is to cause change: to sway opinion, encourage shopping, alter a company image, or capture a direct order. The process begins by connecting.

As a marketer, you are in the business of snagging **attention**, provoking **interest**, orchestrating **desire**, and inducing positive **action**. The task has been embraced for years in the marketing profession by the acronym **AIDA**. This creative and business challenge requires common sense and keen insight into the human condition. The way to the buyer's heart is through his head, and vice versa.

Great copywriters tend to be prolific learners. Bill Bernbach, one of the visionary leaders of advertising's creative revolution in the Sixties, scanned countless magazines, novels, business books, and trade magazines. He filled his head with knowledge that nourished his brilliant copy through cogent human insights. I also recommend prolific reading to all writers contemplating the challenge of motivating Boomers.

This book is one view of the Boomer Generation. Truly committed marketing thinkers will also learn about this generation through the formative literature and art the generation consumed during late childhood through their young adult years. Here are several examples of books and movies that will help you achieve greater insight about Boomers and their unique place in history:

Books

To Kill a Mockingbird by Harper Lee

Storyline: An outspoken and literate six-year-old tomboy by the name of Scout Finch tells the story of growing up in a small Alabama town with her brother Jem and her widowed attorney father Atticus. The children have an intense curiosity about a reclusive neighbor while their father defends a black man against charges of raping a white woman.

Boomer implications: Many Boomers read this book in junior high or high school and through this Pulitzer Prize–winning novel learned about the injustices of racial prejudice and stereotyping.

Catch 22: A Novel by Joseph Heller

Storyline: This bizarre comic novel tells about the audacious adventures of Captain Yossarian, a bombardier based in Italy during World War II. The young Captain tries everything possible to avoid flying missions while his zealous commander keeps increasing the quota needed.

Boomer implications: This novel's title has become a metaphor for a no-win situation. The book satirizes military logic and self-aggrandizement among leaders and taught many Boomers early lessons about the potential weaknesses of military service, the failure of war to provide a panacea for resolution of human conflict.

Tropic of Cancer by Henry Miller

Storyline: Miller's autobiographical novel paints a rich tapestry of the challenges of life in Paris during the early 1930s. The story tells of his poverty, reading, relationships, and growth during this formative era.

Boomer implications: Miller's strong language and explicit sexual descriptions gave Boomers prescient glimpses of coming adolescent splurges into "sex, drugs, and rock'n'roll." In spite of many challenges faced by the protagonist, the book nevertheless instilled a quixotic appeal of European travel, a clarion call answered by millions of Boomers during the late Sixties and early Seventies.

1984 by George Orwell

Storyline: The year is 1984; the scene is London, largest population center of Airstrip One, part of a vast political entity called Oceania. This is a society perpetually at war with one of two other mega-societies.

Winston Smith is responsible for making sure all official records reflect the ruling party's version of the truth. The party understands that truth is propaganda: "Who controls the past, controls the future: who controls the present controls the past."

In this stultifying time when Big Brother is always watching, Winston is in danger because his memory still functions. He knows the Party's official image of the world is dynamic fiction. Drawn into a forbidden love affair, Winston finds enough courage to join a secret revolutionary organization called The Brotherhood, dedicated to destruction of the Party. Together with his beloved, he undertakes a dangerous confrontation with the Party.

Boomer implications: Required reading for most Boomer high school students, *1984*, Orwell's totalitarian and frightening view of the future, imbued distrust of the government.

Boomer mistrust also became evident in a prevalent anti-corporation attitude, as well as a strong tendency to disassociate from other traditional sources of authority. This undoubtedly helped influence "the generation gap" with their GI Generation parents who had learned to respect and trust authority during The Great Depression and World War II. Disgust with the potential evils of technology and information gathering by the government also influenced some Boomers to withdraw from mainstream society and join communes or escape to rural America. A minority of males viewed their ubiquitous military draft card as tangible equivalence of subjugation portrayed in Orwell's novel.

Movies

One Flew over the Cuckoo's Nest, based on the novel by Ken Kesey

Storyline: A long-term Indian inmate of a mental institution relates the story of a futile struggle for control of the ward. The hateful, domineering head nurse attempts to break the spirit of a new inmate as this iconoclast imaginatively inspires the drive for liberation and self-expression among his fellow inmates.

Boomer implications: Kesey's story presents a shocking view of mental health institutions and how eccentric people can too easily be labeled as crazy and unfit to live as part of society. Many Boomers identified with the protagonist portrayed by actor Jack Nicholson because of his defiance of authority and the creative, often humorous ways he attempted to overcome "the establishment." Viewers experience viscerally the ultimate consequence of subjugation and institutional control when Nicholson's character is finally lobotomized.

A Clockwork Orange, based on the novel by Anthony Burgess

Storyline: In a convoluted view of the future, a hooligan by the name of Alex roams the streets of London with his gang, terrorizing citizens at random. He is arrested and subjected to corrective brainwashing with unanticipated results. The author adds a flavor of reality to his prophecy of future life in

London by inventing the teenage dialect of *nadsat,* suggestive of a Boomer lexicon . . . *groovy, baby!*

Boomer implications: In spite of its portrayal of senseless violence, and the offensiveness of this way of life to most viewers, this movie powerfully directed by Stanley Kubrick explores alienation felt by youth and stifling, sometimes arbitrary oppression by authority. The movie further characterizes a growing gap between youth values and those of their parents.

The Godfather, based on the novel by Mario Puzo

Storyline: This movie presents shocking glimpses into the lives of a family headed by a powerful Mafia Godfather. Complex characters reveal the paradoxes of their lives, ranging from religiosity and benevolence to brutality and violence.

Boomer implications: Although most Boomers could not identify with the lifestyles revealed in this movie, many became attracted to a culture within a culture, a counterculture with its own standards, rituals, mores, and loyalties—a powerful sense of brotherhood and sisterhood, of bonds that defy external control.

Empathy is the wellspring of powerful communication, and we often discover our most powerful empathetic connections through literature and cinema. If you doubt this, dig out some old love letters or poetic musings of your youth. In these expressions of your own art, you reached into your heart to find exactly the right words and ideas to express fully your passion. Successfully marketing to Boomers demands the same skills.

How two words captured volumes of Boomer memories

Consider this: The average American is exposed to over 2,500 advertisements every day. When you put these commercial interruptions into the middle of our busy days, we have very little time or attention span to digest advertising messages.

Unless they are being paid to search for a product or service, such as would be expected of a buyer for a company, most people make choices based on very little factual information. They rely more on the image of a product established with advertising over a period of time. Our understanding of most products or services is cursory at best.

True copywriting talent manifests itself through a writer's ability to encapsulate the bundle of values to be found in a product. Emphasis is on the force and brevity of words, not details.

Some of the most compelling advertising of the last thirty years is notable for extreme brevity of word choices.

Where's the beef?
You deserve a break today.
Just do it.

Another hallmark of brilliant copy targeting Boomers is clever use of language, nuance, connotations, and multiple metaphors.

I developed a marketing communication campaign for Orange Glo International, a Denver, Colorado, based manufacturer and marketer of natural cleaning products with familiar brand names such as *Orange Glo Wood Polish & Cleaner* and *OxiClean*.

We developed a direct mail and advertising campaign to target Boomers, particularly women aged 40 and older. The central photograph depicted a beautiful, oyster-colored Victorian chair with a glass of spilled red wine staining the seat cushion. The headline evoked Boomer music culture: "Rescue Me."

Aretha Franklin popularized these words with her hit song, "Rescue Me." The lyrics written by Carl William Smith and Raynard Milnar promised a form of interpersonal salvation: "Rescue me, and take me in your arms; Rescue me, I want your tender charms . . ."

This two-word headline also captured the sales proposition.

We aren't just attached to our possessions because of their tangible form and function. A chair given to us by a grandmother has much greater emotional value. Most would cherish grandma's chair more than all others in their home. We personify the chair, adding our own psychic value to real market value with memories of the gray-haired lady. When grandma says, "Rescue me," the need to resolve a crisis becomes much greater. A cleaning product brand that promises rescue becomes all the more reassuring.

As I developed this marketing program, I knew that the campaign headline would stop many prospects and cause them to think for just a split second. The headline was intentionally evocative of the popular Rhythm & Blues song that Boomers heard when they were just discovering the opposite sex and the mysteries of romance.

As your marketing communication writing becomes more polished, look for novel ways to say something in the simplest language possible. Seek brevity and always try to appeal to the deepest possible levels of emotional response.

The nuances of media in Boomers' lives

Magazine advertising is a medium well suited for Leading-Edge Boomers, because, as a generalization, this group tends to be dominated by prolific readers and news junkies. In this medium you have a chance to make a powerful impression with details and even give an "editorial look" to your layout, as has been so effectively demonstrated by The Sharper Image and Bose Audio. If your ad solicits direct orders, you can also expound upon all the complex features and benefits users will derive.

A radio advertising message compels copywriters to think and write visually. Radio is often called "theater of the mind." Where else can you describe a legion of tin soldiers carrying a banana split into the gaping mouth of a giant rhinoceros?

This medium begs for hyperbole, absurd juxtapositions, and situations never possible in the real world. State Farm Insurance recently challenged radio-listening Boomers to consider the disparity between their idealistic dreams of life as a Garden of Eden when they were young, to the potentially bleak contrast of financial realities today as they confront under-funded retirement accounts without the security of State Farm annuities.

Television forces brevity. One mistake beginning copywriters often make is to cram too much information into too little time. Boomers were not raised during a time when television commercials presented fast cuts and a cacophony of lightning-fast concepts, an approach in vogue today among those targeting Generations X and Y.

The Boomer mindset welcomes greater simplicity, linearity, and focus. For this reason, it's usually more effective in television advertising to follow the dictum developed by advertising guru Rosser Reeves: a Unique Selling Proposition or USP. The TV ad features one dominant, unique benefit offered by the product or service and portrays this benefit with a creative idea.

Direct mail may be the most powerful medium of all, especially when it comes to selling complex products and services. Boomers were taught in school to read in a linear fashion; educators in the Fifties and Sixties emphasized analytical thinking and critical interpretation of written matter. Thus, Boomers can and do react favorably to well produced, in-depth marketing communications, a hallmark of direct mail. The medium allows for presentation of nearly unlimited details and enables the marketer to create a variety of selling messages within the same mailing package.

Defining your primary goal based on advertising purpose

Marketing communication through copywriting can be classified into four broad categories, and each category presents a different writing and creative challenge.

Image Advertising

Image advertising rests on copy oriented to the likability, reliability, or fashionable nature of a product or service. This approach is the choice of those who sponsor products and services that are similar to many other offerings in a crowded category, and the buyer makes a selection based on intangible brand qualities.

Image advertising often relies on associations between unrelated or tangential ideas. For example, consider a comparison between an idea taken from popular culture and a financial product for Boomers.

Recall the popular 1996 movie *Jerry McGuire*, directed by Cameron Crowe. Actor Cuba Gooding, Jr. portrayed Rod Tidwell, a quirky black football player who famously and memorably urges his sports agent, played by Tom Cruise, to "Show me the money." Then consider the potential brand-building power of connecting this prominent, pithy admonition to services offered by a wealth management company (assuming no trademark violations). Suddenly the wealth management company takes on Tidwell's persona, an intense, focused, competitive, self-confident athlete who is also full of heart and compassion.

Brand comparisons may also come from exaggeration and hyperbole, such as giant adults playing volleyball while towering over snow-capped Rocky Mountains, a memorable visual technique employed by Coors beer.

You've seen image advertising used frequently by perfume, beer, and soft drink manufacturers. Marketing professionals sometimes label these product categories as "undifferentiated" until they ply their brand wizardry skills. The most successful products in these categories often succeed because consumers latch onto one important brand image concept or idea about the product, whether it's "the choice of a new generation," a "silver bullet," or "the real thing."

Image advertising is most effective for large and financially strong companies capable of delivering frequent television or magazine advertisements. Although some of the most memorable advertising ever conceived can be classified as image advertising, most consumers would not have been able to associate many of these successful ads with the correct sponsors had the advertisers not spent heavily and inundated target audiences with commercial messages in high-impact media.

Image advertising is also a favorite approach used by companies when establishing a corporate brand. Rather than promote specific products or services, corporate image advertisers strive to associate their company names with positive good human character attributes and beneficent business values. This might be "the power to be your best" as conveyed by Apple Computer or a company focused on bringing "good things to life," a long-term brand image promise promulgated by General Electric.

Awareness Advertising

Awareness advertising, although often similar to image advertising, takes an additional step forward by offering prospective customers a clear-cut benefit, sales point or unique selling proposition.

One of the major assumptions supporting the efficacy of awareness advertising is the nature of contemporary society: harried consumers rarely have time or mental capacity to remember more than a single unique point about a product or service. However, their understanding of a unique sales point is critical to marketing success; otherwise, they'll just select whichever brand is readily available for the least amount of money at the point of purchase.

Because of powerful awareness advertising, many won't buy just any toothpaste. We want a strong "decay preventing dentifrice" approved by the American Dental Association. We won't accept just any paper towel in our kitchens; the paper towel must be "the quicker picker-upper."

Awareness advertising is the most effective approach to achieving differentiation from competitors. It's not enough to say your organization is "setting the standards for quality"—that's braggadocio at best, unsupportable at worst. The promise needs to be unique and specific to the needs of prospective customers. For instance, Del Webb, the nation's foremost builder of homes for retirees, doesn't just construct houses similar to thousands of other builders across the nation; this company builds retirement "communities for living."

Direct-Order Advertising

Direct-order advertising attracts marketing practitioners who want measurable results, not just a superlative brand image or differentiated awareness. Direct marketers demand sales, and they derive those sales from each ad or direct mail solicitation.

Some businesses use direct-order advertising to offer products through magazine and newspaper advertising. Perhaps you have been lured by an advertisement in a Sunday newspaper magazine supplement offering a limited-edition Norman Rockwell plate, or guaranteeing a firmer abdomen with exercise equipment, or promising the most beautiful garden in your neighborhood.

Businesses can engineer elaborate and complex product appeals through direct mail by including the entire sales presentation in a single package. The envelope becomes the store window display, luring the prospect to enter the store. The letter becomes the sales executive offering the best arguments in favor of buying the product. The brochure becomes the sales presentation. And the business reply card becomes the purchase contract.

This type of advertising is not for the timid of heart. It's the most exacting form, requiring a unique product offer, a strong sense of emotional and rational selling arguments, and a willingness to risk enough in multiple ads or mailing packages to learn which "hot buttons" pull orders with the greatest frequency. The medium demands continuous, rigorous testing.

Database-Building Advertising

Database-building advertising has the clear-cut goal of influencing prospective customers to identify themselves. Ads in this genre don't always attempt to close a sale; rather, these ads encourage people to give up their anonymity by requesting more information, perhaps in exchange for a "freemium."

Properly motivated prospects may be willing to tell an advertiser much more than just basic demographic data such as name, address, and telephone number. Motivated by the promise of an incentive or offer, prospects may provide further insights into their preferences, lifestyle choices, and affiliations. Then, supplied with insightful data, an advertiser can become better focused on how to match services and products with the unique needs of discrete market segments.

Receiving information from customers and prospects implies that the advertiser is not just thinking short term: an instant sale, the quick deal, slam-bam, thank you, man. It implies a commitment to relationship building.

When a prospect raises his or her hand for your attention, you must be willing to cultivate this relationship with timely follow up, careful communication, and a steadfast commitment to keeping the prospect as a customer for life.

There is more to this challenge than simply attracting attention and response. It's easy to attract window shoppers with a free offer. You achieve mastery of this advertising approach when you attract potential customers who are ready, willing, and able to purchase your products or services.

As with direct-order advertising, inquiry advertisers tend to be the more scientific in their approach to the medium.

The smart marketers always test, test, test. Many magazines, for example, allow advertisers to test multiple versions of the same ad in a single issue. Half of the subscribers get version A; the other half get version B. A key code on the reply form verifies which of the two ads pulled the most qualified prospects.

How to write effective, Boomer-focused copy

Do your homework

Copywriters often face the "white bull." This is how Ernest Hemingway once described the daunting challenge of an empty sheet of typewriter paper, beckoning him to begin assembling words into sentences, paragraphs, and novels. Today we stare at a blank computer screen. The challenge is no less.

Great writing is hard work, and any writer eventually becomes acquainted with writer's block. Whether words fly from your fingertips or you pace your office carpet threadbare just to begin, the task is always easier if you prepare ahead. Here's how.

Learn everything about the product or service

In our information rich world, you can find volumes of information about everything. If you have spent time surfing the web, you know this point is an understatement. You can search countless information resources from your office or home.

If you can't find specific information about your product or service category, perhaps because it is new, you can find information about products similar to yours. For example, DVD players are supplanting compact-disc players, but the music video-loving market remains similar. Early adopters—those people willing to sample a new product shortly after it's introduced—have motivational characteristics in common that you can discern by studying widely available data.

You may be so overwhelmed by the amount of information available that the deluge will either confuse or discourage you. To prevent information overload, you need to define your information needs as specifically as possible.

For example, if you are interested in understanding Boomer

wine connoisseurs, are you most interested in people who prefer French wines, California wines, or both? Are you interested in true hobbyists or those who imbibe primarily because they have a passion for gourmet food?

By narrowing your information search, you will be better equipped to follow an internet search-engine trail through the maze of bewildering options.

One of the best places to start developing industry savvy is through a trade association that serves the industry. Associations often commission research studies for members and then sell their findings to nonmembers. If you query a trade association, and it has research available but charges nonmembers, then try to network with one of the association's current members. Investing in an association membership may be justifiable for those who intend to be long-term players in an industry. There is much you can learn by developing relationships with other members.

Finally, spend time at your local library and ask the reference librarian as many questions as you can. These people are a conduit to a plethora of reference resources, and I have found them to be more than helpful. They usually enjoy plying their skills to help a bewildered patron.

Your objective is to inundate yourself with information about the product category, market segments, and economic factors that influence the product category. You should also look for futuristic projections about what to expect.

Study the competition

The richest source of insights about how to market to Boomers is to explore how competitors are doing it. You'll learn from their successes and mistakes without investing much more than time. Questions to answer:

1. How has this competitor created emotional ties with Boomers?

2. What are the core marketing messages that this competitor is trying to communicate?

3. What metaphorical images and connotations does the competitor employ to create psychic connections with Boomers?

4. Does the competitor reveal prejudices or Boomer stereotypes?

5. Is humor being used appropriately or does the competitor portray negative images of Boomers?

6. In what ways can we improve on this competitor?

The Four Cs

In a marketing research context, Boomers freely discuss their needs and wants and how their wishes align with products and services. The focus group approach evolved early in their lives. So did unsolicited surveys by telephone. Today Boomers are canvassed about almost everything under the sun.

It's one thing to survey prospective Boomer customers for their opinions and attitudes. It's another challenge to put this information into a powerful context that leads to successful marketplace performance. For this reason, I've adopted a different approach to a classic marketing paradigm that helps copywriters stay focused on what's critical during the information gathering phase.

College students will recall the Four P's of marketing: **Product, Price, Place** and **Promotion**. It is the role of marketers to manipulate these four variables to meet business and sales objectives for companies. A newer framework, in an era of more autonomous, individuated older customers, can be called the Four Cs:

Consumer Wants and Needs vs. Product

Your discovery of how best to communicate your selling argument to prospective Boomer customers can be facilitated by answering these questions:

1. What innate needs or desires does the product or service fulfill?

2. What are the buyer's expectations of the product?

3. What are the exclusive emotional benefits/features?

4. How is the product positioned against competitive brands?

5. What are alternatives for products and services other than your product?

This shift away from a traditional product focus asks you to better define your product from the perspective of deep-seated motivations and underlying emotions held by customers. What psychic and functional needs does the product satisfy? As a mentor once challenged me, "What's the question behind the question?" The more you understand how prospective customers will integrate your product or service into their lives, the more likely you'll be to craft resonating selling messages.

Consumer's Cost vs. Price

The price of a product is never just the price. Boomers have learned this lesson many times as they've adopted new technologies. For example, we all appreciate the marvelous printing quality of today's inkjet printers, which can produce documents as crisp and colorful as the best professionally printed brochures from a decade ago. But the price of the printer is hardly the cost. Replacement ink cartridges often cost as much as the printer itself. So, when framing your sales proposition, never forget that veteran consumers know a thing or two about cost versus price. Address all cost points up front, and you will travel a long way toward the ultimate business goal of establishing a trusting, long-term relationship.

Convenience to Buy vs. Place

Since the advent of the internet, the evolution of investing presents an excellent demonstration of the emergence of customer convenience in today's context: 24/7/365: businesses open 24 hours a day, seven days a week, 365 days a year.

Smart companies are making it easier than ever for Boomers to engage in a business relationship. This includes on-line purchasing, overnight shipping, and consistent customer dialogue to evaluate customer satisfaction.

Convenience is more than creating a variety of purchasing options for the customer. It means giving Boomers access to information about products and services when they want the information. Online knowledge banks and click-through customer service representatives underscore the growing demand for "convenience my way, every day."

To make purchasing convenience a cornerstone of your marketing communication campaign, and therefore your copy platform, here are a few questions to consider:

1. How many different channels can be opened to make it easy to buy the product?

2. How can these channels be integrated across media?

3. What are the seasonal considerations and the special occasions most likely to inspire shopping?

4. To what extent are purchasing decisions impulsive or premeditated? How can we address both types of purchasing approaches?

Communication vs. Promotion

Finally, consider in what manner you are communicating with targeted buyers, not just promoting to them. When you can successfully answer the following demographic/psychographic questions about customers, your marketing messages will resonate:

1. What is their generational group? Leading-Edge Boomers vs. Late Boomers?

2. What is their typical level of educational attainment?

3. Where do they live?

4. What are their lifestyle habits and interests?

5. What are their media tastes and habits?

6. What are some of their characteristic buzz words?

7. What do they know about the product?

8. What common and relevant historical events do they share that might relate to the product or its market positioning?

9. What is happening right now in mainstream culture and society that is deeply affecting potential customers? What are they thinking about?

Boomers have learned the lessons of powerful communication, so they prefer advertisers talking *with* them rather than those talking *at* them. Recall the Flower Power-inspired ad for VW mentioned earlier in this book: "Less flower. More power." This message communicates volumes about shared Boomer values. It goes beyond simply promoting the more obvious functional benefits of owning one of those iconic little cars.

Special copywriting issues regarding electronic media

Radio Copywriting

Radio is an excellent medium to reach Boomers. Middle-aged adults commute millions of miles every year from home to office and back. Radio is often a captive medium as we listen in our vehicles during errands and road trips. Talk radio listeners tend to skew demographically older to people in their forties and fifties. Moreover, there are some special marketing challenges presented by radio:

1. Listeners are distracted and therefore half-attentive.
2. The human mind is usually incapable of absorbing as much through the ears as through the eyes.
3. Radio does not allow you to illustrate or depict your product visually.
4. Clutter is very problematic with radio.

There are a number of strategies that copywriters employ to overcome these limitations:

1. Become a storyteller and help your listeners see the wonders of other lands and peoples. Stories captivate imagination and compel active listening.
2. Write for the ear. This means using clear and simple language and managing the pacing. Frenetic radio copy loses listeners.
3. The distracted mind can usually grasp only one or two simple selling ideas in a one-minute radio commercial.
4. Avoid tongue-twisters such as: "The tremendous team gave a standing ovation to its confused coaches."
5. Use short words, and avoid words containing three or more syllables. Avoid words that are hard to pronounce.
6. Use short sentences.

7. Use conjunctions (such as "and," "but," and "so") to keep copy moving, conversational, and to connect thoughts.

8. Use contractions; non-contracted copy sounds like prose, not conversation.

9. Repeat important words, elements, and names, especially your brand or product.

10. Avoid words that sound similar to other words with different meanings: "chief" could mean "main" or "Native American Chief" or, worse, "cheap."

11. Avoid too much alliteration: "Prize-winning pears presented in perfectly proportioned pairs."

12. Write transitionally: each sentence should connect and flow from the preceding sentence.

13. Capture attention in the first few seconds and maintain it.

TV Copywriting

Television advertising, whichever age group you're targeting, has a universal maxim: the visual solution should carry the message. Show rather than tell. Use visual images, non-verbal messages, sound effects, and music to say as much as possible. Let the spoken word complement non-verbal messages.

The best television commercials combine video and audio to create something greater than either separately. For example, a recent television commercial for IBM's Linux featured some of the greatest icons of the Sixties and Seventies.

The 90-second TV spot depicts a young boy about nine in a futuristic setting reminiscent of the Stanley Kubrick movie *2001, A Space Odyssey*. Two scientists are out of camera view and are observing this tow-headed youngster being tutored by a number of different mentors successively seated next to him.

The respected list of teachers includes boxing legend Muhammad Ali, actor/director Penny Marshall, *A Beautiful Mind* author Sylvia Nasar, and Harvard professor and African-American community leader Henry Lewis Gates, Jr.

During the lessons, one of the scientists inquires, "Does he have a name?" His companion answers, "His name is Linux."

Simple but dramatic visual presentation of great contemporary adults teaching an innocent boy helps IBM communicate the power and flexibility of its open source operating software—a software solution that learns from great minds and then stores this knowledge for younger generations to retrieve on command.

Of course, with Boomers, the power of the visual message may be enhanced with background music featuring a hit rock song from the Sixties and Seventies. GM's Cadillac brand has demonstrated the power of this technique by using music of Led Zeppelin with a communication theme line, "Break Through," evoking the title of The Doors' hit song: "Break on through to the Other Side."

Hopefully you now agree that copywriting is an exacting craft, dependent on both precise analysis and imaginative thinking. Effective copywriting creates the essential empathetic connections with customers, creates loyalty, builds brands, and engenders mutually beneficial, long-term business relationships.

CHAPTER 43

So You Want a Revolution?
Target Boomers on the Internet

SLIDE rules beget the handheld calculator. Calculators beget the TRS-80. The TRS-80 beget the IBM PC and Apple MacIntosh computer. Rudimentary personal computers beget the screaming-fast desktop supercomputers of today.

Along their way to technology nirvana, Baby Boomers have discovered and adopted push-button telephones, answering machines, cordless telephones, VCRs, ATMs, cable TV, CD players, microwave ovens, photocopy machines, faxes, cellular telephones, DVD-players, personal data assistants, email and the internet. Except for the few Luddites among us, Boomers have not had too much difficulty adopting new technologies and taking them in stride.

The digital communication revolution is also a Boomer revolution. Contrary to the popular perception and historical documentation that technology affinity decreases with age, recent evidence suggests that Boomers have a strong propensity to use the internet with nearly as great of a frequency as younger generations.

According to the National Telecommunications and Information Administration (NTIA), internet use is heavily correlated with exposure to the internet at work, and nearly 77 percent of those who use the internet at the office will also use the communication technology at home. Since most Boomers are still working, most have daily contact with the ubiquitous communication medium. Thus, for a sizeable majority, the internet learning curve is now behind them.[65]

The digital communication revolution is also a Boomer revolution.

Furthermore, with employment rates of those aged 50 and over likely to increase relative to previous generations, due in part to a workforce shortage and under-funded retirement accounts, more Boomers will become internet savvy because more will remain in or return to the workforce than typical of older generations. Traditional age barriers to technology adoption will also diminish as the internet evolves to include voice-activated applications, faster transmission bandwidth affording more television-like web pages, and web cams to facilitate full audiovisual communications.

Two other demographic factors that influence steeper rates of internet usage among Boomers are the generation's higher per-capita incomes and the large number of Boomers who have attained a college degree. Both affluence and higher education are lifestyle factors that correlate positively with computer and internet usage.[66]

Something else remarkable about Boomers will increase their propensity for internet usage: social networking. Boomers are the first generation in which peers, separated by decades, routinely find each other through today's extraordinary internet search engine capabilities. The emergence and success of such websites as *Reunions.com* and *Classmates.com* attest to this phenomenon.

Imagine this scenario, for example. Two former college roommates have lost touch with each other since graduation from college in 1972. Pete is awful at keeping in touch, and his world travels as a petroleum geologist made him often inaccessible. Charlie, the other roommate, is more sentimental and tried to stay in touch with Pete through periodic Christmas cards, but years of ignored communications finally convinced him to give up. This may have been the end of the story for Pete and Charlie except for the phenomenon of the internet.

One Saturday following a televised basketball game, Charlie's beloved alma mater won a Sweet 16 victory, and he reminisced about Pete and the great times they used to have together at Saturday basketball games. Charlie sauntered over to his home computer and entered Pete's full name into Google.

Suddenly, Charlie was assailed with several pages of listings and web links to Pete's new oil exploration consulting company. It had been almost twenty years since their last conversation, but on this

Saturday in the new millennium, the digital smoke signals rose with global impact. Charlie dispatched an email to the address offered on the "Contact Us" page of the website; Pete replied within three hours; and the sentimental relationship that began in college found a new mature context.

Now these middle-aged men, with career climbing and child-rearing mostly behind them, have more time for communication and a greater sense of commitment to staying in touch. Their renewed relationship begins with frequent catch-up email communications, then a telephone conversation from cell phone to cell phone, and finally they agree to meet for a basketball game at their former university—hopefully during the championship game.

This story is a typical analogy, and it is being played out daily across the nation. Old friends, former lovers, and previous classmates are getting in touch after years of separation. The internet, with its powerful search capabilities and instantaneous low-risk method of communication, has created an unprecedented interpersonal connection channel not possible before 1995 and the advent of the internet. It has never been less risky, less costly, and more possible to reconnect with special people from the past.

The enabling power of the internet will continue to make this technology all the more omnipresent among Boomers and thus potent for marketers. Staying in touch with loved ones and getting in touch with former loved ones are powerful motivators, especially during the mature years of midlife and beyond.

In addition to the social attraction inherent in internet communications, the rapid deployment of the medium has created a vast knowledge warehouse to serve Boomers' changing lifestyles. Boomers can now research and find almost unlimited information to meet their evolving needs, from searching for details about an adventure-travel vacation in Peru to seeking health information about a sudden onset of shingles (a disease related to chicken pox that often appears suddenly in adults over 50). As the world's greatest library the internet offers another compelling benefit to lure Boomers online.

Although traditional media will continue to connect with

Boomers, the internet deserves special consideration by marketers. However, effectiveness at using this medium for customer prospecting begins with developing sound insights about competitors—competitive sleuthing.

Tips to plan and research strategies for marketing to Boomers online

Begin at home

It's obvious that your major competitors often use their websites to strut their stuff. You can probe backgrounds of key executives, evaluate product and service positioning strategies, and anticipate new-product introductions. You can glean strategic weaknesses by what is missing.

The key is to focus on minutiae. Corporate websites often mislead with announcements for phantom-ware, new markets never to be entered, and less than believable financial projections. However, if you pay attention to details, you'll have a few "ah-ha" experiences that lead to sound predictions about how your competitors are using the internet and are likely to be engaging Boomers though e-strategies.

Think global, sleuth local

When IBM's Chairman and CEO Sam Palmisano sneezes, his cold is likely to become a discussion item in his local newspaper. Once you've amused yourself with IBM's voluminous website, visit the Home Page for the Westchester County newspaper. You'll be amazed at what local media reveal about corporate potentates and their grand visions for the future. You'll be amazed at what senior managers confess to local reporters that never gets printed in national trade media.

If you want a swift and decisive way to find local media that have joined the internet—and virtually all have—visit *www.newslink.org*, which connects you to more than 3,600 newspapers, magazines, and television and radio stations. This powerful media guide is searchable by state.

Keep looking for a job

One of the major Achilles' heels for companies using the internet is the business intelligence that can be surmised from their help-wanted ads. These human resource appeals offer wonderful insights about where a company might be heading in pursuit of Boomer markets and enabling technologies. The two most valuable sites are *CareerPath.com* at *www.careerpath.com* and the *Monster.com* at *www.monster.com*.

Wag the search engine

Gaining competitive intelligence on the web is synonymous with mastering the ubiquitous search engine. Most web veterans are familiar with the process, but search engines are continually adding advantageous performance enhancements. For example, Google lets you start with a broad search then drill down. If your search discovers a number of interesting alternatives, but you want more titillation, return to the beginning page of your search and click "I'm feeling lucky" to instantly discover compatible kissing cousins. Google has also added a phenomenal new service entitled Google News Alerts.

You can sign up for this service at *news.google.com* and click on the link to "News Alerts." You can store any search terms you want, and Google will send you daily email summaries of all major media communications appearing that day on the specified subjects. So, for example, you can set up a Google News Alert using the company name of your competitor and the word "boomer." You'll be amazed about what you can learn from this daily digest of breaking media stories.

Searchers beware. I have asked search engines to find information with exactly the same query on different occasions. The outcome is not always the same. So, if you don't get what you seek on first query, try again at different times of the day and using other search engines such as Ask Jeeves! and Yahoo!. You'll be pleasantly surprised.

Turn on, log in, and connect out

Finally, if you need to expand your search for competitive intelligence beyond the boundaries of logical space and time, look at my two favorite portals to information overload.

Ask Jeeves! (*http://askjeeves.com*) is a marvelous butler ready to answer your every question. Type in search information and Jeeves visits all the major search engines and gives you loads of mesmerizing options with titillating questions to further inspire your search. CEO Express! (*www.ceoexpress.com*) is an intelligent site organized by a female CEO who has put on a single page almost every link you could ever need to learn almost anything of value about everything corporate.

Next time you become more determined to bump up your Boomer marketing research, gather competitive intelligence first. There are few satisfactions greater than preempting myopic competitors by introducing their next Boomer marketing strategy ahead of them.

Marketing to Leading-Edge Boomers in the future will clearly involve multi-channel, multi-media strategies that integrate email, websites, direct response webcasts, online affinity groups, and wireless internet appliances. This is a wired generation that will stay wired as it ages, not only because the medium itself will continue to evolve but because Boomers need to stay connected as they grow older. Maintaining interpersonal connections becomes a core motivator during later life.

CHAPTER 44

Reconciliation

MANY Baby Boomers confronted society's wrath as they struggled with, and then challenged, traditions of preceding generations. For many complex reasons, a bad taste in the collective memory of the nation still lingers.

Boomers certainly experienced their share of dismissive indictments from the GI Generation as it struggled to confront a massive youth cohort set on doing its own thing. Younger brothers, sisters, and even Boomers' children also sometimes nurture unresolved resentments against such a brazen, outspoken generation, willing to risk everything in confronting the establishment.

Some of the most outspoken critics of the generation are of the generation. Younger members of the generation, those born between 1956 and 1964, do not necessarily identify with their older brothers and sisters who experienced the cultural revolution first hand.

Some older, Leading-Edge Boomers are also outspoken against Baby Boomers.

One younger Boomer born in 1962 (Late Boomer) has been outspoken in his criticism of Baby Boomers, preferring to consider himself an elder statesman of Generation X rather than a Baby Boomer.[67] Another equally passionate Late Boomer has set up a website dedicated to carving a separate identity for her more socially subdued, but in her opinion, economically viable segment of the Baby Boom.[68]

Some older, Leading-Edge Boomers, aligned with conservative ideology, are also outspoken against Baby Boomers.

Joe Queenan, a regular contributor to *GQ* and *Forbes*, believes that Baby Boomers are "a whiny, narcissistic bunch of paunchy, corporatized losers." Queenan does not pull any punches in his commentary; he sees his generation as self-centered, rude, and obnoxious. He dismisses all but perhaps an elite few, (such as himself?) as "fakes, hypocrites, cop-outs and, in many cases, out-and-out dorks."

As mentioned earlier, Daniel Okrent presented his excoriation of yuppie Baby Boomers in a June 2000 *Time* article entitled "Twilight of the Boomers." Okrent concludes that Boomers are fatuous, self-important, and lazy.

David Brooks, author of *Bobos in Paradise*, suggests that many Boomers are hypocritical sellouts racing toward a collective self-loathing.

Then, there is Dr. Ken Dychtwald, the best-selling author and gerontologist, who is not necessarily conservative, but is an articulate, visionary leader of the aging population segment. In his book, *Age Power*, he predicts that the generation's tendency toward self-centeredness could devolve into a future "Gerassic Park," where younger generations rebel, perhaps violently. Fortunately, Dychtwald does not believe that this outcome is preordained; rather, how the generation manages its social agenda in the next few decades will determine the intergenerational consequences.

No matter what age or disposition that the critics are, Baby Boomers are growing weary of their maligned status. Call us sensitive, but no generation deserves to be dismissed as "self-absorbed" or some other sweeping invective. A generation by definition is too large, too complex, and composed of too many unique individuals. Additionally, generational bias is simply another form of prejudice, just a different verse and chapter of the primordial thought processes that foster sexism or racism, homophobia or xenophobia.

When bias focuses on a generation quickly growing mature and confronting the challenges of being old in America, prejudice morphs into ageism almost overnight.

When this bias focuses on a generation quickly growing mature and confronting the challenges of being old in America, then prejudice morphs into ageism almost overnight.

Boomers want and expect a chance to right the record and overcome damage wrought by their protest and political movements during youth. Many want to confront adversaries with the force of reason and debate. Others prefer to triumph over the negative stereotypes by doing "good works," by reinvesting time and commitment for nonprofit organizations and philanthropic causes. Still others hope for a fuller, more balanced reporting of their challenges and constraints when they began young adulthood during a time of war, assassinations, racial unrest, and a highly segregated society. Finally, many Boomers want to update the record with greater commitment to giving back to their communities during retirement.

"The 75% Factor: Uncovering Hidden Boomer Values," a report addressing this point was released in June 2002. It was co-authored by demographer James V. Gambone Ph.D., author of *ReFirement, a Boomer's Guide to Life After 50*, and Erica Whittlinger, noted investment expert, and 17-year contributor to Public Radio International's *Sound Money*.

A summary of the report posted on *Retirement.com* paraphrases Gambone and Whittlinger's primary observation:

> When men and women of the Boomer generation face major life-changing moments in the over-50 stage of life, they begin to look within themselves to ask the all-important question, Who Am I Really? According to the report, the good news is that millions will answer this question from a core value perspective that will include the importance of feeling a sense of belonging, and needing to give something back.[69]

What does this mean to marketers?

Well, for one thing, a deficient generational image presents an exceptional opportunity for farsighted companies to do a better job of being fair, even a bit generous. Rather than taking the cynical path adopted by Pepsi-Cola during its Woodstock II television commercial, lampooning washed-up old hippies, how about positioning products around the beneficent attributes of the generation?

This could lead to stories about individuals who continue to answer the call of idealism that Boomers all shared when they were young. These are *not* the stories of angry radicals, dedicated to sparking a revolution. These are *not* the stories of self-centered people wanting nothing more from society than what society will give them for narcissistic gratification. These are *not* the stories of dropouts, dilettantes, and dangerous people on the fringe. These are *not* the stories of materialistic, self-conscious, overdramatic, melodramatic people who lament the passing of youth. Neither are they the stories of ridiculous, Austin Powers' characters.

Within the generation's ranks are millions who signed up for public service and a life-long commitment to helping others. These are career social workers, union leaders, small town doctors, school teachers, political activists, inventors, scientists, nurses, firefighters and police officers, university educators, and spiritual leaders. The stories of these real Boomers reach into the heart of humanity, its compassion, nobility, and selflessness.These are the stories of myth, dreams, and the universal yearning for a better life.

As any marketer will quickly learn by peering under the sometimes-maligned veneer of the generation, the stories about community service are true stories, and their revelation can lead to something miraculous. Gambone and Whittlinger conclude in their report:

> If 57 million of us decided to raise up the values of belonging in a society suffering from the pains of isolation—to give something back, because we have been given so much, and take risks to age maturely and cooperatively with all generations—we would change America in ways we could only have dreamt about in the 1960s.[70]

Annie Gottlieb, an articulate observer and critic of the Baby Boom Generation, is a contributor to major magazines such as *The New York Times Book Review* and *Mother Jones,* and is author of a late 1980's book entitled *Do You Believe in Magic?,* a story about the generation's troubled passage to a more promising middle life. She shared her thoughts about Baby Boomers in middle life and, by implication, the heritage the generation begets to its future:

The amazing changes happening now were born then. The environmental movement wouldn't have burgeoned without the environmental crisis, but thanks to our seedtime, the seeds were there to grow—otherwise there'd be no movement. Every mass demonstration, in Manila, Tiananmen Square, Prague, Sofia, goes right back to 1968 and 'the whole world is watching.' What happened in the former USSR and between them and us was powerfully influenced by citizen diplomacy. And on and on.[71]

This is the essential message: Baby Boomers are moving into a late-stage period of life that portends extraordinary social activism, community service, and intellectual accomplishment. Smart marketers who understand this unique developmental and generational dynamic, and who have cast away long-held prejudices, can hit a wellspring of economic opportunities.

Marketers can develop and sell products and services as responsive to a deepening need for community engagement, in the many forms it will soon take. Companies can position other products as ways to solve problems that impede Boomers' abilities to remain so engaged—products that restore health, liberate calendars, ignite passion, and promote insight.

Marketing programs for still other products and services can shine a guiding light for those seeking the beneficent goals of philanthropy, public service, and principled politics. Marketing communications can pay tribute to those who give back with genuine acts of selflessness and courage.

Those enlightening messages and tributes can become the fountainhead of future sales and profits. Who knows? A miracle might happen.

CHAPTER 45

Boomer Brass Tacks:
Some Cohort Marketing Highlights

THROUGHOUT this book, I have provided marketing insights and recommendations, some of which I distill here for future reference and easy review. Below is the "lite" version of the book. It will give you some of the essence, but none of the depth. You can review basic concepts here, but you will need the benefit of the full discourse about each subject to appreciate the subtle implications.

- Boomers' youthful ideals persist, as well as the expression of those ideals, and will emerge again as the generation faces the challenges and conflicts of aging.

- Wouldn't it be interesting if a brave marketer actually undertook a different approach to the Boomers and their wrenching civil disobedience toward Vietnam War policies? How about a strategy recognizing that many people made sacrifices with the goal of creating a more egalitarian and inclusive society?

- The time is coming when Boomers will not only react to negative stereotypes, even communicated in jest, but will also take aggressive actions against companies dimwitted enough to advance such offensive images.

- Baby Boomers will seek youthful attractiveness through chemistry and surgery, and when that fails, they will absorb youth by associating with icons, values, contemporary culture, and continuing engagement with their world.

- The question all marketers targeting Leading-Edge Boomers must answer is: "How can we enhance the experiential benefits of our product or service?"

- When designing new products for Baby Boomers, think smaller, think lighter, think multi-function, think high-quality construction, and think long-term value.

- Baby Boomers will struggle harder and more vociferously than did their parents to protect freedom and remain in control of the course and quality of elder housing and late-stage care.

- Show Boomers as cynical of the status quo and passionate about positive change, and you will reach into the deepest crevices of the generation's collective motivations.

- "The Golden Rule" will become fashionable again as a measure to differentiate a company from its competitors. Companies targeting Boomers that receive negative publicity for corporate abuse may find it difficult to recover; Boomers can be unforgiving.

- Appealing to the Boomer sense of generational community can become a powerful motivator for marketers selling lifestyle housing communities, recreational facilities, entertainment events, and educational conferences.

- Make your product relevant, a way of bringing together communities and causes, and you will create a more loyal following from a generation willing to reward understanding of—and loyalty to—its ideals.

- As retirement comes closer, many Boomers are changing their focus from "success to significance," where they hope to get back in touch with youthful idealism, and perhaps rekindle a belief that they can positively change the world. Participation in philanthropic causes is destined to become fashionable again.

- Rock and roll is the unifying thread that ties together the complex tapestry of the Baby Boom generation. It presents the most common of shared experiences.

- Any business that seeks to win their long-term patronage and loyalty must recognize Baby Boomers' penchant for cultural diversity. They experiment, explore, and express themselves through a multiplicity of influences, and they respond best to companies willing to embrace a culturally inclusive worldview.

- Marketers hoping to build stronger ties with Baby Boomers would be well advised to remember their environmental concerns and desire to contribute to a more sustainable, healthier planet. This will become more intense as Boomers' remaining time on the planet ebbs.

- The challenge confronting those who market to Baby Boomers is to integrate understanding of the target audience with the secondary influence any marketing medium might have on awareness, motivation, and ultimate purchase behaviors.

- As Boomers grow older and enter their retirement years, many will come to appreciate companies, and their products and services, that portray the generation's role in advancing many areas of human thought and exploration.

- A new kind of hero-worship, featuring real people who've given significantly to their professions and communities, will demonstrate your organization's commitment to balance and fairness. Balance and fairness are the central pillars of Boomers' social and political views. Balance and fairness will win loyalty; their absence will drive Boomers away.

- If you want to reach Boomers by appealing to major developmental influences that recall comfortable memories, focus on the cultural phenomena that punctuated early childhood and adolescence: the late 1950s through the mid-1960s. That is when Boomers worried the least and expected the most from life experiences.

- Many marketing communication programs are monologues. The advertiser talks through a broadcast commercial or print ad about a unique product benefit, ostensibly one that meets the customers' needs, and customers simply purchase the solution. The advertiser does not nurture and reward a feedback loop. You will be successful with Baby Boomers, and all age groups for that matter, to the extent that you create meaningful dialogue.

- The passionate quest for creative immortality is likely to become a powerful trend during the next few years, and this driving fervor will open new doors of opportunity for marketers. The most important question that you can ask is this: "How can our product or service be adapted to meet the needs of a market that is becoming ardent about self-expression and invention?"

- Purchasing products will no longer be just a matter of acquisition for the sake of necessity or social status. Discretionary purchasing will also be motivated by deeper needs to express innate human potential and achieve spiritual and religious congruency.

- In the next twenty years, companies that have earned a special relationship with their loyal customers may be able to develop profitable lifestyle communities with their products as the centerpiece.

- Companies engaged in marketing travel, leisure, and lifestyle products should demonstrate the pace-slowing attributes of their products and services. Show Boomers taking leisurely walks around the neighborhood, or gathering in groups to reminisce over café lattes, or enjoying peaceful time with nature. This is not to contradict recommendations elsewhere suggesting that Boomers should be depicted as active and engaged.

- This generation seeks both high-adventure leisure experiences as well as low-key lifestyles, where retirement homes and neighboring communities become havens for relaxation, contemplation, and socialization.

- Creative integration of youthful icons into the experience of your product or service, in a way that does not summon conscious attention, can reach into the deepest wells of Boomer's collective experiences and their most cherished remembrances.

- Anger remains in the soul of the generation; although this powerful emotion's collective manifestations have become dormant during the previous three decades. The generation that spawned the youth culture in America will not accept humiliations and affronts to dignity that typify some of today's eldercare services and facilities.

- A deficient generational image presents an exceptional opportunity for farsighted companies to do a better job of being fair, even a bit generous.

- Marketers of spiritual products, and those who wish to influence Leading-Edge Baby Boomers through spiritual messages, first must take for granted a dominant religious and spiritual pluralism. For many in this cohort—all but the most religiously dogmatic—the path to salvation has few conceptual barriers.

- Spiritual concerns have, at their roots, a collective desire for community, abundant health, brightening horizons, and, ultimately, life satisfaction. Finally, spirituality is the wellspring of character and an integrated awareness of the inner self. The questions your marketing messages must answer are of temporal proportion, nonetheless as wrenching as what happens after the end of life:

  Who will care for me?
  Will I be able to provide for my family?
  Who am I?
  Where am I going?
  Could there be more to life than this?

- Boomers are moving into a late-stage period of life that portends extraordinary social activism, community service, and accomplishment. Smart marketers who understand this developmental and social dynamic, and who have cast away long-held prejudices, can hit a wellspring of economic opportunities.

- Consumers aged 50 and beyond tend to choose products and service providers that are environmentally responsible and committed to human health; they buy from companies that share the same long-term values; and they choose products manufactured from sustainable resources.

- Businesses interested in developing products and services to target adults age 45 and older have a significant business opportunity when targeting the Boomer/LOHAS (Lifestyles of Health and Sustainability) consumer. Product development, marketing communication strategies, and corporate goals can be aligned with values held by this vital lifestyle and attitudinal cluster, embracing their bedrock standards of health, self-development, environmental sustainability and social responsibility.

- Once people arrive at the middle years of their lives, they have amassed a backlog of experiences. Most, if not all, of the powerful life experiences we remember have emotional overtones. The more life experiences we have, the more we can provide our own emotionally-driven interpretations of what we see and hear in the context of the present. When an ad triggers positive associations with remembered experiences, the featured product passes the first critical obstacle to a purchase decision.

- Ads can be successful by communicating much with few words when they make strong metaphorical appeals to Boomer nostalgia, a sense of shared history, and lingering warm feelings about the halcyon days of youth.

- As people mature, they withdraw from the pack instinct that characterizes young people. Styles become more fluid. Group-think, more common in youth, dissipates. Marketers can address this hallmark of aging by appealing to a middle-aged sense of individuality. People at this stage of life are much more comfortable with images of aloneness and contemplation. A developmental hallmark of middle age includes the desire for an identity apart from the pack, as opposed to being viewed as part of the pack.

- Mature consumers have greater reverence for marketers who respect their intelligence, who honor their maturity by creating marketing dialogues rather than monologues. A mature relationship is one that embraces reciprocity, with both parties giving and taking. The one-sided sales argument is never a reciprocal interaction; it is rarely a show of respect by the marketer for her customer. Successful businesses targeting Boomers recognize that relationships should precede selling. Trust precedes commitment.

- Once emotional ties between a brand and target customers have been fostered, Boomers tend to become information junkies. Many want to know everything possible about their purchases, especially for products requiring a large capital investment such as automobiles and high-end computer technology. Again, because they are less reliant on pack mentality, Boomers seek lots of information to mitigate the financial risk of a large purchase or to justify further an emotionally-driven decision. They are less enamored of brand appeals without the availability of substance or logical support.

PART 4

PREDICTIONS

I guess I don't so much mind being old, as I mind being fat and old.

—Peter Gabriel

Few can believe that suffering, especially by others, is in vain. Anything that is disagreeable must surely have beneficial economic effects.

—John Kenneth Galbraith

Most people die before they are fully born. Creativeness means to be born before one dies.

—Erich Fromm

CHAPTER 46

Seven Prophecies

WHO could have foreseen the events of September 11 twenty years ago?

Some were aware of the possibilities of this tragic day, given longstanding hostilities with a few Middle Eastern countries—especially as the cowardly terrorist attack came closer to reality. Nobody predicted the horrific details, from hijacked commercial airliners to determined suicide squads, to the structural collapse of two World Trade Center monoliths. In addition to painful loss and then anger, a typical reaction to this day was shock. We didn't see the low-blow coming until we were doubled over with heartache.

This bellwether occurrence in recent American history also demonstrates the risks of forecasting the future. Unpredictable events frequently change history, social context, and the nation's character.

I reflected upon this dilemma when considering whether or not to lead this section with a short chapter offering a few predictions for the next life stage of an already unpredictable generation.

Nobody can see 2025 clearly, but demographic and social trends reveal some realistic possibilities. Therefore, with the inherent limitations of prescient thinking in mind, here are seven prophecies for significant trends likely to factor into upcoming marketing analyses and strategic plans.

1. An Aging Generation in Conflict

By 2025, the oldest Boomers will be 79 and the youngest will be 61. With most of the generation squarely in retirement, or trying to be in retirement, federal and state governments will be confronting extraordinary fiscal pressures to balance the needs of a massive population of older citizens with the needs of the rest of America. This could lead to unprecedented social and political friction between generations. Today's established entitlement programs most certainly will undergo dramatic reinvention, or nullification. Millions may be forced to discover creative, sometimes pathetic economic survival strategies that don't exist today. Some of those strategies will harken to times past, from bartered goods and services to self-help communities akin to bygone tribal village— maybe even indentured servitude. Naturally, new products and services designed to ameliorate conflict will springboard from the economic and social tension growing between generations.

2. Breakdown of Mass Marketing and the Traditional Consumption Paradigm

Since the early 1980s, America has endured an increasingly unbalanced distribution of wealth between the super-rich and the lower- and middle-class population, carving a growing economic rift and creating a society that might eventually have just two classes: the rich and the rest of us. Our current path toward a plutocracy ruled by a mere handful of extremely wealthy individuals almost guarantees a growing economic fissure. With one-third or more of all Boomers unable to pay the costs of healthcare, and an overstressed Medicare system, American businesses targeting this segment may no longer be able to rely on traditional mass consumption patterns and the underpinning democratic values involved with America's distribution of wealth. If, for example, healthcare commands from one-fifth to one-half of the average retirement monthly outlay, including increasingly expensive health and long-term care insurance, there will be greater competition for what's left of Boomers' limited discretionary dollars. Only the elite will be able to afford many luxury purchases designed for broader mature market segments, including proactive and preventative medical care.

3. Expanding Social Stratification Begetting Alienation

Boomers have popularized individualism since their emergence from childhood, sometimes to the ire of their critics: that threadbare myth of a self-absorbed narcissism whereby each individual's needs are the only priority. This stereotype, combined with a wider acceptance of individual social choices within a multicultural context, could collide with economic pressures and accelerate social stratification. One result could be an accelerating loss of our national identity. Another byproduct could be isolation of America's oldest citizens. This could also lead to more mean-spirited marketing communications by those targeting youth segments to help dramatize significant differences between the hip and young and the staid and old. In turn, social alienation and stratification could engender more defensive and even offensive awareness advertising campaigns created by those organizations serving older markets, as well as Boomer advocacy groups. Society is becoming dangerously polarized.

4. Extraordinary Advancements in Direct and Relationship-building Marketing Strategies

Advancing media analytics and database marketing technologies will increasingly allow marketers to employ traditional national mass media (television, radio, magazine, and outdoor) with the targeting and cost efficiencies of local media. In the future, within minutes of a commercial message transmission through national media channels, marketers will understand subsequent communication impact on Boomers, from advertising recognition and attractiveness, to repulsion, to direct-purchase behavior. The evolution of digital entertainment media, merging with computer technologies, will allow multinational mass marketers to engage in refined direct marketing and relationship-building strategies not available today.

5. New Survival Strategies for Widowed and Divorced Women and those without Male Partners

Women have always had greater longevity than men, and this will not change with the aging Boomer population. Because many Boomer women will eventually face a period of life lacking the traditional social model typified by heterogeneous pairings—a man and woman in a single household—newer forms of Boomer consumption and lifestyle strategies are forthcoming. For example, mature Boomer women will engage and develop their networking and support communities into communal living arrangements, cooperative buying clubs, and asset protection circles. Red Hat gatherings, simultaneously whimsical and serious networking, portend this emerging trend.

6. Increasing Demands for Experiences Reflecting Changing Late-Life Needs

As documented elsewhere in this book, experiences take priority over possessions in later life, especially when Boomers confront inevitable serious losses—from the death of parents and peers to debilitating diseases, and failures in careers and long-term marriages. Introspection and reflection spring from loss, leading to heightened interest in learning for its own sake; travel to gain more of a global perspective; mental stimulation from infotainment; creative experiences and artistic production; and soulful searching by way of traditional religion and alternative paths to spiritual awareness. Boomers have traditionally been a searching generation, amplifying their experiential quests beyond the boundaries and benchmarks set by today's older generations.

7. Stubborn Unwillingness to Surrender to the Aging Process

It is not in the Boomer nature to surrender to authority, especially the domination of the aging process itself. Their primary survival strategy will be adaptation and this will manifest through reinvention of identity, both individual and institutional. Many will invent new ways of life, underpinned by dramatic physical changes, from major geographic relocations to appearance makeovers. With a growing sense of global connectivity, many exotic outposts such as byways in South America and Australia could become late-life havens for economically strapped Boomers. Furthermore, so-called anti-aging medicine will continue to challenge the nation's health-care system as it becomes more proactive about functional restoration and intervention at earlier stages of the disease process. Thus, we can expect to see much more aggressive mitigation of degenerative diseases such as arthritis, heart disease, and diabetes. Emerging medical technologies such as organ cloning and biogenetic engineering could lead to surprising and drastic physical changes preferred by the generation's elite, especially those with the resources to pay for optional surgical and genetic intervention. Furthermore, the aging process, coupled with the significant social pressures mentioned earlier, will lead to formation of new institutions that foster and exonerate aging and act as strident political action committees to make preventive and restorative care more readily available to the aging masses.

The following chapters continue this speculative thought process about what might be. These possibilities always begin with Boomers, who they are now, what they believe, and how they adapt to change. Finally, the book closes with a short story that attempts to package Boomers' lives tomorrow with the metaphors and values important to this generation.

CHAPTER 47

Baby Boomers at Midlife

The following essay predates the rest of the text for this book, yet it rings true in its metaphors and vision of Boomers' unique brand of middle aging. It originally appeared in the respected national writing competition held by *Writer's Digest* magazine, where it received critical recognition.

Baby Boomers at midlife: coming of age revisited

When a middle-aged individual struggles with aging, it is called an identity crisis. When a generation struggles with the same fact of life, it is called a zeitgeist—a shared feeling for an era, a spirit of the times.

As the leading edge of the Baby Boom—the so-called Sixties Generation—passes into midlife, millions must struggle with the dissonance between the idealism of youth and the nihilism of middle age. The iconoclasts who spawned the youth culture of the Sixties and Seventies look backward from the beginning of a new millennium to reincarnate flickering vestiges of youth. Rock singer and Boomer John Mellencamp laments, "It's a lonely proposition when you realize that there's less days in front of the horse than riding in the back of this cart."[82]

The first wave of the Baby Boom Generation is on the threshold of a major value shift, a bellwether social trend, the outward appearance of which could seem like a mass midlife crisis. For some anguished Boomers, the crisis may rekindle the most immature and frivolous moments of adolescence. Most will be more subdued.

Nevertheless, because of the imposing size of the population of older Boomers and their historically significant impact upon the national agenda, this zeitgeist could explode into social and political upheaval reminiscent of the Sixties. In the words of Dennis Hopper's cynical hippie character from the movie, *Flashback*, "the next decade will make the Sixties seem like the Fifties."

The first wave of the Baby Boom came of age at a volatile point in history. As a member of that leading-edge wave—those Boomers born between 1946 and 1955—I was 13 when Soviet Premier Nikita Khrushchev and U.S. President John F. Kennedy locked horns over the Cuban missile crisis, 14 when Lee Harvey Oswald shot and killed Kennedy in Dallas, 18 when the streets of Chicago became a war zone during the 1968 Democratic National Convention, 20 when the war casualties in Vietnam peaked, 21 when 300 civilians were massacred by U.S. troops in the Vietnam hamlet of *My Lai*, and 24 when President Richard Nixon resigned in disgrace for a political espionage cover-up called Watergate.

As German psychologist Karl Mannheim observed, social upheaval during the impressionable years of adolescence can foment and congeal a generation. Just as the lessons of depression-era economic deprivation live on with the children of the Twenties, the Sixties Generation carries with it an indelible sense of intra-generational connectivity, a psychological ball and chain that was attached during those impressionable years when effusive societal change was the norm. Shared volatile experiences of a generation are, however, both weights and magnets.

The coming-of-age period of their lives—the fragile years that fell roughly between San Francisco's Summer of Love in 1967 and the end of the U.S. involvement in the Vietnam War during January 1975—are a haunting attraction to those who find disenchantment in their contemporary lives. Careers in crisis, mid-life economic shortcomings, unsatisfying marriages, waning physical prowess, and widespread boredom can foster musing daydreams about Vietnam protest marches, backpacking sojourns to Europe, bare-butt swimming parties, LSD mind trips, first love affairs, unfettered road trips, and Woodstock.

The quest to return to more vigorous and vital times of life can become unrelenting to people who find their middle years empty of meaning or value, and short of expectation. Adolescent memories become idealized.

"The days of our youth are the days of our glory," wrote Lord Byron.

In his book *The Baby Boomers*, author Paul C. Light exploded many myths about the generation, including the false belief that this generation retains one distinctive identity; but he also revealed several salient, overarching themes.

Today, many older Boomers' lives fall short of the ebullient expectations they held during the *Age of Aquarius*. A sizable segment of the generation is financially unable to pursue the American Dream, which has traditionally been defined as a home, financial security, and quality education for children. Boomers have been forced to accept job market overcrowding, downsizing, and career ladder limitations as an unpleasant fact.

Many older Boomers feel politically alienated when confronted by the juggernaut of two political parties, now converging to become two sides of the same coin. These themes form to reveal the face of disenchantment, an omnipresent undercurrent of disfranchisement. Today's economic realities—in contrast with the idealistic expectations of forty years ago—are precursors to restless stirring, the renaissance of experimentation, value conflicts, erratic behavior, role playing, depressive moods, grief reactions, and profound anxiety states.

Coincidentally, these psychological struggles are also hallmarks of adolescence. Just as the new teenager reluctantly lets go of the idealized aspects of early childhood, the inner battles of middle-aged adults are reflective of persistent efforts to relinquish the past, but never fully let it go.

That the generation is recalcitrant when it comes to discarding the tangible metaphors of youth has been widely documented. The health food and vitamin craze of the early Seventies led to the jogging and fitness crazes of the early Eighties, and the Nineties demonstrated robust sales of age-masking cosmetics and plastic surgery. Oldies radio formats—once the domain of Benny Goodman and Frank Sinatra—have transformed into audio museums for vintage rock and roll artists such as The Byrds and Buffalo Springfield. Contemporary women's fashion designers have resurrected miniskirts and platform shoes, and middle-aged men more frequently sport shaggy silver mop-tops and salt-and-pepper beards. A succession of movies, from *The Big Chill* to Oliver Stone's *The Doors*, pay homage to an era that just won't die in the hearts of middle-aged men and women.

Some pundits attribute these generational obsessions with the symbols of the Sixties as simply pedestrian nostalgia. It is true that every generation likes to return to its time of *arrogant naïveté*, to relive those deep and persistent moments when they captured a full view of the world and gained a sense of control over destiny, but nostalgia is not pedestrian when viewed as a method of coping. Nostalgia, though mere expressions of fantasy, can make a positive contribution to later adult life.

Louise J. Kaplan, Ph.D., author of *Adolescence: the Farewell to Childhood*, said it succinctly: "Nostalgia softens grief. It takes the sting out of the sense of loss. Grief empties the soul. Nostalgia replenishes." Nostalgic memories ignite passion, affirm evolving priorities, incite new learning, revive visionary gleam, and enhance wisdom. They represent the universal yearning for a better life.

Perhaps this generation, like all generations, outwardly pays tribute to the past as a method of adjustment to present and future realities. But perhaps, for the Leading-Edge Baby Boomers, there is also a deeper, hidden agenda driving the urge to return.

William Wordsworth looked upon youth as a time of fresh vision. He wrote:

There was a time when meadow, grove, and stream,
The earth and every common sight,
> *To me did seem*
> *Apparel'd in celestial light,*
The glory and freshness of a dream.

If the impetuous youth of the Sixties is rediscovering that beauty is truth and truth is beauty, then truth endures as an indelible caricature and perpetual quest of the generation.

Annie Gottlieb, a coherent writer about the Sixties Generation, observed in her book, *Do You Believe in Magic?*, "If there is one theme that runs like a red thread through the fabric of our generation, it is an obsession with the truth: finding the truth, telling the truth, not lying to oneself, or others—honesty, authenticity, integrity."

It is hard for me to deny that the vanguard of the Baby Boom is coming of age again in middle age. Too many people I know are searching for nostalgia, freeing long buried dreams, coming to terms with failures, viewing consumption as meaningless materialism, creating more congruent personal and work lives, and setting new fulfillment goals beyond wealth. And many look back pensively, considering the gaps between dreams and realities.

One consequence of a return to adolescence is anguish. Coming of age—a second time—means a painful coming to terms with the past and exorcising the tenacious demons that spawned youthful idealism. Coming of age begs Boomers to renew their disdain over lingering social injustice. It forces many to take an accounting of their progress in building ethnic harmony. It raises the specter of environmental pollution and their personal responsibilities to protect the natural world. It is all about unfinished agendas. But coming of age, while tumultuous, can also be a harbinger of a more satisfying future.

Once again, it means honoring the nobler ideals of world peace, economic equality, egalitarian civil rights, human potential, and spiritual enlightenment. It means sharing a new, perhaps revitalized generational zeitgeist—that tenacious obsession with the perfectibility of the human condition. The stuff of truth.

CHAPTER 48

Becoming Digital: A Boomer's Trip

ARGUABLY, Professor Nicholas Negroponte is the high priest of digital discourse. I met him at a symposium in Colorado Springs, Colorado, and he intractably altered my view of Net reality.

Founder of MIT's vaunted *Media Lab* and co-founder of *Wired* magazine, Nicholas reminds me of Timothy Leary, the 1960s guru who advocated "turn on, tune in, drop out."

Although Leary influenced the Baby Boom Generation with some astounding, mind-altering thoughts about *being*, now Nicholas is handing another youth vanguard the consciousness-raising precepts of *being* **digital.** Digital reality has a tune in, turn on, drop out quality to it, so I instinctively tuned in to Nicholas with rapt attention.

He says *bits* are replacing atoms as the DNA of human interaction. The internet is about global movement of 1s and 0s at the speed of light.

I get it! Bill Gates demonstrated this. Recently, when I ordered computer software from Microsoft my order went through the internet as *bits*, and I received the software via a computer modem download. It took two hours to transfer roughly 80 million bits from Bill to me. Thus, I avoided dealing with the old-fashioned atoms of an order form, and Bill avoided mailing me the costlier atoms of computer disks. We exchanged electrical signals, and the invoice zipped to my American Express card as bits. I paid the credit card bill via an electronic bank funds transfer.

The day-to-day implications of this could have less reality grounding than flying cars and teleportation. Upon further thought, however, I put Nicholas' revelations into a meaningful construct: my experience with the last major communications revolution—the emergence of broadcast television.

You see, bits do not just take us into a new era of global trade. Media companies are rushing to the internet as their new market-place with one critical difference in their business plans. Instead of pushing bits at people through broadcast or cable programming, they will soon allow us to pull at bits, meaning you and I and our computers will compose our own programming, at times most convenient to us.

That is powerful stuff, and ironic.

As an early-arriving member of the Baby Boom, I recall the moment that I discovered a spellbinding distraction from real life wistfully referred to as *Howdy Doody Time*. I remember becoming entranced by a toothy, freckle-faced puppet after seeing him on a tiny black and white screen, with my mother in the background commenting to a neighbor: "He just loves TV. He runs to the set every day after nursery school."

The tone of her voice, even as interpreted through the ears of a four-year-old, suggested her belief that my enjoyment of this diversion was a very good thing—it freed her to concentrate on bridge club and her women's service club, P.E.O.—as if my adaptation to broadcast entertainment would be anything other than addiction.

Television dominated our childhood, as it became the focal point and cultural force of my generation. Few Baby Boomers can think about early black and white television without recalling sweet memories of Matt Dillon and Miss Kitty in *Gunsmoke*, Beaver Cleaver, or the momentous occasion of The Beatles debut on the *Ed Sullivan Show*.

These heroes and televised moments shaped us, bound us together by the shared experience of watching them, and cata-pulted us into adulthood with an unprecedented mass-media ori-entation to the world. We became slightly obsessed with *Gilligan's Island* and *Stalag 13*, decay-preventing dentifrice, bulbous Speedy Alka-Seltzer, and Senator John F. Kennedy, a presidential candidate who looked better in front of a television camera than his unshaven opponent, Richard M. Nixon.

Not only did network television forge a common bond that made the brainless icons of sitcoms and advertising common parlance, but also it affected the way most thought about our nation and its collective march through history.

Baby Boomers were—and to a lesser extent, still are—an idealistic generation. When you have been raised on a *Have Gun—Will Travel* attitude about life, you tend to see conflict as solvable in twenty-two minutes or less. The world is nefarious, but good always prevails, just as televised heroes spewed cliché tomes while settling disputes with a quick draw and precise aim, delivered before a "message from our sponsor."

Back to Nicholas. During a ride from the airport, he confided that his seminal bestseller *Being Digital* was dated before the publisher had shipped it to bookstores. In the book, he did not even predict a tidal wave of companies and individuals rushing to the internet with the same intensity that Baby Boomer males once flipped on *The Mickey Mouse Club* and brooded for Annette Funicello.

Nicholas envisioned the advent of digital connectivity and its profound ramifications, but even the "High Priest of the Bit" did not predict how rapidly this communication channel would overwhelm society and inexorably shift the balance of human interaction to a medium measured not by gross rating points, but by the number of website hits.

Actually, society has moved beyond this "threshold of a dream" within a span of months. The world is connecting through its desktop computers faster than my generation rushed to watch Boris and Natasha attempt their subversive, clandestine plots against a cartoon anti-hero, Bullwinkle the Moose. It is no longer a question of how quickly corporate America will get the website up—because most corporations already have. It is now a question of how much larger the percentage of Americans will be who are on line in time to trade sodden opinions about George W. Bush's most recent lambaste of his non-conservative critics.

"Computers are no longer about computing," writes Nicholas, "they're about living."

Whew! If television was slightly revolutionary to American society and culture—"the way it ought to be"—then we are talking staggering influence for these bits.

We are talking about a digital culture using its own language, like *spam* and *flame* to describe social affronts. We are talking about an omnipresent global network, but perpetually local, whether digital communicators reside on opposite sides of the Pacific Ocean or the same city block. Local connectivity is more about shared interests, expressed by exchanging sanctimonious keyboard taps through web servers, than it is about geography.

Silly Putty was something I learned about through television. Suddenly, we all had to own a plastic egg full of amorphous stuff that could lift a colorful image of Charlie Brown right off the Sunday cartoon section of the newspaper. Television introduced the product, and our collective broadcast consciousness produced the fad. Now the rush is to share personal philosophies, opinions, and life stories by publishing *blogs* on the internet.

America Online makes it oh so easy by offering subscribers as much as two megabytes of webserver space at no additional cost above monthly connect fees. That is almost greater computing-power-per-individual than governed the on-board computer systems responsible for putting Americans on the moon and trumping the Russians.

Instead of publishing one fleeting, rudimentary impression of *Snoopy* on a gooey brown hunk, I can now scan my family vacation photos, upload them to the AOL server, and share our beatific moments at Atlantic City with an appreciative global audience.

I cannot help wondering about today's youth. One friend, now twelve years old, views the internet as a given in his day-to-day experience, as much as I once expected *Andy Griffith* to fill my weeks with the simple, down-home wisdom of a small town sheriff. Except there is one major difference: My sentient buddy can, with the twitch of his index finger, click a colorful, underlined word *babes.com* and summon steamy manifestations of adult experience. Instead of receiving the calming influence of Aunt Bea, my protégé (if his parents aren't watching) can spend digitally produced moments with *Bedroom Brandy*.

The emerging DNA of information is without boundaries. Bandwidth, or pipeline delivery capacity, is not an issue. We will get plenty more of that soon enough with fiber optics and satellite links to our homes. America's youth are already empowered beyond Boomers' wildest flights of fantasy during our youthful power reveries. Forty years ago, what budding Davy Crockett, sitting Indian-style too close to the phosphorescent tube and garbed in a coonskin cap, could imagine his fingertips accessing the *whole* world, or the potential of creating a global network next Saturday afternoon?

Meaningful interaction is transforming into glib, often poorly constructed sentences dispatched by unseen contemporaries through digital Chat Rooms to suit every persuasion—even *Brandyholics*.

Will cyber-kids become constructively idealistic with all the barriers removed between them and the body of human thought and action? Will these kids become possessed by shared indignation that leads to social revolutions such as women's rights and the environmental movement, or greater racial equality?

I wonder, but I do not have time to wonder too long. I have emails to answer and Hypertext Markup Language to learn. There are many people, anonymous and physically far removed from me, whom I am eager to enliven with keyboard-generated smiley faces. There is the occasional jerk in cyberspace with whom I must take my stand by dispatching incendiary bits, the *Colt 45* revolver of today.

I have much to do, and I do not even have to leave this keyboard or put on clothes to do it.

CHAPTER 49

Baby Boomers, 2028

WHAT could be the American Experience in 2028 if the public fails to accommodate an aging population, with more than one-fifth over 65? What might be the consequences of ageism upon a denigrated generation?

The following story reveals one courageous woman's struggle with an intolerant society. She has built a successful San Francisco law practice by fighting for women through landmark court battles, but this legacy is no longer enough to satisfy an impassioned activist.

The dignity and security of her generation are at stake.

Again, Sam

Courage is the price Life exacts for granting peace.

It was 2028 when, as if an epiphany, I recalled those words by Amelia Earhart, hurled to me from childhood, long forgotten. The sky was cloudless, neither foggy nor polluted, making this September day a phenomenon. Then a shadow rushed over me from above, one of those old-fashioned Lear jets used by corporate potentates to survey their kingdoms, and it was at that moment that I thought of the indomitable spirit of a woman who, through her courageous, early twentieth century transatlantic flights, had come to symbolize women's liberation, my passion and purpose.

I had been sitting at the top of Mt. Tamalpais above the San Francisco Bay for at least two hours, thinking about the true significance of my 78th birthday. From below, the Bay glared back at me; tiny waves flashed in my eyes as if dozens of camera strobes.

I had been there a long time, waiting for a dull headache to pass.

My name is Christi Sedgwick. I am a woman marching ahead of her retirement years, although I keep myself fit and look ten years younger than my real age. Believe it or not, I still turn men's heads, a blessing and a curse for being what they used to call a *blond fox*. The smarter men learned quickly to gaze beyond my face and see seething strength in a trial attorney on a mission. I own controlling interest in my firm, which I started right after Washburn University Law School and have built for over fifty years. We have a national reputation for our successes in representing women and defending sisters who have been maligned by male-dominated businesses and the paternalistic political system. Even fifty years after the women's movement kicked into overdrive, there remain many challenges ahead for women: paternity cases, custody battles, sexual harassment—you name it. You'd think men and their subjugated women would get it by now.

My wealth includes a Victorian house on Market Street, a white Acura Legend with hybrid solar/Eco conversion, a few high-growth mutual funds, and a son named Keef. He hates his given name and prefers to be called by his nickname, Ken.

I savor driving through Mill Valley and up to the top of that mountain. For years, it has lured me to the summit where I can gaze upon the Bay and Pacific Ocean. Often I have taken a long lunch hour and gone there just to be alone. On this provident day, however, the sun wrapped my face with soft chamois and held back chilly west wind, allowing me to sail the sea of possibilities.

The issue of my thought was—courage. I pondered for a long time how courageous my life had been since the Seventies, when I was a more committed activist and not as materialistic. I have to tell you, it is a thorny issue for me to put the record of my life before my heroine, Amelia. My headache fought with ambivalence and self-consciousness. And, above all else, I knew Keef wouldn't let it happen unchallenged.

"Once a flower child always a flower child." He might say something like this with irony and an air of futility. Even when he had been a small child, he loved to be my father. Daddy died from a cerebral embolism before Keef was born, and sometimes I wonder if Daddy reincarnated as my son. Like Daddy, Keef's words are always sensible: opinionated reasonableness is one byproduct of being raised by fourteen fathers and nineteen mothers during our mourning commune days. He grew up with full voting privileges. He would say something obvious and mitigating; I would feel guilty; and he would try to yank away my sense of clear purpose . . . again.

The ocean brought Sam nearer to me as usual, and again I thanked him for inspiring me to give back as much as I could. I don't have anything to be ashamed of—I know this—and I have contributed more than many people my age, but what I have accomplished in the courts for women's causes is no longer enough, not anymore. Watching the distant surf and thinking about him made my decision easier, although changing course so dramatically after fifty years cannot be ill considered.

• • •

Sam tossed another Budweiser can onto the pile next to the blanket—making five, I think—though he had not seemed drunk. It had been his final day before shipping out, and he insisted that we spend the day near Point Reyes. He wanted nothing fancy—just a picnic dinner, a cooler full of cold beer, and me. Keef had stayed with my mother. I remember thinking that we should be more formal about this—perhaps a fine dinner at *Ernie's* with Dom Perignon. Sam had simple tastes. He wanted to remember our beach and a peaceful day. For a man disappearing to Nam, peace was his priority.

"Nothing like our sunsets . . . not anywhere," he had said.

Feeling at once poetic and shallow, I offered, "They set beautifully over there, too."

He leaned back in his lawn chair, folded his arms, and gazed at the incoming surf. "When I see those sunsets, I'll think of you. Right now." Then he looked at me again . . . the whites of his eyes red from too much sun and beer—maybe a tear. But the way he looked at me, I knew he had meant it. He didn't have to say anything. I thought the same.

"Sam, it will pass," I said later, sounding too much like a pop philosopher.

"It'll be a year in hell. I just hope it's a round-trip ticket."

"But I'll be there. I promise."

He said, "As best you can."

"I will, in my heart." It did not occur to me how illusory this sounded.

He issued a loud sigh and said, "Let's walk."

Grabbing my hand, he pulled me to the surf. We walked for hours, long after moonrise, and into the lonely hours before dawn. We talked about our lives, our rather significant accomplishments as student activists at the University of Kansas, and our hopes for a future without the military draft, undeclared war, or complicated U.S. foreign policy, obfuscated by *Domino Theories* and *The Red Scare*.

"The ocean clarifies everything," he said after making love, at sunup. "The sea makes life's purpose so much easier to understand. Christi, we're here to prevent senseless aggression, to end oppression and war. That's our mission, no matter what distractions life throws in our path."

He looked toward the waves beginning to sparkle with the sun rising behind us from the east. "You know why I'm really going?"

"I don't know for sure . . . your dad?"

"Look at the bigger picture. Why am I *not* dodging and escaping with you and Keefy to Canada?"

"Patriotism?"

"Hell, no. It's my patriotic duty to defy this insanity."

"Then what, damn it? We can be packed by tonight."

"I'm going because I want to stay in politics, and few will vote for a draft dodger. I need a clean record and the legitimacy of military service, an Honorable Discharge. Otherwise, my career will be over before it starts."

There was nothing I could say then, not my fear of his never returning, or my doubts that he had made the right decision for Keef and me. My last words to him on that beach: "I'm proud of you, Sam-Man. Just come back to us."

• • •

When I felt the sun swallow gulps of deep ocean fog and interrupt its warmth, I gave up my perch above the Bay and drove back to the office. The carved oak doors guarding *Sedgwick, Samuels, and Barkley* met my elevator on the sixteenth floor. They looked like trap doors, and I pushed angrily through them.

"Finish the brief by tomorrow morning," I said brusquely. With Richard, my favorite paralegal, I liked taking the upper hand. He resented my bossiness, but respected my conceptual skills. He'd malinger if I didn't bully him now and then.

"Not *completely* fleshed out!" Richard whined. "For goodness sake, Christi, not by tomorrow!"

"Rich, it's got to be done. You have my rough . . . check it against citations, put it in our format, and port it to my desk mind-pad by 7:00 a.m. for editing. Judge Bayliss has no patience for tardiness. He said by end of business tomorrow. Your deadline is 7:00 a.m."

Richard growled but hung his head closer to the computer terminal, a sign of acquiescence. I punched his pudgy stomach now and then. It worked for both of us when I reminded him of possible alternatives.

I shut my office door and walked to the west-facing window. The sun was falling beyond the Golden Gate Bridge, sending pink orchid light across the horizon. Blue-gray fog crawled under the bridge. My high-rise office in the Financial District, a comfortable consequence of many favorable court decisions, afforded me an expansive view of the Bay. Buddy lived next to my office. I sensed his presence seconds before he tapped on my door.

"Come in, Buddy."

"Hey, Christi, how was your excursion to David Crosby Land?"

His jokes were always weak, especially the ones about my favorite Seventies rock group, *Crosby, Stills, Nash & Young*, but he thought of himself as the Court Jester of *Sedgwick, Samuels & Barkley*. He is Barkley, one of only twelve men in the firm, now pushing a staff of 48 attorneys.

"I didn't see any *Wooden Ships*," I said, flatly. "But I did make a decision. Sit down."

He raised his eyebrows in a wide expression. He sat at a small conference table next to my desk, and I slid into a chair next to him. "The last time you looked at me this way was when you asked me to reassign a client to one of the younger *women* attorneys."

"It's not about giving up turf, Buddy. I'm retiring."

He gasped. "Hold on a minute, Christi. This is too much. We're doing great. You're doing great. What's happening?" He stared at me with the bulldog glare that had intimidated many corporate ass-holes presuming that women deserve second-class pay, token job titles, and reassuring pats on the butt.

Strangely, my heart began pounding as if this was my first job interview. "It's time for me to leave."

"Christi, you're the Sedgwick on the door, and it's your rep that has built our firm into a powerhouse. What do you need?"

"Freedom."

"We can cut your hours back. But we need you to haul in the big discrimination suits. Without you, our firm would never have attracted Jane Sander and her lawsuit against her board at GE. Remember, this is about litigating for justice, but it's also about big bucks." He reached into his suit pocket and pulled out a Waterman pen, ready to sign another separation agreement.

I felt anger at his predictable reaction. The cowboy-boot-wear-ing Harvard law student of the Eighties had become the financial wizard of the twenty-tens. He is always so arrogant when he thinks everything is negotiable. I hate that part of his transformation from a pothead to a pompous defense attorney.

"Buddy, I'm bored. This career isn't a challenge anymore. For God's sake, I'm in my late seventies, and though I might feel younger, I need to take a different path now."

He sat furtively on the edge of his chair. He pulled at his salt and pepper beard like Socrates. Silence prevailed for a minute, and he didn't look me directly in the eyes. He knew I could hold his silent stare for as long as he could take it.

"Okay. You got a sabbatical. Take as long as you want. We can lean on the Seven Sisters more than usual. I want you to think this out."

"I've thought it out. You're wasting time trying to convince me to make this a short-term thing. I empowered you five years ago to run this firm and take our mission forward when I pull out."

"I was thinking maybe when you're in your mid-eighties . . . "

"You've got the team; we've earned the reputation. You knew this was coming, and it's time for me to go."

My heart slowed to silence.

"Christi, you've been our vision, my friend, and trusted advisor. I need you to be here tomorrow . . . and tomorrow. We just turned the corner with the third righteous quarterly in a row. The law journals are coming in quarts."

"All the better for your status . . . "

". . . And we're going international. Wow, just think about suppression of women in the Middle East!"

He stood and walked to the window. A Nino Cerutti suit draped around his shoulders, with the perfect tailoring borne by a movie star. Long-forgotten sexual memories filled me with remorse as I recalled the time business had become pleasure. I will never understand why I let Holly have him. I struggled with the forbidden memories, and I stared past him through the window. Stars popped from the dark blue sky above. The Golden Gate Bridge had become two long strings of white Christmas tree lights arching above a puff of cotton fog.

He swung back around and stabbed me with squinting eyes. "Not the *Great Gray*'s? You're not going over to them?"

My ears burned. "Christ, Buddy, I'm moving to the Institute."

"Institute . . . you mean that commune in Oregon . . . that paranoid group trying to refocus the federal budget on the elderly? Lady, I thought you closed the last chapter on Sam and grew out of that phase a long time ago."

"Don't call me lady, and don't call us elderly, damn it. It's not a phase, and it's not a commune. It's an institute for spiritual growth and to advance more enlightened understanding of the meaning of aging . . . *The Institute for Human Ascendance*."

"What the hell do you expect to do there?"

I stood and walked over to him. Relying on instincts honed over thirty plus years, I positioned myself squarely in front of him so he could not look away. I could count on this tactic to garner undivided attention and sometimes empathy.

"Emotional and spiritual growth ended for me after we punctured the glass ceiling in the auto industry. Intellectually, I've learned much. I'm proud of my accomplishments ... the ABA award and all."

I pointed to my head. "What I've gained has been here."

I pointed to my heart. "What I need is fulfillment here. You're right behind me, just thirteen years younger. What I do next may even impact your old age."

He gave me his stupid macho-man grimace.

I crossed my arms defensively. "Damn it, I'm seventy-eight years old and the clock is ticking. Age-extension therapy has its practical limitations."

"You could be the cover photo in a magazine ad!"

Ignoring him, I pressed my point. "There was a time when we shared idealism. Remember when we were going to change the world? Sure, we've won some high-profile cases against companies and the government. But, you know what? Little has changed. Bitterness swells as fast as the population of people over 65 enlarges."

"*Bitterness* may have some foundation. Look at the federal budget for senior entitlement programs!" Buddy started warming up for a pre-trial debate.

"Bullshit! Stop using that word . . . senior!"

"Okay, okay. You're right."

"A powerful ascendant lobby doesn't justify violence. Last month the age war led to that bombing of the Flint Hills Residence in Topeka, Kansas, and the deaths of 214. Two of those people were my law school classmates!"

"Okay, I'll give you that point."

"Then consider the algorithmically exploding statistics on mugging and violent crimes against ascendant people. *Liberators* are pushing euthanasia legislation through Congress and would have us put to sleep when we become over ninety and irreversibly disabled. ·

"Keef is just as screwed-up about money and material things as we were before the Cultural Revolution. Nothing has changed."

"I've got to say it . . . for one, *you've* made a shit-load of money."

"Damn it. We're allowing society to turn old age into a crime."
Before he could speak, I grabbed both of his hands.

"After I become a part of the Institute, I'll do just what I'm doing here."

"Scare them into submission?"

"Asshole. I'll fight for ascendants with all the passion I've given women's issues. I'll get the word out that there's still a chance for people to grow, to become more inclusive, to benefit from the wisdom and energy of the majority. It's time members of our generation stop being victims and start fighting for our rights."

Something changed in his expression. His eyes grew softer. He wrapped his large, warm hands around my icy fingers. "I won't hold you back. You're too . . . important. But I'm still your partner. We'll call this a leave-of-absence until you tell me, unequivocally, that you're not coming back to the firm."

For the first time in years, he embraced me. My back stiffened, but gradually I let my muscles relax under the even pressure of his reassuring hug. I placed my hands tentatively on his hips. "There's no point in talking you out of an attitude," I whispered. "You resolute shit-head. I guess you'll have to get the message your way."

● ● ●

My only son Keef, large, muscular, intense, stood at the doorway to my house, hesitating, as was his custom, until I welcomed him heartily. He needed reassurance.

"Come in," I said with a smile.

"Hi, Christi. What are we having?" He always calls me by my first name, although he knows I hate it.

I walked toward the kitchen and Keef followed me.

"Pasta and marinara sauce. Sit down. You want a drink?"

He sat heavily at the breakfast table. "You got any Corona?"

"Out of beer. How about a glass of Chardonnay?" I am *still* getting used to serving alcohol to my fifty-five-year-old. Parts of him are like a comfortable youngster, someone I will not, or cannot let grow up.

I poured a glass and pushed it in front of him. Meticulously dressed in a blue double-breasted suit, he was boldly handsome.

He pulled a Stimuhaler from his coat pocket and took a thoughtful drag. "Okay. What's this about moving?"

Like his grandfather, he used a minimum of words to get to the point. I smiled at the thought and answered, "I'm quitting SSB, selling my house, and moving to the Institute in Oregon. Wanna come?"

"Hell no, I don't want to come. Didn't you get enough of that hippie lifestyle back in the Seventies?"

I looked up from the sauce, determined to remain calm. "I'm not trying to drop out this time; I'm dropping in. This change is about activism."

"Give me a break . . .'dropping in'? Old people are becoming more rebellious than teenagers."

Ignoring him, I slid two pounds of fresh pasta into a large steel pot full of boiling water. I could hear the French bread sizzling in the broiler. I removed the pan of garlic toast and set it on the counter. I knew he wouldn't let things go.

"Come on, Christi. Let me have it."

"All right, Keef." I drained the water from the pasta, divided it into two portions: a small helping for me and a huge serving for him. I smothered the spinach linguini with sauce and shoved a plate in front of him, served myself, and joined him at the breakfast table. "Stop sucking on that Stimuhaler first."

He took two huge drags, knowing my disdain, stashed the portable fix in his suit jacket, and mixed up his plate of pasta and sauce. "Go on," he said emphatically.

"It's as simple or as complicated as you want to make it. Our society is unable to evolve beyond discrimination. As it stands today, the target of aggression has shifted from minorities to the oldest . . . the *ascendants*."

Rolling his eyes, he said, "That word again."

"Then there are the possible euthanasia laws. And voting disempowerment—clearly unconstitutional. But still, there is a growing cohort of young people who want to take away voting rights from anyone over 85. Politics today is about aggression and power over people in my age group, the Baby Boomers, not about equal justice."

"Don't you yet believe that 'equal justice for all' is just a threadbare American myth?"

"A myth? Perhaps. But it's still in the fabric of our democratic principles, and I'm sick of the growing ageism agenda. I'm tired of seeing us maligned everywhere I turn. I think I can do something about it."

"I guess if anyone can, you can. But . . ."

"That's why the Institute."

Keef thoughtfully shoveled pasta into his mouth. He glanced down at me with his father's intense blue-gray eyes. "I can't win once you've made up your stubborn mind, can I?"

"I'm tired of playing attorney for a group that clearly has few major issues today. We're winning! Young women can barely comprehend how far we've come. They consider their equality in society as a given, and here's the rub: few truly understand that if any group is maligned as a group, it makes no difference if it's women, African-Americans, homosexuals, or Hispanics."

He shoved his half-empty plate to the side. "Christi, isn't it time for old people to retire and step aside, just as they have for generations?"

"See, you've adopted some of *their* myths. It's best to separate us from the herd . . . institutionalize us, disembowel us . . . ultimately, get rid of us."

"I didn't mean it that way."

"Yes you did. Get this: It's about creating a future that means something by attacking back, by using my knowledge and experience to fight against those who would bury us."

He swallowed a slug of wine. "Part of you has always lived in the idealized past. The Seventies were just too much."

"That's not where I'm coming from. Sure, those were the days of my youth. The commune helped me say good-bye to Sam . . . after so many years M.I.A . . . wherever he was . . . or is. They helped me put *that* war into perspective. But it took five long years for me to let your father go. Emotionally, they helped me heal."

Keef looked frustrated. "The Settlement was an extended family, and it helped us both. I'm thankful for that. But, Jesus, those people moved on. I moved on. Why can't you?"

"You're not listening. I'm not trying to recreate the Seventies' experience. This is different. What's happening today is genocide.

We've been through this . . ."

He pushed away from the table and stood. Edging over to the sliding glass doors next to the breakfast table, as if transfixed by the twinkling lights of Bernal Heights, he said, "Look, Christi, this is a little hard to handle. Jason just graduated from Harvard, and I was hoping he could work with his grandmother and learn from the best. Now you're leaving the firm."

"It's time for me to live my life again. You have a good job. Your kids are all on their way to promising careers. I've done the grand-mother thing while staying focused on my law practice. Now it's my turn."

"Hasn't it always been *your turn*?"

"I've been the outraged defender of women's rights for years. Now I must be the defender of a generation once again as they face another cold, condemning time. History is repeating itself."

"I'm sorry, but I think this all sounds paranoid."

I walked over to him and put my head on his chest, surprised to feel the strength and development in his pectoral muscles for a man settled firmly into middle age. "This is Vietnam revisited: an out of touch government, and a dangerous voting block filled with untrue beliefs about the enemy. It's no longer enough to make good money. Things have to change."

He brushed my silver-blond hair with his fingers. "Christi, I'll never figure you out. It's not my job anymore. Just be practical about one thing."

"And that is?"

"Keep your house. You may be back."

I pinched his butt the way I used to when he was a kid. I looked up at his frustrated, loving eyes, smiled, and said, "Don't call me Christi. I'm your mother."

"OK. Mom. Don't call me Keef or Keefy. For God's sake, I'm Ken."

• • •

The drive up the Coastal Highway felt invigorating. I left for the Institute before sunrise on a Saturday in early December of my seventy-eighth year, feeling at once emancipated and youthful. I

had packed my Acura with winter clothes, books, treasured photographs, framed awards for my office at the Institute, two lamps,
a stuffed Granny Goose, and my mind pad. Those possessions made
me feel whole; every important treasure surrounded me. The wind
felt chilly, but by noon, I opened the sunroof and let the sun toast
my face. I felt changes moving through me in cadence with the
westerly winds pouring from the ocean across the highway.

Sam had given me a solid gold peace symbol that last day
together. I still wear it around my neck. Although it has become
unfashionable then fashionable then unfashionable again, I have
always worn it, but I keep it hidden below my business clothes.
When alone, I often find myself playing with it as if a worry-stone.
As I zigzagged along Highway 1, the *Rune of Peace* appeared in my
left hand before I knew it.

"Peace is not just a symbol," Sam had said to me. "It's about sacrifice."

Accepting the evanescent gold trinket from him, my eyes filled
with tears. As the sun lifted from the eastern horizon, sending ten-
drils of golden light across Point Reyes, I answered, "It's about loving all people—all races, religions, cultures, ages . . ."

"It's about having the principles to set people above politics," he
said. "It's inclusion over differences. It's honoring the cycle of life."

We were so young and naive.

Although I planned to stop early for the night near the Gold
Coast of southern Oregon, the day had unfolded so seamlessly as I
glided from one little town to the next. Layers of defensiveness
peeled from me. While I drove slowly through coastal villages, I
considered several possible motels, but each time I reached the city
limits, I pressed on. Darkness had preceded me when I arrived in
Florence, Oregon.

I admit that I have become fearful of solo night driving because
ascendant women are being targeted and few passersby will stop to
aid *ticks,* as we have come to be called. So, I pulled off the highway
at the Holiday Motel, a huddle of white cottages. They are clean,
quaintly cozy, and best of all—they sit next to the beach. After
checking in, I snuggled into my parka and Airlocks. I danced
quickly down a sandy trail to the oceanfront.

The beach is so ambiguous. Simultaneously it is pristine, quiet, soft, and bold, salty, and empty. There is clarity in the air. There is connection beyond temporality or necessity. The litter is splendid.

This night was thick with fog. A cold breeze had rushed across the tides to fill the mood with wet brine. The sea brought freshness to my flaring nostrils. I knew a careful God had organized the beach. The birds scoured the wave-swept tide line for every edible nuance. Broken sand dollars, crab exoskeletons, and algae remained.

I walked and walked and came upon a clutch of crows consuming a seal carcass, and my teeth chattered as I thought about roving hordes of young men who specialize in mugging ascendants. They also dress in black. I broke silence by yelling at the bellicose flock and chasing it from a morbid feast. The image of scavenging disgusted me, but I reminded myself: to the wildlife inhabiting these beaches, survival does not find sympathy. It is a kind of courage.

I thought about the survival of my generation at the end of its cycle, the debatable failures of its agenda, the antagonism that had been distilling for decades, and not unlike the low tide, the ebbing possibilities for dramatic social change. It is failed courage. No peace.

And I discovered again my loneliness—"the livid loneliness of fear," as she called it—the fifty-six years I had pressed forward without the love of my life. I passed along that beach in my shell, doomed to the same mortal uncertainty as sea creatures. The black swishing waters triggered introspection and a complex awareness of the world around me. The ebb and flow of change had become frenzied.

At once, I had an awareness of the rich transcendental opportunities waiting before me, and the hopeless limiting barriers presented to me by life on earth in a degenerating body. Sam had understood all these barriers when we were young and had inspired me toward a lifetime of legal activism, the bitter joy of the *fight for right*, as he had called it. This same sea now became my metaphor for a final change. I could taste the salt air and fly away as Amelia to my Sam and his spirit, wherever it waited for me.

Suddenly, I felt old again, but not too old to mount one more struggle for justice.

• • •

"Hi, Keef."

"Christi . . . Mom. Where are you?"

"Florence, Oregon."

"You okay?"

"I wanted to tell you that I love you."

The telephone fell silent for a few seconds. "Are you sure you're all right?"

"I'm fine. Couldn't be better, actually. I'm standing in a phone booth near a small grocery store. I have a cute cottage next to the . . ."

"You don't sound okay. Why aren't you using your bracelet communicator?"

"I'm okay, really. I just wanted to say hi to my son, even use an old phone to express an old-fashioned sentiment. I know I don't say 'I love you' enough. How are you?"

"Great, couldn't be better. Why don't you forget this odyssey, Mom?

"We've crossed those murky waters, Keefy. I'm gone. I'm surer of it than ever. Crossing over is not a cakewalk. But it's the right path for me now."

"You have a good life here in The City." There was another long pause.

Perhaps also a sob?

"Christi, will you say hello to Dad when you get there?"

"You're reading it wrong. Sam and I aren't ready for an eternal reunion, but it is in his memory that I won't live another day without fighting for the convictions we shared."

"That's ridiculous. He believed in stopping an insane war more than half a century ago."

"No, you've missed the point. He believed in justice for all, and that the voice of the people must shout louder than any hegemonic force."

". . . And so my idealistic mother wants to swim against the tide of popular opinion once again?"

"Tonight it became clearer. Listen to me."

The sigh sounded as if a gasp, but now he listened.

"There was an ancient seagull hobbling on the beach, trying to find a dead fish or perhaps a discarded sandwich. It looked as if it had seen it all, traveled a thousand miles, maybe to Howland Island and back. It found something to eat, but two younger gulls landed next to it and while one distracted the old gull, the other stole its food. The young birds flew off while the old gull kept struggling.

"Then it found something else to eat, and the two juveniles swept in and stole the food again. This time there was a violent confrontation and a young gull attacked the old one, putting it down."

I could hear Keef clicking the projected keyboard connect to the *Universal Mind*, and I knew he had stopped listening or was sending that message. "I'm going to hang up now. Goodbye."

"Christi . . . Mom, I'm listening. The young gulls beat up the old gull, right?"

"You're missing the point again. Damn it, this is important! Quit typing!"

Silence again on his end.

"The young gulls assassinated the old gull because he was vulnerable. That's what America has become . . . young attacking old."

Still silence.

"When I approached the old gull, mortally injured I'm sure, I felt the presence of your dad as if this instance had become a psychic link to the moment he may have become mortally injured in Vietnam."

"Uh, huh."

"But he wasn't young anymore. His spirit felt older, wiser, and he implored me, through the manifestation of this bird, to rescue those who have been fighting ageism and an unsympathetic youth ready to pluck away our sustenance and spirits."

"Spirituality has always played a major part in your decision-making style. But come on . . . an old gull? Sam?"

"Aging is a state of being and a metaphor. Though our scientists are doing a great job extending health into the nineties and beyond, we haven't evolved to cherish ascendants, to protect them from opportunists, to let them be relevant until the end. Our hearts haven't become wiser as lifespan has widened."

"Okay, I get your parable."

"You do and you don't. The old gull is ignorance and a pathetic decline of compassion."

A long sigh issued from the other end. Daddy was in him again. "Then soar, Christi. Fly away if you must."

"Keefy, I shall."

And that is how I, Christi Sedgwick, found the courage to join the fight to end ageism and renew hope among America's most reviled generation, my generation, the Baby Boom. Ever since, my days have been full of anger, conflict, and confrontation, balanced by a clear and persisting inner peace.

You see, my mentor had asked the right question long before her final flight from New Guinea to Howland Island. She wrote: *How can life grant us boon of living, compensate for dull grey ugliness and pregnant hate unless we dare?*

Now for some answers.

How to Create, Organize and Manage a Great Boomer Promotion

WHAT constitutes a great Boomer promotion? A great promotion impacts would-be customers or clients positively. It causes them to feel good. It gives them a memory that will endure for years. But that's not enough.

A great promotion has a demonstrable long-term impact on your business. Though you may achieve short-term benefits, it's the long-term, relationship-building capacity of the promotion that makes it great. A good promotion makes customers feel better about your brand and more connected. Through the promotion your brand has become more tightly woven into the fabric of their lives; it becomes an extension of them; it better defines who they want to be today, and it also sets a target for their future. But even that is not enough.

A great promotion excites the media. Bored with covering and reporting soft news (and generally your promotion will be classified as soft news), the media needs to find something intriguing about it. Perhaps it has a twist that will help disadvantaged people. Maybe it breaks through banal promotion boundaries and stands apart from the slew of telethons and running races that vie for consumer attention. Perhaps your promotion becomes a metaphor for the struggle between good and evil. Perhaps it promises a large gathering of people, reminiscent in its context of Woodstock. With the help of ideas presented in this section, your story breaks through the clutter of daily news and ends up as a main news story or on the front page of one of the newspaper's major sections. Great media coverage is a hallmark of a great promotion, but that's still not enough.

Not only does a great promotion engage a substantial segment of your primary business market, it also reaches a narrower but highly important group of influential people known summarily as community leaders. If your promotion attracts the mayor of your city or representatives of the city council or national political leaders, then you know your promotion is on its way to being great. A great promotion needs and usually gets the flattering glow of luminaries. But, you may have guessed, even that is not enough.

The last person this promotion must infuse with energy and pride is you. Yes, you'll work your butt off. If you have a normal psychological make-up, you'll have a few moments of intense anxiety about the details. You might even lose a few nights' sleep. Anything worth your best will steal some easy-feeling-peace-of-mind. But if you come away from your promotion with a sense of accomplishment unrivaled in your past promotional experiences, if you look back on that chapter of your life with ardent pride, then, finally, you'll know you've staged a great promotion.

This section is a straightforward "how to" guide for the novice or professional promoter who wants to have maximum impact on Boomers.

For the novice, this chapter will give you the confidence you need to plunge into the process. As the proverb goes, "A journey of a thousand miles begins with the first step." This guide gives you a roadmap through the ambiguous routes along the course of a major promotion.

For the veteran promoter, this chapter will help consolidate what you know and, by drawing on your own experience, give you a clearer understanding of how to elevate your brand and let it shine brighter to the 37 million Leading-Edge Boomers. By revisiting basic concepts in a complex discipline such as sales promotion, I believe you add mortar to a stronger foundation. Concepts that may have passed over your head when you were just learning can crystallize in the presence of greater experience.

This is knowledge and when knowledge meets experience, you have wisdom. And, quite simply, my goal is to help more people become wiser promoters, not only for their benefit, but for the enrichment of all who attend a great promotion.

The Big Idea

Creative thinking: turning the box inside out

Perhaps your most difficult challenge is creating an original promotional idea. As Thomas Carlyle aptly observed, "The merit of originality is not novelty, it is sincerity."

There are few truly original ideas. Almost every type of gathering under the banner of a promotion has been tried by someone, somewhere. Almost every athletic competition, from badminton to a wheelchair race, has been attempted. How can you create a truly original idea?

You can't and you can. Although your idea may not be completely original, it can build on a time-tested concept and add a unique twist: wheel chair races at an ice skating rink, for example. Or a bluegrass jam at an art gallery. Or a beach party in a hotel lobby. Or a Seventies Retro party at a Chinese restaurant. The secret to developing a great promotional idea is to meld divergent ideas.

To set conditions for creative thinking, I recommend you pick a quiet time in your home or office and sit at an empty computer screen or put a blank yellow legal pad in front of you. Type or write down as many associative ideas as you can think of related to the general subject of your promotion. Brainstorm. Don't be critical, let ideas flow. Be silly. Be cynical. Be ostentatious.

Let's take a typical example to illustrate this process.

Junior Achievement helps children learn about business and the importance of staying in school. To fund the organization, most JA franchisees conduct an annual Bowl-a-Thon. Bowlers receive pledges from friends and associates then bowl on a given Saturday and donate their pledge money to the organization. This tested fundraising method has certainly worked for JA, but how can you infuse it with more novelty and make it appeal to Boomers?

Bowlers could be given a theme such as the 1950s and be asked to wear period costumes to the Bowl-a-Thon. The 1950's dress theme ties nicely to bowling because we think of bowling as a recreational innovation from that decade. Many Boomers include bowl-ing alley experiences among their earliest recreational memories.

Another idea would be to form one team comprised of local celebrities. This group could include a local television anchor, the mayor, a member of city council, and a prominent business exec-utive. Since this group is already high profile in the community, they could be used to provide advance publicity for the event through friendly jostling and public challenges. Of course, they would dress for publicity opportunities and look like Elvis, Buddy Holly, James Dean, and Sammy Davis, Jr.

The most critical challenge is to add magic to your promotion. Magic means excitement. Excitement is contagious and usually begins when a few opinion leaders in your community or industry throw their support to the promotion. Your challenge is to create an opportunity for them to say yes.

Making more out of less

Converging once divergent ideas has another positive effect: less becomes more. That is always a goal of a great promotion: to build a critical mass where the resulting effect is much more dramatic than the weight of the component parts. Think of this concept as you would an atomic explosion. You build on a basic concept to reach a critical mass of fissionable material. Once you do, your pro-motion detonates with a force much greater than would be expected from the ingredients. You create a chain reaction, but instead of fissionable material, your chain reaction is energy trav-eling through people by spreading shared excitement and delight.

Critical mass, or making more out of less, can be achieved by continuing to add what I call "promotional extensions." Take the bowl-a-thon idea discussed above. Now that you've added the ele-ment of 1950's period costumes, and you've recruited community leaders to dress as 1950's celebrities, what else can you do to bring excitement?

You could invite a local vintage car club and have members bring their restored cars to the bowling alley parking lot. Now you've reached the hearts and minds of another segment of poten-tial bowlers and Boomers—classic car enthusiasts. The auto show adds an extra publicity angle. Plus the cars help you create an ambiance suited to the theme of your bowling fundraiser.

Here's another idea: Every community has a musical group that plays songs from the era of Elvis Presley. In Colorado Springs where I spent fourteen years as a marketer, the most popular show band was Flash Cadillac, a retro-1950's group that you may have seen on the television show *Happy Days* or in the movie *Apocalypse Now*.

Perhaps one of your local Fifties-era bands is still playing together. You could contact a band member and convince his group to play a special gig for the bowl-a-thon. Now you've added 1950s music to expand the ambiance, which leads me to another point to consider during the idea generation stage.

Appeal to all five senses

I have been told that Walt Disney and his colleagues recognized the value of building an entertainment environment that engaged all five senses. Disneyland and Disney World are both examples of this understanding. Like the Disney organization, you should attempt to satisfy each of the five senses with your promotion.

You satisfy the sense of hearing through music or sound effects: Olympic theme music for an athletic event or classical music for a promotion involving the arts. Sound can be generated by live musicians, recorded music, singing tropical birds, digital sound effects, or other forms of musical media, always taking into account what would appeal to your target audience, Leading-Edge Boomers.

When I set out to attract new members to the Colorado Springs Fine Arts Center campaign, mentioned earlier in this book, I wanted to create a special reward for membership—an offer, as direct marketers call it. So I offered anyone who joined the Fine Arts Center before a cut-off date free admission for two people to a party. The party was staged at the Fine Arts Center, but we transformed that staid, traditional building into a "be-in" right out of the late 1960s.

For music, we put together special tapes featuring some of the best bands from the era. The sound system, a work of art in itself, came from a high-end stereo speaker manufacturer. The tunes were terrific.

To satisfy the sense of taste, the most obvious solution is food. Which foods you select make a difference to promotional ambiance.

During the gathering of community leaders selected to recreate The Beatles' album cover (which occurred about eight weeks before the new-member party) we served food popularized during the 1960s. If you're old enough, you'll remember the popularity of cookouts, and on a large scale there was no more popular way to cook out than to roast an entire beast, usually buried underground and slow cooked over smoldering charcoal. So we roasted a pig. There were also small frozen cups of ice cream with wooden spoons similar to those handed out at "ice cream socials" when I was in elementary school. It wasn't easy, but we found a dairy capable of supplying the ice cream cups. We used this same culinary approach at the new-member party, and what a hit the food was with Boomers.

The sense of smell is a little trickier to address, but smells constitute some of our most powerful memories. For a Sixties' party, how about sandalwood incense? For a bowl-a-thon with a 1950s theme, how about dousing all your male food servers with a liberal dose of Old Spice cologne?

The sense of touch is also sometimes difficult. No, we didn't have a Wesson Oil party during the Fine Arts Center new-member party. We did park a 1969 Volkswagen van covered lavishly with pop art in the lobby and allowed people to sit in it and, for the more intrepid souls, to languish on the interior shag carpet.

Setting the stage

Writing your promotion proposal

The first major step toward turning a big idea into reality is to convince partners to climb onboard the bandwagon. (Again, I allude to the bandwagon metaphor, which I believe is the essence of a successful promotion: Build an attractive bandwagon and people will jump on.)

When approached with a new promotional idea, most business executives ask to see something written. Some will ask for a written proposal to test your sincerity and to determine if your idea has concrete form. Others use this request as a put-off, knowing from experience that lots of people have great and not-so-great ideas, but few have the organization and implementation skills to see ideas through to fruition. Still other executives want something written to share with decision makers in the same organization. A major promotion is rarely approved by an established institution, such as a radio station, without internal collaboration.

To address these needs, I have developed a written summary approach that I use as a leave-behind. My promotional summaries break down into five sections:

Objectives

Succinctly state what you intend to accomplish, usually four or five major objectives. I always separate my objectives into distinct statements and, as a matter of style, begin them with the word "To..." Here's an example of an objective I used to describe what I planned to achieve in direct sales impact with a self-liquidating premium promotion for an oil company:

1. To offer prospective customers value-added business incentives, thereby stimulating incremental mid-grade gasoline usage by 10 percent over comparable sales during the previous year.

As you can see, this objective is specific, measurable, and oriented to the bottom-line impact of a promotion. This approach also sells well to senior executives. With few exceptions, they are interested in improving shareholder equity and profits. If your promotion is for a for-profit business, you are well-advised to keep this in mind.

The objectives section includes a statement about the impact you intend the promotion to have on your product's image. In this vein, here's what I wrote for the oil company promotion:

2. To further develop positive brand perceptions among consumers in Oklahoma City, thereby increasing unaided brand awareness, unaided advertising awareness, and favorable predisposition to buy, as measured by pre- and post-promotion telephone tracking surveys.

Strategies

Objectives state what you want to accomplish. Strategies delineate, from a big-picture point-of-view, **how** you intend to accomplish your objectives. This section of your proposal summary is critical to your success; it's the nuts and bolts section where you describe your big idea and the steps you propose to realize your objectives.

To make writing the strategy section easier, the first paragraph is always a capsule statement about the entire promotion. If I stopped you in a hallway, ostensibly in a rush, and I asked you to tell me in a very concise way what you're doing in your promotion project, your terse answer would convey what you need to communicate at the beginning of the strategy section.

The next few paragraphs elaborate on your summary statement by answering some important questions:

1. Who are the potential partners in the promotion and what are their roles?
2. In general, what do the partners bring to the promotion (facilities, media, in-kind creative services, etc.)?
3. When is P-Day (Promotion Day)?
4. Who benefits and why?

The strategy section should be no more than 300-400 words. Think of it as an executive summary. Your goal is to entice busy executives and help them understand the promotion with no more than five minutes of reading time.

Another way to develop the strategy section is to write a succinct, paragraph-length strategy for every objective. You tie strategy number one to objective number one by answering this question: "If my first objective requires me to accomplish this, how will I go about it?" When written in this style, each strategy statement begins with an active verb, such as develop, create, organize, foster, join, or facilitate.

Tactics

Here's where it gets a little fuzzy. The difference between a strategy and tactic is elusive and often up to interpretation. I view the tactical section as a more specific representation concerning the strategies of your promotion.

For example, in the strategy section you may have identified the role of a radio station partner for cross-promotion and as the primary conduit to get the word out. In the tactical section, you might include an actual media plan that delineates when and how frequently promotional spots will air, when and where remote broadcasts will occur, and how the radio station will broadcast live on event day.

. While these details are critical, this information may be more than most people will want when they are analyzing their decision about potential involvement. However, by having details presented here, you demonstrate to even the casual reader that you've thought about your promotion at every level.

Other areas usually covered in the tactical section include a list of goods and services you'll need. If you're planning an athletic competition, you might include the rules of play and how the contest will be judged. If you're organizing a fundraiser, your tactical section might include a description of how monies will be distributed and to whom.

The tactical section usually describes promotions within promotions. For example, if you are planning a softball tournament between media celebrities to draw attention to your Over-50 Olympics promotion, then the details of the media contest would be described in the tactics section. (The softball tournament serves as a tactical method of achieving the broader strategy of pre-publicizing your Olympics.)

Timetable

This is the section where you break your promotion down in terms of the calendar. It's easiest to work back from P-Day, or the date your promotion will happen. Let's say your promotion will happen on August 15 and today is March 1. You should create an overview summary of the hallmark dates and what you need to accomplish by those dates. For example, by March 30 you will have submitted your proposal for consideration by your local Pepsi bottler, with a decision due from the bottler by April 15.

This first level of time planning should be macroscopic—only key points of accomplishment. We'll get much more detailed in the next section.

Responsibility chart

Next you should include a responsibility chart. The responsibility chart does just what its name implies. It lists, usually in spreadsheet format, critical tasks, due dates, and who is responsible for making sure each task is completed. If you have not yet identified all of your partners, you can leave the responsible entity or individual in a generic form: "radio partner," for example. The chart usually includes a blank space by each responsibility to allow for notes.

I have found that when I create a responsibility chart and give copies of it to everyone who has any role whatsoever with the promotion, we literally and metaphorically get on the same page. The chart serves as a very polite way to make sure my partners understand their responsibilities and my expectations for their contributions.

Budget

This section is where you warm the hearts of "quants"—quantitative types or those people who live and die by the numbers. The most effective budgets are those that categorize cost centers in a logical, easy-to-follow layout.

If your promotion includes paid radio media, you might break down these costs by actual costs of radio spots and the costs of producing the spot. When you break down each of your promotion's cost centers in this manner, you make it easy to follow and you tie your costs conceptually back to your strategies.

Methods of evaluation

These measurable factors are usually stated in the "Objectives" section of your promotion summary, but here you re-state critical objectives and add how you propose to measure their attainment. If improving a brand's positive perceptions among a defined target audience is your primary goal, then how are you going to measure changes in perceptions? Pre-post telephone surveys? Event exit interviews? A follow-up mail survey to registrants? An on-line evaluation form, disseminated through an email and Web link?

It is important to determine how you measure success and set this out in your proposal document. You not only avoid subjective debates after it's all over, you also show your partners and bosses from the first impression that you are plugged into achieving something bigger than just another trophy for your portfolio.

Selling your Big Idea

If you have been moving through this chapter in a linear fashion, then you are already on second base. You have created a great promotion idea, and you have developed a promotion proposal, which is your primary selling aid. Now comes the fun part: convincing others to jump on your bandwagon.

It is outside the scope of this chapter to provide a full tutorial on the art of selling. I'm convinced that if you have a great concept and have put yourself through the discipline of creating a promotion proposal, then you don't need to personify superstar salesman Zig Ziglar to sell your promotion. Your passion for your idea will take you far. However, I have learned a few sales tricks that should be helpful. These, of course, apply to all promotions, not just to those for Boomers.

Media momentum

First, begin by soliciting a media partner or partners. Once you have received a commitment from a media partner, it will be much easier to solicit and receive support from other organizations. How do you convince a prospective media partner?

Give them time. Don't expect a local radio or TV station to jump on your bandwagon at the last minute.

As with all important business negotiations, request a face-to-face meeting with the highest appropriate authority. I write "appropriate authority" and literally mean it. Perhaps you can win an audience with a station's general manager, but do you risk alienating the promotion director or general sales manager? You probably should avoid meeting exclusively with lower-level sales personnel because, although you may get some positive buying signals at that level, these non-decision makers may end up inadequately pitching your idea to people higher up in the organization.

Present to both sides of the brain. Selling to a business decision maker is inherently a left-brain/right-brain process. Begin with the right brain, the locus of creative and intuitive thinking: Sell sizzle. Your initial goal is to sell the dream, evoke the vision, and paint the picture in glowing, metaphorical colors. Remember the overriding goal with all promotional events: *Promotions are temporary dream states where we create a reality different from, more transcendent than, everyday experience.*

The goal, then, is to help this critical media decision maker "see" your promotion on several levels.

First, you want her to experience the fun of participating. Any savvy executive knows how much work goes into a major promotion. You don't want her to dwell on that; you want her to see herself back stage meeting Joe Walsh, the lead guitarist from The Eagles, or sitting in a VIP tent at the finish line, or publicly thanking her listening audience from center stage.

But you must not forget the left brain. That's where your promotion summary comes into play. When you present the details through a crisply worded summary, you show and tell the media decision maker that you have your act together. You also overcome one of the most significant obstacles, the perception that this promotion is just pie-in-the-sky daydreaming. A promotion in the hands of a disorganized person is headed for disaster. When you demonstrate your organizational skills, you rarely have to address this concern.

The left brain will be looking for objections and justifications to say no. It's much easier for a decision maker to say no to an idea than buy into your vision and join the party. So you clearly need to think through some of the most probable objections and answer them before they even surface.

Use your organization's advertising budget. There is no question that if you're armed with an advertising budget, and the authority of how and where to spend it, you will have the decision maker's attention. Don't bludgeon her with the budget, but it is fair game to suggest how your discretionary spending authority may work to the station's advantage over its competitors.

Connect with their causes. If you're not armed with an advertising budget and you don't have a long-term relationship with the potential media partner, then your promotion clearly needs an angle that will fit the interests of the station's senior managers.

When I was the advertising and sales promotion manager for a petroleum and convenience store company, I was not buying a lot of television commercials in a mid-western city that I had targeted for a cause-related promotion. Nevertheless, I wanted a television station to participate in the promotion to increase its reach and add credibility. When I interviewed the station's community affairs manager to find out which nonprofit organizations and community causes were important to the station's top management, I learned about an organization set up to provide nourishing evening meals to underprivileged children who might otherwise not have a balanced dinner. This "cause" tapped the heartstrings of the station's general manager. So—no surprise here—the children's food bank became the recipient of funds raised through my promotion. The television station became an enthusiastic partner, and its participation encouraged other prospective media partners to rally under the same banner.

If appropriate, involve a nonprofit organization. Most nonprofits are eager to be included in any effort to help them raise funds. There is hardly any reason not to involve a cause in your promotion at some level, even if the cause is not the focus or intent of your promotion. Once a nonprofit organization will benefit from your promotion, the news-reporting-side of media has found a legitimate reason to get involved. A good philanthropic cause— something worthwhile and highly relevant to the community— brings status to a promotion. It taps a deeper, nearly universal human need but one that especially resonates with Boomers: the desire to help others less fortunate, to give back.

A note of caution: Give from proceeds and give generously. It will pay off in the long run.

Once you've won the support of a key media organization and/or a quality nonprofit, you'll have enough of the bandwagon built to entice other partners.

Follow up and follow through

Once you've engaged key decision makers in discussions about your promotion, follow up and follow through aggressively. If someone asks for more detail, get it to them, if possible the same day. Use technology to your advantage through faxes, email, and telephone voice mail.

Again, you need to be careful about being aggressive to the point of making yourself unwelcome, but look at every request for information as a way to demonstrate your sincerity, your organization skills, and your own critical commitment to the promotion.

Casting

Deciding on the right number of partners

The first question you need to ask yourself when approaching other companies is how many partners do you really want? Resolving this issue is critical to the equity position you'll retain in the promotion.

Bringing in partners has the effect of slicing a pie; you don't want to cut the slices too small. Everyone has seen a promotional advertisement in a newspaper with ten or more logos at the bottom of the ad. Although there is usually a primary or presenting sponsor and this is usually the company with the largest logo in the ad, the impact of this promotion for any one company can be weakened by a smorgasbord of sponsors.

From experience, I believe the cut-off point is one or two other for-profit companies, one nonprofit organization, and one to three media partners. Any additional participants and you may get more confusion than you get positive results.

When I recommend from one to three media, I am looking at

your potential media mix from a multi-channel point-of-view. Usually I negotiate for title sponsorship with one key media sponsor such as a daily newspaper. I then add a radio station and a television station for media balance. Few media willingly join with other media in their same category, but they are often willing to forge cross-promotional alliances with media in non-competing categories. That's why I have had much success convincing dissimilar, non-competing media to forge co-promotional partnerships.

You can tie-in with a nonprofit organization that already has established relationships with other community-spirited companies, thereby attracting those companies to your project. Or you can leverage your media relationships to entice other publicity-seeking sponsors.

Finding another for-profit partner or two may be in the best interest of your promotion, especially if other partners are willing to bring value to the table. "Value" can be cash, in-kind services, retail distribution outlets, or product samples. Finally, a promotional partner can tag his own standard advertisements with promotional mentions, which, of course, extends the reach of your pre-promotion advertising.

Birds of a feather . . .

The best place to go hunting for partners is to begin with those companies that traditionally promote aggressively: Pepsi, Coke, Coors, Budweiser, McDonald's, Starbucks and other major retail-focused marketers. These are companies that consistently lead in the discipline of promotion. They invent events, concerts, festivals, fairs, competitions, and bizarre experiences to keep consumers cheerfully aware of their brands.

The problem with these partners is also a consequence of the opportunity they present. They plan their calendars well in advance; they're approached by many promotional suitors; and they usually like to be in a controlling position. However, a good idea and plenty of advance notice can win you a terrific partner with a healthy marketing budget and a clear understanding of the value of promotion.

There is a basic issue you should be prepared to discuss when you meet with one of these potential partners. Beverage companies want to sell cases of their product, and retail organizations, such as fast-service restaurants, want to generate store traffic. Rarely does one of these companies agree to a promotion just for awareness or image enhancement. So, you must think through your marketing strategy carefully and be ready to suggest how your promotion will benefit bottom-line sales or store traffic. Since you are working on Boomer promotions, you also need to make sure the potential partner wants to target Boomers.

The important point here is that you consider the needs of your potential partner and frame your promotion strategies to help him sell more goods or generate greater store traffic.

Everybody needs a Mary Lee

You have conceptualized, written and presented your promotional strategy to several partners. You have commitments. Now the nitty-gritty work begins. This is where Mary Lee comes in.

Mary Lee is someone from my past who was the quintessential implementer. She was a stickler for details and could keep track of a hundred issues at one time. Under the pressure of deadlines, she always kept a sense of humor. She had fun working with people, and other people enjoyed working with her. Not only was she a good facilitator, she anticipated problems before they occurred.

I suggest at this point in the evolution of your promotion that you find your own Mary Lee. Perhaps your temptation is just to take care of everything yourself. Maybe budgetary constraints prohibit you from adding a support person to your team. If that's the case, then you have my sympathy.

Even if you are an extremely detail-oriented person, you still can benefit from off-loading a lot of the follow-through work on someone else. The best argument in favor of this is to give you more time to stay focused on the big picture. When people get too wrapped up in the details of a promotion, they lose sight of what is important. They concentrate on tactics rather than strategies.

You should stay in the driver's seat of your promotional bandwagon, not fixing it every time a wheel breaks. Find a Mary Lee or Johnny Ray to help you out of the ruts.

Star Power: pros and cons

Over the years, I've worked with notable personalities such as Robert Stack, Joe DiMaggio, David Cassidy, Chris Burke (Corky in the TV series *Life Goes On*), best-selling author Nicholas Negroponte and a slew of professional and Olympic athletes. There is no question that a celebrity brings your promotion vitality and a greater probability of publicity. It's also fun to meet and associate with these people. They live at a different pace than most of us, and they are afforded a place in our society akin to European royalty. They are often just nice people who happen to have special talents. Because of these positive attributes, involving a celebrity in your promotion makes a lot of sense.

If your promotion is primarily a fundraiser for a nonprofit organization, then you may attract a celebrity for just expenses. Unless the charitable cause is the celebrity's own passion, you should expect to pick up airline tickets (usually for a minimum of two, and usually first class seats), hotel (usually a suite), transportation (usually a limousine), meals, and incidentals.

While this may seem like a small price to pay for the glowing aura of a celebrity, some quick calculations will show you that you're still looking at an investment of several thousand dollars. You must decide if the additional cost of a celebrity, talent fees notwithstanding, weigh favorably or unfavorably against the extra mileage you'll get with a celebrated personality drawing larger crowds.

Unfortunately, there are other issues to consider. If you're not paying talent fees, then you have a nebulous commitment. It's much easier for the celebrity or his handlers to back out at the last minute. Furthermore, you are probably aware that some celebrities can be a little eccentric. Thus, you will be forced to pander to special dietary requests or go out of your way—usually during the busiest hours of your promotion—to take care of unexpected demands.

I've never had unreasonable difficulties with celebrities, but some of their handlers are a different matter. Let's be blunt: The people surrounding celebrities—agents, managers, publicists— are sometimes highly paid jerks. Their jobs require them to get maximum benefits for their clients with minimum investments of time and effort. If you encounter obstacles, these are the people most likely to get in your face. Therefore, you may want to judge the usefulness of bringing in a celebrity based on your intuitive sense of the attitude of the celebrity's intermediary.

My final recommendation concerning using a celebrity is to treat her as such, especially if you are borrowing her image and reputation without fee compensation. She has earned her elevated station in society, and you need to follow commonsense and standard protocol in handling every aspect of her visit to your community. Start with excellent first impressions.

When my team met a rock star at the airport to kick off a fundraiser, we were waiting at the gate with a limousine—naturally. The star was weary from an early morning flight and also hungry. So we had stocked the limousine with an elegant fruit basket, coffee and juice. When we arrived at the hotel and checked her into a suite, we made sure to allow over two hours on the agenda for her to rest and freshen up before the first press conference.

The balance of her trip went the same way. We anticipated every need, and we gave careful thought to details. Accustomed to special handling, the rock star was still impressed with our thoughtfulness and consideration for her comfort and satisfaction during the visit. This buoyed her enthusiasm and energy. We made a friend and concluded the promotion feeling very justified with our investment.

Where are they?

Although celebrities often live in seclusion, they aren't as hard to track down as you might think. Their self-interest is tied up in being accessible to the right people. You just need to be resourceful. If the celebrity is a recording star, you can find his agent through the record company. If she is a television actor, you can contact the company producing the show or the television network on which she appears. If he is a sports figure, that's easy. Just contact the team and get a referral to the agent. If you're interested in a writer, contact him through his publisher or agent who is usually mentioned in the introductory credits of the book.

Eventually you'll track down an agent or manager, and this is the person who usually screens your initial proposal. Most agents will carry proposals, even ones where compensation is not involved, to their clients. If a client is not currently "hot," you are in a much better bargaining position. Sometimes ebbing popularity is just the period in a career when a celebrity is most willing to contribute to a nonprofit cause. So I recommend that you be creative about who you target, and consider quality people not currently riding the popularity tide. Fading stars still attract attention, especially in smaller communities.

Products as stars

There are other kinds of celebrities beside media stars. Many products have earned star stature in the eyes of certain audiences. What does Harley-Davidson represent to the avid biker? How about Budweiser to the motor sports enthusiast? Or Apple computers to the graphic designer? Products are images, and images are perceptions.

When you enter into a partnership arrangement with another company, you are often enlisting the support of its star products. This can be highly advantageous in helping you attract the right people to your promotion. If your organization or product is low-profile, the partnership can elevate the status and visibility of your brand.

As in all marketing endeavors, it is beneficial for you to understand your customers or constituents. This means getting inside their heads and learning about what they need and want, their lifestyle choices, and the products they choose to reflect the way they live. When you achieve this kind of intimacy with your target audience, then you are equipped to solicit support from companies with products and services of exceptional value to the people you most want to influence through your promotion.

Pre-production

Pre-production meeting

Once you have succinctly and brilliantly summarized your promotion, met and concluded your negotiations with partners, and begun implementation, your next most important task is to call a pre-production meeting with your organizing committee.

I recommend a bribe such as the proverbial free lunch. Everyone in business today is over-taxed, and your promotion—while perhaps at this time occupying the center of your life—is just one more distraction to many if not all your partners. But you need them to jump on your bandwagon and start moving in the same direction. An enticement is a good starting point for this critical first meeting because it represents a tangible expression of your appreciation for their time.

At a pre-production lunch or breakfast or dinner or pizza party or whatever, you begin the critical task of delegation. This is when you must gently transform from a sweet suitor to a benevolent dictator. Your job is to get other people to help you do the work.

The pre-production meeting should include an agenda that you have sent to each participant in advance. Start the meeting on time and keep the meeting focused with the agenda. You must insist on a meeting time and location that virtually guarantees attendance by all critical participants. If one key individual is absent, then you may end up hosting several disjointed pre-production meetings.

The centerpiece of the meeting should be the responsibility chart that you designed when you were developing your promotional summary. If you use this tool as it was designed, then you take your team through each item, step by step, so that everyone understands exactly what is expected and who is going to take care of what.

As the meeting facilitator, allow enough time at the end of the meeting to summarize all commitments and assignments. Set a firm date to meet again, a time that should be consistent with the demands of your promotion timeline. Finally, update your promotion responsibility chart to reflect changes and commitments made by team members and send the revised chart as soon as possible to all participants.

Promotion Theme

Many people believe that a promotion theme serves as the organizing focus of a promotion. It's the peacetime equivalent of a battle cry. You give people an idea to rally behind and become passionate. You may want to spend some time in your pre-production meeting discussing a promotional theme.

Your theme should be simple to express and succinct. From two to eight words is probably the ideal length. The theme should evoke a goal that most people understand, or will come to understand once your pre-promotion marketing begins. I like themes that have several levels of meaning, all equally positive in interpretation. If possible, your theme should include a visual graphic. The words and graphic work together to form a positive impression. Don't get too hung up in a theme line. It can facilitate your marketing, but it isn't essential for a successful promotion. Themes I've used in the past include:

Colorado Springs Ahead (A community-based effort to revitalize a sagging economy in Colorado Springs)

Get More Smiles per Gallon (A fund-raiser for a petroleum company designed to raise money for three nonprofit organizations dedicated to helping underprivileged children)

High Technology . . . The Next Generation (A community economic development promotion centered on high technology careers and youngsters)

Silver and Strawberries on Ice (A promotion for The Broadmoor Hotel's World Arena, featuring Olympic Silver Medalist figure skater Brian Orser and the children's animated character Strawberry Shortcake)

Accountability

Holding people accountable for their commitments without alienating them is one of the most difficult challenges of promotion management. A lot of this delicate balancing act depends on your personality and the interpersonal dynamics between you and other promotion team members.

My advice is just to use common sense. Praise team members frequently. Always take time to share your appreciation. Recognize extraordinary effort with small gifts such as promotion T-shirts, hats, and other merchandise. Give extra tickets to members of your organizing committee for family members and friends of the family. Be generous.

On the other hand, constructively criticize privately. Most people respond to gentle prodding without feeling offended.

However, if you notice one of your promotion team members failing to follow through with commitments, you need to address the situation immediately. Promotions have one important human characteristic—they are mortal. You only have so much time to get it right; then the promotion is over, and it is dead. You have an obligation to give your partners plenty of opportunities to air grievances, blow off steam, and stay connected with you and your mutual goals.

But just because a partner was once someone you had to woo and cajole—to win over—he nevertheless has made a commitment and both of your careers have something to gain or lose as a result of promotion performance. You must feel self-confident enough to challenge results while avoiding the nasty trap of micromanagement.

If after careful, compassionate communication with a partner, the individual still performs as a slacker, don't hesitate to escalate your concerns to a higher court. You may need to meet with the slacker's boss. You may risk alienating a team member, but if you stay focused in your criticism on performance of the task at hand and avoid the temptation to analyze a personality, most people will reorganize their priorities with a little pressure from the boss. Although this is a situation most of us will do anything we can to avoid, you owe it to yourself and the success of your promotion to make sure an individual doesn't destroy your hard work. I've seen it happen.

Just remember this: Long after a promotion is over, most people will recall the outcome of the project—whether it was a success or failure—rather than short-term divisiveness between a team member and you.

VIP involvement

Hospitality planning

During the pre-production phase of a promotion, you need to pay special attention to hospitality, particularly VIP hospitality. Most promotions establish two social classes, the "haves" and the "have mores."

The "haves" are those people who comprise your primary target market: customers, members, media audiences, ticket holders, etc. The "have mores" are those people who are special because of business or community status—your company's biggest customers, the CEO and board of directors, top managers working for your partners, and elected representatives. It is the "have mores" that I'm focusing on in this section.

It is normal protocol to plan special food and beverage functions and staging areas apart from the rest of the audience. This is akin to the backstage area of a rock concert: lavish food packaged with special access privileges. The backstage area also allows VIPs to meet and greet entertainers and celebrities in an atmosphere of special inclusion. It's a place of relaxed energy where your select group can kick back a little without being on stage and on guard.

Your initial planning group should include an individual assigned to the task of developing a hospitality plan for the elite: where, when, how much, and how often. This individual's goal will be to plan official involvement with VIPs before, during, and, in some circumstances, after your promotion. The planning process should be constrained by a realistic budget and an overall vision about how these special people should experience the promotion.

I recommend you find someone who loves parties, perhaps an active socialite who is always the first to volunteer when a party is on the horizon. I've had exceptional success with gregarious members of the Junior League, women who are well trained in the mechanics of planning and organizing but also know how to have a great time. Find the right person for the task of VIP hospitality, and you'll give this important responsibility very little additional thought.

Who's Who

Your goal is to create a unique experience for opinion leaders in your community. The value is obvious: Opinion leaders pave the way for a more successful promotion; they also pave the way for its return the following year. Who are they?

They appear regularly in your local newspaper. They are elected officials, prominent home builders, Chamber of Commerce board members, volunteer executives helping important nonprofit organizations, journalists, homegrown business owners, and tourism officials.

The membership directory for your Chamber of Commerce is a great place to start. That list will capture many of your community's most successful and visible business leaders. If your city also has another organization that focuses on economic development, see if you can get a copy of its membership roster, too.

I mentioned the Junior League in the previous section. If your community has a chapter of this organization, then get a copy of its membership roster. The women who belong have several things in common: young, successful, passionate about volunteer work, connected to community issues, generally prosperous, efficiently organized to get projects accomplished, and many are married to successful men in the community.

If your focus is long-term success, not only for the promotion that may have inspired you to read this chapter, but throughout the coming years, then I recommend you begin compiling a mailing list of local opinion leaders. Once you put this list together, and keep it updated on a regular basis, you will have a valuable resource to aid your long-term business success.

What VIP's expect

Let's start with what VIPs generally don't expect. They don't care to associate with sycophants and social climbers focused on ostentatious pandering to their egos. They don't want to be treated so differently they may appear to be elitist. That doesn't work in today's culture. Even the very wealthy want to maintain some of the outward manifestations of simple, wholesome, everyday-people values.

Therefore, your VIP party should focus on three things. First, the food presentation should include an attractive variety of light fare that is easy to eat standing up. Second, the party should be staged in an environment conducive to socializing; they are social people, so make it easy for them to network. Finally, the party should evoke the theme of your promotion through staging and decorations. If you have included a guest celebrity or celebrities, then of course this is the time for a cameo appearance.

Keep your VIP event low-key but classy. VIPs are weary of stuffy, formal occasions. Like any other person, they just want to have fun and experience the sizzle of a promotion.

The secret of a successful pre-event

Once you've decided who is coming and what they will discover when they get there, you need to determine the best way to get them there. Much depends on the size and relevance of your event. If you're getting lots of pre-publicity and there is generally a buzz throughout the community about the promotion, then your major problem will be how to exclude people rather than how to get the right people to your event.

But if your event is a little more obscure, then you may need to determine a very creative way to beckon movers and shakers. A lot hinges on your invitation and how it's presented.

One time I faced the task of bringing key members of the media to the kick off celebration for a new nightclub in an established hotel. My client was most generous in making sure there would be a tremendous food buffet and an open bar. His business is food and beverages. However, media people tend to be rather fickle, and, for obvious reasons, they are often targeted for grand opening celebrations.

We decided to take advantage of a current television hit and use it to our advantage. Perhaps you remember the *Miami Vice* television series starring actor Don Johnson. The show created a fashion rage for unstructured, loose fitting silk and natural fiber clothes—a distinctive *Miami Vice* "look." The show inspired a very vogue new look emphasizing hot colors and cool whites.

My team found two models—college students, actually—who looked as if they belonged in the TV series. We dressed the male and female in *Miami Vice* clothes and sent the couple around town to hand-deliver party invitations to media personalities. The young couple delivered each invitation to a key member of each organization's staff, such as the television anchor, including written instructions for the recipient to invite nine more people from the staff as guests. (Notice how this trick created a demand to be on the "A-List," and we didn't have to undertake the delicate task of making final selections.) We didn't stop there.

Our *Miami Vice* couple delivered a large piece of a jigsaw puzzle. The full puzzle was poster size and depicted an airbrush illustration of the client's new nightclub logo. The deal was this: If you come to the party and your puzzle piece finishes the puzzle, you win a two-hour complimentary cocktail party and lavish buffet for the rest of your staff—up to 200 people.

I don't think anyone missed the grand opening party, and for the next several months this new nightclub had a line of people waiting for admission every night. It was a fun nightclub, and that stimulated attendance, but it was through the influence of opinion leaders that we were able to make sure this new hot spot became "the place to be" in town.

Media and publicity

The media plan

If you've been successful in your front-end work with media and have enlisted the cross-promotional support of one or several media organizations, then your media plan is half finished. You know which media will be advertising your promotion, and you have a good idea about the level of their broadcast airtime and print space commitments. The major task ahead is to develop the creative message and work with promotion directors to get TV and radio spots scheduled and print ads placed.

However, even with media as partners, I've found it extremely useful to work with a media specialist and actually develop a media plan. This is because a media plan commits everybody. They know what you expect, or at least what you aspire to achieve.

The Media Plan is a formal document that defines how much media you need to successfully promote your event. The levels are usually expressed with two key media terms.

"Reach" describes the percentage of people in a certain target demographic, such as adults 40 to 60, who will be exposed to at least one advertising message during your pre-promotion advertising. "Frequency" describes the average number of times this same group will receive the same message, possibly through different media channels, during pre-promotion advertising. A media plan describes all media you will be buying as a composite and sets forth how many ads will appear on each station or in each print medium to achieve your overall goals.

Details of media strategy are outside the scope of this discussion. However, as a generalization, you want to "reach" as many people as possible in your preferred target demographic. Between 80 percent and 90 percent is usually the goal for ambitious promoters, with an average frequency between three and seven messages in a two to four-week period. These "ideal" media objectives can be very expensive if you are buying your media, so you'll need to adjust your goals based on either your budget or how much promotional advertising you have negotiated with media partners.

There is always a trade-off between reach and frequency. The higher the media reach—or percentage of unduplicated audience members—then the lower the frequency with which audience members will be exposed to repetitive messages.

Few advertisers can afford both high reach and high frequency. My recommendation is to emphasize reach: You want to get the word out to the most people possible during your pre-promotion advertising. If your promotion is steeped with exciting potential, people won't need many repetitive messages to remember your advertising. We all go where the action is.

Many event promoters with slim budgets concentrate their advertising messages in a short period so they can assure high reach while accumulating a few impressions per individual. They treat their promotion as a new product. New products require less frequency to achieve communication objectives because new products are "newsworthy," and people pay closer attention to news. Established products, such as toothpaste, need more frequency because we pay less attention to things with which we are already familiar.

I recommend that you solicit support from a media specialist to help you find the right balance between reach and frequency within the limits of your budget and allocated promotional air time and print space.

Although you can hire an advertising agency to do this, a few inquiries with your contacts in the media will lead you to one or several freelance media buyers. You can either negotiate with the freelancer for a nominal fee to help you put a media plan together, or influence this individual to kick in his or her support for your nonprofit cause. In the several community-oriented promotions that I've led, I have always included a media planner or buyer on my organizing committee.

Some promotional pundits will be dismayed at my suggestion that you even bother developing a media plan for a nonprofit promotion that relies heavily, if not exclusively, on donated media. When media donate time and space to support a nonprofit cause, they usually pick the times and places your advertising will appear. Of course, in the spirit of partnership, you may be able to influence these decisions, but some media might resent being handed a document that defines the delivery weights you expect. It's somewhat akin to accepting a gift and then telling the giver you really want something more.

Even with nonprofit promotions, I have still created a media plan. When presenting the plan to media who are donating promotional time and space, I suggest that the plan is only a guideline for their consideration to help us all succeed. The plan suggests times of the day (day-parts), number of days (flight duration), and proposed programming where the ads might appear. This document will help the station achieve its part of the overall media objectives, and the tactic has always served the larger interests of the promotion. Media partners have inevitably become more focused in trying to schedule the best times and places for my ads to appear.

The role of the press release

There are two avenues through the media to reach your target audience. The first is paid advertising or promotional time and space donated by media partners. The second is through the news-reporting side of the media. There is always an invisible wall between the two sides of media, and you should never expect your promotional partnership with a television or radio station to guarantee automatic news coverage. You have to deal with both sides of the media within their own paradigms. I've already discussed the role of the media plan and its function with the promotional side of media. A press release is how you deal with the news-reporting side.

A standard press release follows a fairly rigorous style developed over the years between those who pitch the news and those who cover it. Break the rules of form and style, and you'll risk someone tossing your press release into a circular file. To help you write a press release according to the needs of the media, there are plenty of reference resources. However, the two most important parts of the standard press release that I will mention here are the headline and lead paragraph. How well you write these two major points of reference in your release will usually make or break its success.

The headline serves the same function as the headline in a newspaper article. It should attract attention and be larger than the typography on the rest of the page. It's a good idea to print the headline with bold-face type. The best headlines cause curiosity: "What's going on here?"

Study headlines in major newspapers, and you'll get the basic idea. Then test your draft headlines—and you should write several—with members of your organizing committee to find out which headline compels those people to want to read the release.

Your lead paragraph usually answers the six most typical journalistic questions. Who? What? Where? When? Why? How or how much? In fifty words or less, the lead paragraph needs to sum up the news. The crisper you write copy, the more professional it'll look to journalists, and the more likely they'll read on for details.

The balance of the release gives details and usually includes a quote by someone who is influential and connected to the event. Of course, the release emphasizes what is new, different, exciting, or most stimulating about your promotion.

If you've followed my advice earlier in this chapter and developed a truly unique approach to your promotion, then you have the essential "hook" you'll need to tantalize people with a "nose for news."

You should send your press release to every media organization that can possibly reach your preferred audience. Most communities have a local press association, and you can call the president of this organization to request a mailing list. Reporters are not interested in being secretive about who they are; their success depends on being visible and accessible. If you can't locate a local press association representative—and a good source for this information is one of your media partners—then have someone call every television station, radio station and newspaper in your community

If you do have media partners, this can mitigate coverage of your event by competing media. To address this issue, I recommend that you write two releases: one release will brazenly highlight your partnership relationship (for the reporters working for your partners), and the other release will will focus only on the promotion itself. If your promotion is large enough, such as a citywide sporting event, then media competing with your partners will probably cover your promotion from different angles—perhaps a human interest story focusing on an athlete, for example.

The role of communications technology

Any marketing communications effort to pre-publicize a promotion would fall short without an effective use of technology. That includes the telephone, fax and email. Use these tools to help you with follow up. The more contacts you can make with an individual journalist, without making a nuisance of yourself, the better. People, journalists or not, usually need several appeals to their attention since we're all distracted by multiple priorities and dead-lines at any given time.

You can fax your release if you have inspired curiosity from a reporter. (Sometimes it is better to send an original copy of your release by overnight mail as the first step. One clear exception would be when your promotion is breaking news—such as a fundraising response to a disaster. Then email and faxing become the preferred modalities.)

You should always follow up after mailing your press release by calling each journalist to answer questions. The Internet provides a more immediate channel of communication. Since most journalists have email addresses accessible through the Internet, and they pub-lish these addresses on their business cards and letterhead, or post them on Web sites, you have a more expedient way to dispatch fol-low-up email messages and bypass the paper shuffle. I always include my name and affiliation, as well as the central concept of the promotion in the subject line of my first email contact. Journal-ists are deluged with email, so you need to make sure they instantly recognize your email message as relevant, rather than spam. Even in a follow-up email message, I always include the original press release for reference.

Media discrimination: pros and cons

At some point you must weigh the benefits and liabilities of tying-in with just one or a few media. That decision depends entirely on the size and impact of your promotion. If it's a small promotion with a small budget and likely to be of interest to just a sub-seg-ment of the community, then you may need to align your promo-tion with an individual radio and television station. This will guarantee your promotion some media support, but you'll pay for this in negligible participation by other media.

If your promotion is a huge event with city-wide or industry-wide implications, you may want to avoid aligning with just a few media partners. Media tend to be hard-headed competitors, and exclusive relationships forged by their competitors cause them to ignore your promotion. You are more likely to get their competitive juices working for you on the news coverage side of the equation if you leave media partnerships out of your strategies. Many will be willing to offer you pre-event and event coverage to achieve some measure of event ownership.

When managing large, highly visible events, I've sometimes found a useful path of compromise between these two extremes. I've fragmented the event into discrete, non-overlapping components and handed these components to individual stations on an exclusive basis. For example, during the World Cycling Championships, I gave one television station promotional rights to World Records Night. Another station received exclusive rights to Opening Ceremonies. Although this balancing act required some mediation skills, most of the participating media organizations were happy with their slice and gave it the emphasis of a major promotion.

Media promotion within a promotion

One of the tried-and-true methods to assure media coverage among several competing broadcasters and publishers is to plan an exclusive media promotion within your overall promotion. This tactic works best if part of your ultimate objectives includes a goal to help a charitable cause or nonprofit organization.

During the build up to the World Cycling Championships, for example, we staged a tricycle race between members of the media. Much to my surprise and delight, owners, general managers and reporters showed up in droves. You can imagine the value of this photo opportunity: sophisticated adults trying to maneuver tiny tricycles on a velodrome track. We received great news coverage by making sure the owners of the stations delivered on their commitments to show up. We bugged them incessantly. All of the local network television affiliates sent camera crews to cover the boss riding on a tricycle.

Another promotion that I ran annually for a resort hotel was an all-media ski race to raise funds to help fight children's cancer. Again, the charitable goal of the promotion, plus the lure of a fun competition between friendly rivals, assured excellent turn out and exceptional local news coverage.

The Production

What P-Day looks like

The days and hours leading up to a promotion are at best ambiguous; at worst, chaotic. Most new promotions are tall on organizer enthusiasm and short on human resources. There aren't enough helpers to go around. Thus, some aspects of the promotion get taken care of flawlessly, and other elements are either dropped or overlooked.

Ambiguity is the hallmark of a good promotion because there is always more to do than time and resources permit. If you're a perfectionist—which characterizes many successful promoters, including yours truly—then you must learn to accept non-perfection. Over-planning and over-delivering are two pitfalls you simply must avoid. Your innate perfectionist tendencies, including the planning and organization techniques I have discussed in this chapter, will have helped you anticipate most of the contingencies. Now that the promotion is at hand, you should let go of your tendency to over-manage or micro-manage and allow nature to take its course.

The only way I know to do this is to stay focused on your overall objectives. Take care of what matters and achieve the things you set out to accomplish. If you attract 10,000 spectators, and that was your goal, it won't matter if someone forgot to pick up the balloons. What everyone will remember is your success in delivering the audience you promised.

Promotion Day or P-Day may actually be less frustrating and ambiguous than the days or hours leading up to it. Although promoters cultivate an instinctive skepticism about people following through, particularly volunteers, we are usually pleasantly surprised when P-Day comes and people actually show up and do their jobs. Although you may get nebulous commitments from some of your supporters, when the show finally goes on, those who have poured sweat and blood into the effort won't miss a fleeting chance to be where the action is.

If you've followed my advice, you have handed tickets or invitations to your partners to include members of their immediate families. When your promotion includes their families, it's pretty hard for staff to blow off their commitments.

On P-Day, expect a certain amount of pandemonium. Adrenalin will come to your aid as well as other people. Again, your promotion will not be perfect, but those imperfections will be invisible to most of your guests.

Motto: Be Prepared

Any Boy Scout certainly learned the implications of the Scout's motto: *Be Prepared*. This timeless wisdom pays off big time for promoters. Here are some recommendations concerning how to be prepared on P-Day.

I have learned through experience to bring a backpack to every promotion. The backpack is my survival kit. It always includes changes of clothes and extra shoes, especially to deal with weather changes in outdoor promotions.

There is nothing worse than being underdressed when a cold front moves through during an outdoor promotion. You need to be thinking about more important things than cold, wet feet.

Second, I always bring survival food. Maybe you function best on hotdogs and syrupy beverages, but I need high quality, balanced food to maintain my energy, so I always bring high-quality nutrition bars and fluid replacement beverages. Knowing full well that planning and executing a promotion has taken a toll on me physically I also keep and consume a stash of vitamins.

If you are a high-technology geek, like me, then you certainly want to include your laptop computer in your backpack. That's because your laptop has your planning spreadsheets, timelines, executive PowerPoint presentation, critical contact names and telephone numbers, and all other pertinent information you've put together during the planning phases of your project. A Personal Data Assistant, or PDA, is sometimes sufficient as a lightweight laptop computer substitute.

Technology geek or not, you must include high-technology communications capabilities in your survival pack, and eventually attach this technology to your body. A cellular phone or two-way radio is mandatory. That way you can be at one end of a crowd of

20,000 dancing rock 'n' roll fanatics and still have someone contact you from the other side of the crowd, without the hassle of trying to hunt you down. Of course, your partners need to be equally accessible. Store their cell phone numbers in your cell phone in advance so all you need to do is push a keypad button to call one of your partners or support staff members.

I also recommend that you have several communications devices with you at all times. This could include a pager and cell phone, or a two-way radio and a pager, etc. Don't forget to include fully charged back-up batteries and AC adapters in your survival pack.

Include some drugs in your pack. I'm referring to legal, over-the-counter drugs such as pain relievers, upset stomach medications, and antihistamines, especially if you're prone to allergies. I also recommend that you include Tylenol in your survival pack and take the medication before, during, and after your promotion to counteract muscle and joint inflammation.

Finally, don't forget to include some bandages to cover minor cuts and a product called Moleskin to cover foot blisters that may develop from so much dashing around.

Also, you may need some basic tools such as screwdrivers, pliers, a hammer, and some fastening tools such as a staple gun and industrial-strength tape. There is always a last-minute need to hang something somewhere.

Since you have a detailed responsibility chart, it is always advisable to review this document—which, of course, you've updated on a regular basis right up to P-Day. You may also want to call everyone on your organizing committee who hasn't been in touch immediately preceding the promotion just to make sure things are buttoned down. If you need a parade or occupancy permit, keep it with you and keep it dry. If you have a rental contract for the venue, have a copy ready in case someone erred on a family reunion invitation and the entire branch of the Schmidt family shows up.

The role of the generalist

As the promoter, you're not the ticket taker, competition judge, bathroom re-supplier, or caterer, although special situations may require you to fill in for any of these roles on a short-term basis. You are a troubleshooter. Your role is to deal with whatever requires your attention at the moment and get others to perform their assigned tasks as planned. Micro-management will be your worst enemy; you need to be willing to let others do their jobs, their way, and only correct behavior when it is totally non-productive.

You must stay in a big-picture framework, focused on overall objectives rather than details. If you've organized your promotion effectively and recruited good partners, then your problems will be short-lived and easy to remedy.

And don't forget Mary Lee. Your assistant should be your shadow for most of the promotion and be ready to run quick errands or fill-in temporarily for other workers.

How to prevent a disaster

There is always an element of risk in any promotion; you can't change that. One thing most promotions have in common is the tendency to attract large groups of strangers and gather them in atypical environments. Someone may get hurt or sick. We're mortal, we're fairly fragile, and you can't change that.

The way to reduce chances of a disaster is to anticipate every possible disaster. Your local protective agencies—police, firefighters, medical emergency personnel—can give you lots of advice about the reasonable precautions you should consider, given the circumstances of your promotion.

Simply follow their advice. Have an emergency ambulance team on site if recommended. Be sure you've met all local regulations concerning temporary structures such as bleachers. Hire off-duty police officers to help with security.

These points are obvious but must be included in your pre-event planning. Many protective services are available free-of-charge, particularly if you're promoting a publicly-funded event. But know what's free and what will cost you extra so you can factor these charges into your promotion budget.

A disaster does not always include an injury or illness. What happens if the band doesn't show up? Or the star athlete isn't warming up when he should be? Or the jet fly-by is fifteen minutes late? No easy answers here. But two other preparatory steps on your part will help.

First, make sure people are where they're supposed to be ahead of schedule. This is particularly important if arriving crowds may slow up access for entertainers. Second, make sure you have contingency plans with every key player in your promotion; make sure everybody has multiple ways to communicate.

Documentation

Once in the midst of a promotion, many people go with the flow and stop keeping track of important details. As I mentioned earlier, some of this is good because you don't want details to distract you from larger, more important objectives.

If you plan on repeating this promotion, however, it is very helpful that you document what's happening. Add to your survival pack a digital camera, plenty of the camera's memory cards, and back-up batteries. You may also include a hand-held digital video camera. It's probably wise that you either hire or bribe a professional photographer or videographer to help you document your promotion, but you should carry a compact, hassle free camera with you. Other team members could carry disposable cameras if a snapshot occasion arises when you are elsewhere. A conventional film camera can also provide photographic documentation in the event of injury or damage.

Events and promotions invite "photo opportunities of a lifetime." One spectacular photograph or video clip could be all you will need to keep convincing others in the coming years and guarantee the long-term viability of your promotion.

I also bring with me a micro-cassette tape recorder to take verbal notes as things are happening. Again, if just one note reminds you of a critical opportunity to include in your plans for next year, then the inconvenience will be worth it.

Ego and its aftermath

Promotions are sometimes ambiguous and chaotic, and they do create conflict. Ego often comes to the forefront in a manner more intensified than in normal, day-to-day experience. I have a theory as to why.

A promotion becomes its own temporary society, with new and uncommon rules of conduct. People who intuitively understand their place in the everyday world find themselves in new roles, often with more authority than normal. A servile teenager suddenly controls an admission gate with all the power it implies. A docile senior citizen becomes Attila-The-Backpack-Checker. A high school janitor becomes a referee with an arena full of writhing fans hanging onto his every decision.

Then there is the city council member who, quite full of himself, doesn't get admitted to the VIP area, or the successful business executive who commands a company of more than a thousand employees and can't get through the gate.

Some people who are mostly powerless in everyday life acquire short-term authority, and they like how it feels. Other people who are accustomed to oceans parting before their feet get inadvertently treated as "one of the little people." Promotions magnify egos and invite conflict, usually over who can go where, when.

You can't predict when and where there will be ego conflict, but you must anticipate it happening and deal with it swiftly and diplomatically. Follow tried and true advice: "Commend publicly and criticize privately."

If a gatekeeper gets too full of himself, compliment him in front of others concerning his hard work at keeping trespassers from getting through the gate. Take him aside and privately ask him to be kinder and gentler when someone is clearly confused about admission policies. If some big shot doesn't lighten up because you failed to roll out the red carpet, be firm and direct about your policies, but buy him a drink. You have to find that delicate balancing point between benevolent love of humanity and the absolute need to control the tide of people coming in and out of your promotion. It isn't easy. Just let common sense and a long-term concern for relationships control your judgments.

The Wrap

Not until the paperwork's done

Once your promotion is finished, everyone has gone home, and you are finally alone, take fifteen minutes and write down the names of everyone who made a real difference during your promotion. These are the people who promised and delivered. They're the people who made modest commitments but under the pressure of the moment took extraordinary steps to help you put out a fire or overcome an obstacle.

It's the person who drove back through the line of automobiles coming into the venue to make another thankless, but necessary trip to the airport. Write his name down now. Write down the name of the police officer who tactfully broke up an altercation between two teenagers before tempers flared into an all-out fist fight. And the name of the radio announcer who had to adlib during a live break-in while you shoved a tardy athlete toward the microphone. Don't forget the caterer who at the last minute stretched food for thirty into a substantial meal for forty without anyone being left hungry. Don't forget the person who took care of the indelicate issue of a clogged toilet in the restroom. And, of course, you must include the lonely ticket taker who spent the entire day greeting new arrivals with enthusiasm, while missing all the action.

If you haven't guessed yet, you're putting together a list for thank-you letters. And the best time to compose this list is when the events of the day are still fresh in your memory. I have found that although I'm usually exhausted and emotionally spent at the end of a major promotion, I am also too charged up to rest right away. I always need some time to unwind. I have also learned that this is the time I am most grateful—most clearly aware of all the help and special support I've received from so many people.

Of course, you will eventually compose a form letter that doesn't read like a form letter. It will express your sincere gratitude to everyone on your organizing committee: your partners and vendors and key governmental officials who helped you open the right doors and get approvals. That's just smart business.

But I'm suggesting you also create a custom list to include those special people who "went above and beyond the call of duty." They deserve special recognition. They deserve hand-written, personal thank-you notes. Who knows? These same people are likely to be first in line next time you are ready to create another promotion from scratch. And they've already proven that you can count on them.

Debriefing

Within a few days following your promotion, you should make it a priority to get your support team together for a brown bag, working lunch. Please set positive expectations for this gathering by asking everybody to think back through the promotion and jot down relevant points they wish to make during the meeting. Ask them to include positive comments as well as constructive criticisms in their discussions. Your team should review every detail of what happened and what didn't happen.

Set the mood and tone of the debriefing by complimenting every individual. Don't be effusive to the point of phoniness; the way to avoid an appearance of phoniness is to compliment specific behavior. This is another occasion when your notes during and at the end of the promotion will come in handy. I've found that the responsibility chart serves as a great tool to guide the discussion. With everyone's permission, take copious notes or even tape record this meeting. Try to keep the meeting focused so that you have time to cover every detail, from the pre-promotion build up to the post-promotion clean up.

A presentation

The first time you blaze trails across uncharted frontiers is the riskiest. Building a bandwagon, sometimes without a clear image of how it will eventually appear, is not easy. I have good news for you: You have considerable skill at magic because you have already helped people see what wasn't there. You have helped them suspend the natural tendency to distrust change and new ideas. That's behind you now.

If you have followed my advice about promotion documentation, you have plenty of notes, photographs, videotapes, and testimonials from participants. This raw material will help you develop an outstanding presentation to sell your promotion next time.

Maybe your promotion is a one-time event and won't be repeated, but hopefully your future as a respected promoter is secure and you will want to invent some new promotions. Your decision to capture your experiences in a memorable way may have a great deal of bearing on future opportunities, and I encourage you to create an eye-grabbing audiovisual presentation. Every great artist and promoter needs a great portfolio.

First, develop your presentation using one of the powerful computer-based presentation programs such as Microsoft PowerPoint. Once you become accustomed to using these relatively easy software technologies, you'll benefit from the flexibility, visual power, and portability of this kind of presentation.

As Marshall McLuhan stated, "The medium is the message." A state-of-the-art, computer-generated audiovisual presentation will say volumes about your professionalism.

Second, keep your presentation short: from ten to fifteen minutes. Busy executives cannot maintain their concentration on a presentation for much more than ten minutes. These same people will also appreciate your net-to-net attitude.

Finally, sell to the heart first, and then sell to the head. Give future participants a strong sense of your vision by sharing the images and metaphors from your promotion that elevated the human spirit: the aging nursing home residents helped by the fundraiser, the moments of athletic accomplishment, the coming together of disparate minorities, and so forth. Let them feel the power of your creation.

Then sell to the head. Business decisions ultimately come down to a judgment of the benefits and liabilities of a course of action to the "bottom line." Help your audience members develop confidence in the capacity of your promotion to improve brand image, increase sales, change negative perceptions, and help the community in a meaningful way.

When you distill your promotion and make it a persuasive audiovisual presentation that sells both to the heart and head, then you're on your way to a place in the annals of great promoters.

The Great Boomer Promotion Revisited

Let's review what has happened. After weeks or months, the big day arrived. You remained focused on your objectives and kept a clear vision of what was important. Your colleagues, business associates, friends, and new acquaintances took a ride with you on a bandwagon that you designed and built from scratch. As a newly formed and increasingly powerful team, your group rolled in the same direction toward a destination that transformed normal, day-to-day reality into a supernormal experience. Key media contributed broadcast airtime and print space to help you publicize the promotion. Your team influenced many community leaders to throw their influential weight behind the promotion, and this busy group honored you by eagerly accepting invitations to a VIP gathering, becoming enthusiastic opinion leaders.

You started from nothing, and through the power of persuasion, vision, tenacity, faith, trust, and enthusiasm, you developed an extraordinary social opportunity for your community. Now that your hard work, thought and dedication have focused everyone on that single point in time, the nexus of the promotion, you can take a deep, confident breath and realize the full power of your dreams transforming into a new reality. You did your best, and this time your best was good enough. Your promotion was nothing less than a spectacular success.

Congratulations. You created, organized and managed a great Boomer promotion.

Notes

1. "Not Acting Their Age," by Tim Stewart and James M. Pethokoukis, *U.S. News & World Report*, June 4, 2001.
2. Executive Summary: *The 75% Factor: Uncovering Hidden Boomer Values*, co-authored by James V. Gambone and Erica Wittlinger.
3. *My Generation*, a publication of AARP, January-February 2003 issue, *What's Wrong with This Picture?*
4. Statistics reported on *Baby Boomer Headquarters, www.bbhq.com,* a division of Miracle Productions, Inc.
5. For an interesting timeline of this period, see a thought-provoking analysis at *Baby Boomer Headquarters, www.bbhq.com/Sixties2.htm,* hosted by Herschel Chicowitz.
6. The U.S.Constitution, Article 8: only Congress has the authority to declare war; Congress never declared war against North Vietnam.
7. "Twilight of the Boomers," by Daniel Okrent. *Time* magazine, June 12, 2000.
8. "Baby Boomers Increasingly Victims of Age Discrimination," *Athens Banner-Herald*, March 28, 2002.
9. "When Will the Wall Street Bubble Burst?" *The Washington Times*, August 23, 1998.
10. "When Baby Boomers Grow Old," *The American Prospect*, Volume 12, Number 9, May 21, 2001.
11. "Boomers Hope to Break Age-Old Ad Myth," by Hillary Chura, *Advertising Age*, May 13, 2002, as reported at *AdAge.com*
12. "Challenging Obsession with Youth," by Kelly Greene, *The Wall Street Journal*, April 6, 2004.
13. *Ageless Marketing: Strategies for Reaching the Hearts & Minds of the New Customer Majority*, by David B. Wolfe and Robert Snyder, pp. 140–143, (Chicago: Dearborn Trade Publishing, 2003)
14. For more information and background about Generation Jones, see *www.jonathanpontell.com*
15. From a speech by Ken Dychtwald, Ph.D., at the American Society on Aging National Conference, April 14, 2004
16. *Ibid.*

17. "Challenging Obsession with Youth," by Kelly Greene, *The Wall Street Journal*, April 6, 2004.

18. "Fed Chief: Trim Benefits," Associated Press story in *The Denver Post*, February 26, 2004

19. *Ibid.*

20. Harley-Davidson U.S.A. website: *www.harleydavidson.com*

21. "Jesus Is Just Alright," words and music by Arthur S. Reynolds, September 26, 1967.

22. "Imagine," words and music by John Lennon, September 15, 1971.

23. *National Geographic* Expeditions, Travel Catalog 2003, © 2002, National Geographic Society.

24. As reported on *www.gorving.com,* the official website of the recreational vehicle industry

25. "Baby Boomers Look to Volunteerism," *Oak Ridger Online*, Oak Ridge, Tennessee, March 30, 2001. *www.oakridger.com/stories/033001/com_ 0330010090.html*

26. Statistics reported at Ronald McDonald House Charities website, *www.rmhc.com/mis/rmhs_facts/index.html*

27. "They Just Won't Grow Up," by Lev Grossman, *Time* magazine, January 24, 2005

28. AHHA mission statement, as reported on the organization's web site: *www.ahha.org*

29. "IMC Defined," *Journal of Integrated Communications*, website of the Medill School of Journalism at Northwestern University: *www.medill.nwu.org*

30. Parody lyrics adapted from "Lucy in the Sky with Diamonds" on *Sgt. Pepper's Lonely Hearts Club Band,* by The Beatles, as originally written by John Lennon and Paul McCartney.

31. *Understanding Media: the Extensions of Man* by Marshall McLuhan, Cambridge, Massachusetts: MIT Press, 1994.

32. iConnect technology, Roaring Pine, *www.roaringpine.com*

33. "America's Best," *Time* magazine, August 20, 2001; "Persons of the Year" *Time* magazine, December 30, 2002; and "The Quiet Heroes," *Parade* magazine, March 21, 2004.

34. "The New Retirement Survey," Merrill Lynch, February 2005, *http://www.ml.com*

35. "Sony Targets Boomers-Turned-Zoomers," *Advertising Age*, October 21, 2002.

36. "Message from the Chairman" at *Pfizer.com*: *www.pfizer.com*

37. "Ad Agencies Reap the Benefits of Viagra Battle," by Michele Greshberg (Reuters), August 19, 2003 *www.forbes.com/home_europe/newswire/ 2003/08/19/rtr1061407.html*

38. "Making the Line-up for the Big Game," by Christopher Roland, *Boston Globe* online, January 27, 2004, *www.boston.com/yourlife/health/diseases/articles/2004/01/27/making_the_lineup_for_the_big_game/*

39. "Disease Mongering," by Bob Burton and Andy Rowell, PR Watch.org: *www.prwatch.org/prwissues/2003Q1/monger.html*. The authors noted that more than $13.2 billion was spent on pharmaceutical marketing in the U.S. in 2001.

40. "Saddling Up: Boomers Hit the Road On, Yes, Motorcycles for Charity," *Time* magazine, October 21, 2002.

41. *The American Prospect*, Volume 12, Number 9, May 21, 2001.

42. *Domestic Travel Market Report, 2002 Edition*, Travel Industry Association of America, *www.tia.org/Travel/TravelTrends.asp*

43. "Born To Be Wild" words and music by Mars Bonfire. Copyright © 1968 Songs of Universal, Inc. on behalf of Universal Music Publishing, a division of Universal Studios, Canada LTD. (BMI) International Copyright Secured. All Rights Reserved. Used by permission.

44. *Easy Rider*, screenplay written by Peter Fonda, Dennis Hopper and Terry Southern, released and copyright © 1969 Columbia Pictures.

45. "Not Acting Their Age," *U.S. News & World Report*, June 4, 2001.

46. "Madison Avenue Likes Muhammad Ali," by Stewart Elliot, *The New York Times*, February 23, 2004.

47. Speech by Lt. Gen. Barry R. McCaffrey, (reproduced in the *Pentagram*, June 4, 1993) assistant to the Chairman of the Joint Chiefs of Staff, to Vietnam veterans and visitors gathered at Vietnam Verterans memorial Wall, Memorial Day 1993.

48. "Boomer Bummer: Retirement May Get Ugly for Generation," *The Wall Street Journal*, July 9, 2003.

49. "Despair of The Jobless," by Bob Herbert, *The New York Times*, August 7, 2003.

50. "The New York Times Special Report: The Downsizing of America," *The New York Times* Company, Inc., 1996.

51. "The Boomer Bust," by Radley Balko, *Fox News Online*, *www.foxnews.com/story/0,2933,93337,00.html*

52. Boomer Deathwatch, hosted by Rick McGinnis at *http://www.rickmcginnis.com/boomer/*

53. "Meet the Greedy Grandparents," by Steve Chapman, *Chicago Tribune* columnist, *Slate.com*: *www.slate.msn.com/id/2092302*

54. U.S. Bureau of Labor Statistics, August 21, 2002

55. *The Age Explosion: Baby Boomers and Beyond*, a joint publication of the Generations Policy Initiative and the Harvard Institute for Learning in Retirement, Paul Hodge, founding editor

56. From Campbell-Ewald Health survey of baby boomer caregivers and

elderly parents, as reported on *www.seniorjournal.com*, October 19, 2005

57. Study evaluating chances of obesity in adults, funded by the National Heart, Blood, and Lung Institute, and reported in *Annals of Internal Medicine*, October 4, 2005.

58. Nielsen Net Ratings, week of September 5, 2005

59. Alan Greenspan, then Federal Reserve Bank Chairman at the Federal Reserve Bank of Philadelphia's Policy Forum, December 2, 2005

60. Global View and EarthSeeds Project, co-founded by Mark Joyous and Robert Bogatin, on the foundation's website: *www.earthseeds.net/index.php*

61. *EarthSeeds* website: *www.earthseeds.net/earthseeds/earthseeds.php*

62. *Understanding the LOHAS Consumer Report* ™, published by the Natural Marketing Institute, 272 Ruth Road, Harleysville, PA, 19438, 212-513-7300, *www.nmisolutions.com*. All references and discussion in this chapter pertaining to the LOHAS consumer segment were undertaken with permission of Natural Marketing Institute.

63. "Pushing the Buy," by Clint Witchalls, *Newsweek International*, March 22, 2004.

64. Microsoft Corporation company website, reviewing its 2004 campaign, February 24, 2004, *www.microsoft.com/mscorp/ads/tv.asp*.

65. *A Nation Online: How Americans Are Expanding Their Use of the Internet*, National Telecommunications and Information Administration/Department of Commerce, 2002.

66. "Staying Connected: Baby Boomers and the Internet," by David Lazer *Harvard Generations Policy Review*, Volume 1, Winter 2004.

67. As inferred from an online essay by D. Mary Lasker, *www.american-wasteland.com*, American Beauty: "Reducing the Boomer Infestation, November 7, 1999.

68. As inferred from a Web site dedicated to Late Boomers called *www.late-boomers.com*, edited by Nancy Hill.

69. "The 75% Factor: Uncovering Hidden Boomer Values," by James V. Gambone, Ph.D. and Principal Investigator and Erica Whittlinger, MBA, Baby Boomers and Partners, ReFirement® Incorporated.

70. *Ibid.*

71. Letter from Annie Gottlieb to the author, December 16, 1989.

72. "The Real Life," written by John Mellencamp, *The Lonesome Jubilee*, Riva Music, Inc., Copyright © 1987.

Bibliography

"Baby Boomers Look to Volunteerism," *Oak Ridge Online*, March 30, 2001.

"Baby Boomers Increasingly Victims of Age Discrimination," *Athens Banner-Herald*, March 28, 2002

Balko, Radley, "The Boomer Bust," *Fox News Online*.

Burton, Bob and Andy Rowell, "Disease Mongering," *PRWatch.org*, 2003

Center for Disease Control, National Center for Health Statistics, *Live Births by Age of Mother and Race, 1933–98*.

Chapman, Steve, "Meet the Greedy Grandparents," *Slate.com*.

Chura, Hillary, "Boomers Hope to Break Age-Old Ad Myth," *Advertising Age*, May 13, 2002

Dychtwald, Ken, Ph.D., *Age Power: How the 21st Century Will be Ruled by the New Old*, Los Angeles: Jeremy B. Tarcher, 2000

Dychtwald, Ken, Ph.D., *Age Wave: The Challenges and Opportunities of an Aging America*, New York: St. Martin's Press, 1989

Elliott, Stewart, "Madison Avenue Likes Muhammad Ali," *The New York Times*, February 23, 2004.

"Fed Chief: Trim Benefits," *The Denver Post*, February 26, 2004.

Frank, Thomas, *The Conquest of Cool: Business Culture, Counterculture, and the Rise of Hip Consumerism* , Chicago: University of Chicago Press, 1977.

Freeman, Marc, *Prime Time: How Baby Boomers Will Revolutionize Retirement and Transform America*, New York: PublicAffairs, 2002

Gambone, James V. and Erica Whittlinger, *The 75% Factor: Uncovering Hidden Values*

Greene, Kelly, "Challenging Obsession with Youth," *The Wall Street Journal*, April 6, 2004.

Greshberg, Michele, "Ad agencies reap the benefits of Viagra battle," *Reuters*, August 19. 2003.

Herbert, Bob, "Despair of the Jobless," *The New York Times*, August 7, 2003.

Hodge, Paul, *The Age Explosion: Baby Boomers and Beyond*, joint publication of Generations Policy Initiative and Hard Institute for Learning in Retirement.

"IMC Defined," *Journal of Integrated Communications,* Northwestern University.

Kaplan, Louise J., *Adolescence: The Farewell to Childhood,* New York: Touchstone Books (Simon & Schuster) 1984

Light, Paul Charles, *Baby Boomers,* New York: W.W. Norton & Sons, 2002.

Locke, Christopher, *Gonzo Marketing: Winning Through Worst Practices,* New York: Perseus Publishing, 2001.

McGinnis, Rick, "Boomer Deathwatch," *www.rickmcginnis.com/boomer/*

McLuhan, Marshall, *Understanding Media: The Extensions of Man,* Cambridge, MIT Press, 1994.

Morgan, Edward P., *Democracy in Eclipse? Media Culture and the Postmodern "Sixties,"* Department of Political Science, Lehigh University.

Negroponte, Nicholas, *Being Digital,* New York: Vintage Books, 1996.

Orkent, Daniel, "Twilight of the Boomers," *Time* magazine, June 12, 2000.

Putnam, Robert D., *Bowling Alone: The Collapse and Revival of American Community,* New York: Touchstone Books, 2001.

Roland, Christopher, "Making the Line-up for the Big Game," *Boston Globe Online,* January 27, 2004.

Roof, Wade Clark, *A Generation of Seekers: The Spiritual Journeys of the Baby Boom Generation,* New York: HarperCollins, 1993.

Stewart, Tim and James M. Pethokoukis, "Not Acting Their Age," *U.S. News & World Report,* June 4, 2001.

"The Downsizing of America," *The New York Times Company,* 1996.

Understanding the LOHAS Consumer, Harleysville, PA: Natural Marketing Institute, July 2004.

"What's Wrong with this Picture?" an article in *My Generation,* AARP, Washington, DC, February 2003.

"When Baby Boomers Grow Old," *The American Prospect,* V.12, No. 9, May 21, 2001.

"When Will the Wall Street Bubble Burst?" *The Washington Post,* August 23, 1998.

Witchalls, Clint, "Pushing the Buy," *Newsweek International,* March 22, 2004

Wolfe, David B. and Robert E. Snyder, *Ageless Marketing: Strategies for Reaching the Hearts and Minds of the New Customer Majority,* Chicago: Dearborn Trade Publishing, 2003.

Index

About the Author

BRENT GREEN studied psychology in both undergraduate and graduate school, and spent the first four years of his career working as a counseling therapist, where he honed deeper insights about human motivation and behavior. His counseling practice afforded him an opportunity to work with and help a diverse range of patients suffering from a plethora of mentally- and physically-disabling conditions.

For twenty-seven years, he has worked in the field of marketing communications. In the capacity of a marketing and creative strategist, as well as an award-winning copywriter, he has had innumerable successful business experiences selling a multitude of products and services to Baby Boomers—from real estate to fast food, from a new business radio format to a worldwide cycling event. His marketing experiences cover practically every product and service category. Over fifty regional, national, and international awards acknowledge his creative and commercial accomplishments.

The author also wrote and published *Noble Chaos*, an award-winning novel about Baby Boomers during the Vietnam War era. As with any foray into fiction writing, this challenge forced the author to think intensely and critically about the sociology and culture of this coming-of-age period, as well as to understand the indelible values that persist within an influential generational segment. He received critical recognition from *Writer's Digest* magazine for a forward-looking essay about Baby Boomers in midlife, included in this book.

In addition to formal education in psychology and accumulating real-world marketing experiences, the author has spent two decades reading extensively about Baby Boomer demography, cultural developments, and futuristic predictions. In this book, he has incorporated some of the more significant insights gleaned from many hours spent reading and reflecting.

The author is also a Leading-Edge Baby Boomer. He reached maturity during the critical time when this generation adopted its core values and beliefs. He was part of the party, as well as a curious and critical observer.

Brent Green can be contacted at *www.marketingtoboomers.com*, *www.bgassociates.com*, and *www.managemedia.com*, or visit his blog at *http://boomers.typepad.com/*.